THE GREAT OPERAS OF

Richard Wagner

An Account of the Life and Work of this Distinguished Composer, with Particular Attention to his Operas.

Illustrated with Portraits in Costume and Scenes from Opera

By
GUSTAV KOBBÉ

Copyright © 2018 Read Books Ltd.
This book is copyright and may not be
reproduced or copied in any way without
the express permission of the publisher in writing

British Library Cataloguing-in-Publication Data
A catalogue record for this book is available from
the British Library

A History of The Theatre

'The Theatre' is a collaborative form of fine art that uses live performers to present the experience of a real or imagined event. The performers may communicate this experience to the audience through combinations of gesture, speech, song, music, and dance, with elements of art, stagecraft and set design used to enhance the physicality, presence and immediacy of the experience. The specific place of the performance is also named by the word 'theatre' – derived from the Ancient Greek word *théatron*, meaning 'a place for viewing', itself from *theáomai*, meaning 'to see', 'watch' or 'observe'.

Modern Western theatre largely derives from ancient Greek drama, from which it borrows technical terminology, classification into genres, and many of its themes, stock characters, and plot elements. The city-state of Athens is where 'theatre' as we know it originated, as part of a broader culture of theatricality and performance in classical Greece that included festivals, religious rituals, politics, law, athletics, music, poetry, weddings, funerals, and symposia. Participation in the city-state's many festivals – and attendance at the City Dionysia as an audience member (or even as a participant in the theatrical productions) in particular, was an important part of citizenship.

The theatre of ancient Greece consisted of three types of drama: tragedy, comedy, and the satyr play (a form of tragicomedy, similar in spirit to the bawdy satire of burlesque). The origins of theatre in ancient Greece, according to Aristotle (384–322 BCE), the first theoretician of theatre, are to be found in the festivals that honoured Dionysus. These performances (the aforementioned City Dionysia) were held in semi-circular auditoria cut into hillsides, capable of seating 10,000–20,000 people. The stage consisted of a dancing floor (orchestra), dressing room and scene-building area (skene). Since the words were the most important part, good acoustics and clear delivery were paramount. The actors (always men) wore masks appropriate to the characters they represented, and each might play several parts.

Athenian tragedy (the oldest surviving form of tragedy) emerged sometime during the sixth century BCE, and flowered during the fifth century BCE – from the end of which it began to spread throughout the Greek world – and continued in popularity until the beginning of the Hellenistic period. Aeschylus, Sophocles, and Euripides were masters of the genre. The other side of the coin – Athenian comedy, is conventionally divided into three periods; 'Old Comedy', 'Middle Comedy', and 'New Comedy'. Old Comedy survives today largely in the form of the eleven surviving plays of Aristophanes, while Middle Comedy is largely lost (preserved only in a few relatively short fragments in authors such as Athenaeus of Naucratis). New Comedy is known primarily from the substantial papyrus fragments of Menander.

Western theatre developed and expanded considerably under the Romans. The theatre of ancient Rome was a thriving and diverse art form, ranging from festival performances of street theatre, nude dancing, and acrobatics, to the staging of Plautus's broadly appealing situation comedies, to the high-style, verbally elaborate tragedies of Seneca. Although Rome had a native tradition of performance, the Hellenization of Roman culture in the third century BCE had a profound and energizing effect on Roman theatre and encouraged the development of Latin literature of the highest quality for the stage. This tradition fed into the modern theatre we know today, and during the renaissance, theatre generally moved away from the poetic drama of the Greeks, and towards a more naturalistic prose style of dialogue. By the nineteenth century and the Industrial Revolution, this trend continued to progress.

In England, theatre was immensely popular, but took a big pause during 1642 and 1660 because of Cromwell's Interregnum. Prior to this, 'English renaissance theatre' was witnessed, with celebrated playwrights such as William Shakespeare, Christopher Marlowe and Ben Jonson. Under Queen Elizabeth, drama was a unified expression as far as social class was concerned, and the Court watched the same plays the commoners saw in the public playhouses. With the development of the private theatres, drama became more oriented towards the tastes and values of an upper-class audience however. By the later part of the reign of Charles I, few new plays were being written for the public theatres, which sustained themselves on the accumulated works of the previous decades. Theatre was now seen as something sinful and the Puritans tried very hard to drive it out of their society. Due to this stagnant period, once Charles II came back to the throne in 1660, theatre (among other arts) exploded with influences from France, and the wider continent.

The eighteenth century saw the widespread introduction of women to the stage – a development previously unthinkable. These women were looked at as celebrities (also a newer concept, thanks to ideas on individualism that were beginning to be born in Renaissance Humanism) but on the other hand, it was still very new and revolutionary. Comedies were full of the young and very much in vogue, with the storyline following their love lives: commonly a young roguish hero professing his love to the chaste and free minded heroine near the end of the play, much like Sheridan's *The School for Scandal*. Many of the comedies were fashioned after the French tradition, mainly Molière (the great comedic playwright), again harking back to the French influence of the King and his court after their exile.

After this point, there was an explosion of theatrical styles. Throughout the nineteenth century, the popular theatrical forms of Romanticism, melodrama, Victorian burlesque and the well-made plays of Scribe and Sardou gave way to the problem plays of Naturalism and Realism; the farces of Feydeau; Wagner's operatic *Gesamtkunstwerk*; musical theatre (including Gilbert and Sullivan's operas); F. C. Burnand's, W. S. Gilbert's and Wilde's drawing-room comedies; Symbolism; proto-Expressionism in the late works of August Strindberg and Henrik Ibsen; and Edwardian musical comedy. The list continues! These trends continued through the twentieth century in the realism of Stanislavski and Lee Strasberg, the political theatre of Erwin Piscator and Bertolt Brecht, the so-called Theatre of the Absurd of Samuel Beckett and Eugène Ionesco, and the rise of American and British musicals.

Theatre itself has an incredibly long history, and despite the massive proliferation of theatrical styles and mediums – it essentially owes its existence to the ancient Greeks and the Romans. The three main genres; tragedy, comedy and satyre, continue to influence plot themes, directing, writing and acting, with frequent and fascinating interrelations and overlaps. As a genre, it remains as popular today as it has ever been, and continues as a massive influence on popular culture more broadly. It is hoped that the current reader enjoys this book on the subject.

To my dear father-in-law,
David Lowe,
one of the "greatest generation"

Long my imprisoned spirit lay
    Fast bound in sin and nature's night;
Thine eye diffused a quickening ray,
    I woke, the dungeon flamed with light;
My chains fell off, my heart was free,
    I rose, went forth, and followed thee.
—CHARLES WESLEY, "AND CAN IT BE THAT I SHOULD GAIN?"

"I am an eighteenth-century man."
—D. MARTYN LLOYD-JONES

Contents

1	Eighteenth-century evangelicals as spiritual mentors **An introductory word**	1
2	"A flame of pure & holy fire" **George Whitefield's life & ministry and his thought about the Christian life**	9
3	"Sacramental glory" **The Lord's Supper and the power of the Holy Spirit in the hymnody of Charles Wesley**	37
4	"Guide me, O thou great Jehovah" **William Williams, Pantycelyn and his hymn**	53
5	"Dissent warmed its hands at Grimshaw's fire" **William Grimshaw of Haworth and the Baptists of Yorkshire**	65
6	"The great spiritual director of souls through the post" **John Newton as a spiritual mentor**	81
7	"Co-equal, co-essential, and co-eternal" **Introducing Anne Dutton and her reflections on the Trinity**	101
8	"Eminent spirituality" & "eminent usefulness" **True spirituality according to Andrew Fuller**	119
9	Becoming William Carey **A sketch of his life, thought and ministry**	137
10	The Holy Spirit, the *charismata* and signs and wonders **Some evangelical perspectives from the eighteenth century**	171
	Index	205

1

Eighteenth-century evangelicals as spiritual mentors

An introductory word

> A pitch of profligacy that has never since been equaled.
> —SELINA HASTINGS[1]

The final decades of the seventeenth century witnessed a distinct decline in public manners and morals in England. Attestation of this fact is found in both public documents and private testimonies. Here is the witness of one author, the London Baptist theologian Benjamin Keach (1640–1704), writing in 1701:

> Was ever sodomy so common in a Christian nation, or so notoriously and frequently committed, as by too palpable evidences it

---

1   Selina Hastings, "A peeress with a passion for piety," *Sunday Telegraph* (December 14, 1997).

appears to be, in and about this city, notwithstanding the clear light of the gospel which shines therein, and the great pains taken to reform the abominable profaneness that abounds? Is it not a wonder the patience of God hath not consumed us in his wrath, before this time? Was ever swearing, blasphemy, whoring, drunkenness, gluttony, self-love, and covetousness, at such a height, as at this time here?[2]

Despite the presence of a number of gospel-centred ministries like that of Keach and various societies which had been created to bring about moral reform, homosexuality, profanity, sexual immorality, drunkenness and gluttony were widespread. And the next three decades saw little improvement.

The moral tone of the nation was set in many ways by its monarchs and leading politicians. The first of the Hanoverian monarchs, George I (1660–1727), was primarily interested in food, horses and women. He divorced his wife when he was thirty-four and thereafter consorted with a series of mistresses.[3] Sir Robert Walpole (1676–1745), prime minister from 1722 to 1742, lived in undisguised adultery with his mistress, Maria Skerrett (1702–1738), whom he married after his wife died.[4] As J.H. Plumb has noted of aristocratic circles in the early eighteenth century, the women "hardly bothered with the pretence of virtue, and the possession of lovers and mistresses was regarded as a commonplace, a matter for gossip but not reproach."[5] Not surprisingly other segments of society simply followed suit. Pornographic literature, for instance, multiplied almost unchecked. Newspapers advertised such things as the services of gigolos and cures for venereal disease, and one could purchase guide-books to the numerous brothels in London.[6] It was, as a recent writer has put it well, "an age when atheism was fashionable, sexual morals lax, and drinking and gambling

---

2 Benjamin Keach, *Gospel Mysteries Unveiled* (1701 ed.; repr. London: L.I. Higham, 1817), III, 310.
3 J.H. Plumb, *The First Four Georges* (London: B.T. Batsford, 1956), 39–42.
4 J.H. Plumb, *Sir Robert Walpole* (Clifton: Augustus M. Kelley, 1973), II, 114.
5 Plumb, *Sir Robert Walpole*, II, 114.
6 Roy Porter, *English Society in the Eighteenth Century* (Harmondsworth: Penguin Books, 1982), 279.

at a pitch of profligacy that has never since been equalled."[7]

Social conditions were equally bleak. While many of the rich indulged themselves and all of their whims, the lot of the ordinary man and woman was quite different. For a variety of economic causes, the towns of England mushroomed in the eighteenth century. The population of London, the capital, more than doubled. By the end of the century it contained over a million people and was the largest city in the western world.[8] Many men and women came to these cities from rural poverty, hoping to find a decent living. But adequate housing could not keep up with the demand, and those who most needed the shelter lacked sufficient funds to purchase it.[9] Consequently, houses were desperately overcrowded. In a large industrial centre like Manchester, for example, ten people living in a room was common. Such rooms were often without furniture and even lacked beds. The occupants would sleep close together on wood shavings for warmth. Disease was rampant and unchecked: smallpox, typhus, typhoid and dysentery made death a very familiar figure.[10]

From such a dismal situation many sought escape in drink. Beer had always been a central part of English life. But in the eighteenth century many turned to something far more potent: gin. By mid-century, the consumption of poorly distilled, and often virtually poisonous, gin was eleven million gallons a year. Some idea of the debilitation wrought by this plague may be grasped in terms of a simple item of record. In one area of London, for instance, comprising 2,000 houses or so, 506 were gin shops. One contemporary novelist, Henry Fielding (1707–1754), estimated that in London 100,000 people drank gin as their principal means of sustenance.[11] The sort of suffering that such consumption of gin brought in its wake is well illustrated by a news item from 1748 which reads as follows:

---

7   Selina Hastings, "A peeress with a passion for piety," *Sunday Telegraph* (December 14, 1997).

8   J.H. Plumb, *England in the Eighteenth Century* (Harmondsworth: Penguin Books, 1963), 144.

9   David Lyle Jeffrey, "Introduction" to his ed., *A Burning and a Shining Light. English Spirituality in the Age of Wesley* (Grand Rapids: Eerdmans, 1987), 9.

10 Plumb, *England in the Eighteenth Century*, 12.

11 Jeffrey, "Introduction," 9.

At a Christening at Beddington in Surrey the nurse was so intoxicated that after she had undressed the child, instead of laying it in the cradle she put it behind a large fire, which burnt it to death in a few minutes.[12]

"REVIVE THINE OWN WORK IN THE MIDST OF US"

The Hanoverian Church of England was basically helpless when it came to dealing with this dire moral and spiritual situation. By and large the bishops of the Church of England were, in the words of English historian J.H. Plumb, "first and foremost politicians," not men of the Spirit. "There is a worldliness," Plumb continues, "about eighteenth-century [bishops] which no amount of apologetics can conceal." They undertook their clerical duties "only as political duties allowed."[13] The worldliness of these bishops showed itself in other ways as well. Jonathan Trelawny (1650–1721), Bishop of Winchester, used to "excuse himself for his much swearing by saying he swore as a baronet, and not as a bishop"![14] Such bishops had neither the time nor the interest to promote church renewal. Of course, the decadence of church leadership was by no means absolute; but the net effect of worldly bishops was to squash effective reform.

Moreover, the attention of far too many of the clergy under these bishops was taken up with such avocations as philosophy, biology, agriculture, chemistry, literature, law, politics, fox-hunting, drinking—anything but pastoral ministry and spiritual nurture. There were, of course, a goodly number of Church of England ministers who did not have the resources to indulge themselves in such pursuits, since they barely eked out a living. But few of them—wealthy or poor—preached anything but dry, unaffecting moralistic sermons. The *mentalité* of the first half of the eighteenth century gloried in reason, moderation and decorum. The preaching of the day dwelt largely upon themes of morality and decency and lacked "any element of holy excitement, of passionate pleading, of heroic challenge, of winged

---

12 Cited Porter, *English Society*, 35.
13 Plumb, *England in the Eighteenth Century*, 43.
14 Cited J. Wesley Bready, *England: Before and After Wesley. The Evangelical Revival and Social Reform* (London: Hodder and Stoughton, 1938), 50.

imagination."¹⁵ In a diary kept by a shopkeeper named Thomas Turner (1729–1793) from East Hoathly, Sussex, such preaching was insightfully criticized as an

> idle lazy way of preaching, which many of our clergy are got into, seeming rather to make self-interest the motive for the exercising their profession than the eternal happiness and salvation of men's souls. To which if we add the intolerable degree of pride and covetousness predominant in too many of our clergy, we need not wonder at our degeneracy from the strict piety with which our forefathers worshipped God in the first ages of Christianity.¹⁶

Part of the reason for this spiritual ineffectiveness of the ministers of the Church of England is the fact that, in the year 1662, upwards of 2,000 ministers of the Church of England, the most spiritually-minded group of the established Church at the time, had been expelled from her ranks for refusing to conform completely to the rites and practices of the Church of England. These men, known to history as the Puritans, had sought unsuccessfully for close to 100 years to bring reform and renewal to the Church of England. Eventually they were forced out to join three fledgling denominations: the English Presbyterians, the Congregationalists and the Particular Baptists, also known as the Calvinistic Baptists. These three groups became known as the "Dissenters" or "Nonconformists." Little wonder then that the Church of England found herself at a distinct spiritual disadvantage when it came to leading the nation in moral and spiritual reform in the early eighteenth century.

But, even among many of the Dissenters, the children of the Puritans, things were little better. One knowledgeable observer of these churches bemoaned the fact that "the distinguished doctrines of the gospel—Christ crucified, the only ground of hope for fallen man—salvation

---

15 Horton Davies, *Worship and Theology in England* (1961 ed.; repr. Grand Rapids: Eerdmans, 1996), III, 73.

16 Thomas Turner, *Diary*, entry for January 20, 1758, in *The Diary of Thomas Turner, 1754–1765*, ed. David Vaisey (Oxford: Oxford University Press, 1984), 131.

through his atoning blood—the sanctification by his eternal Spirit, are old-fashioned things now seldom heard in our churches."[17] The Christian life was basically defined in terms of a moral life of good works. Spiritual ardour was regarded with horror as "enthusiasm" or fanaticism. The ideal of the era is well summed up by an inscription on a tombstone from the period: "pious without enthusiasm."[18] The spiritual situation in which early eighteenth-century Dissenters thus found themselves is well described by two Congregationalist ministers in 1737, Isaac Watts (1674–1748), the father of the English hymn, and John Guyse (1680–1761). "There has been a great and just complaint for many years," they wrote, "that the work of conversion goes on very slowly, that the Spirit of God in his saving influences is much withdrawn from the ministrations of his word, and there are few that receive the report of the gospel, with any eminent success upon their hearts." They were thus constrained to pray, "Return, O Lord, and visit thy churches, and revive thine own work in the midst of us."[19]

Now, it is an amazing fact that the revival for which Isaac Watts and John Guyse prayed did not originate in England among the Dissenters, but within that body which had actually persecuted the Puritans, namely, the Church of England. From our perspective, this fact can only be seen as a display of God's sovereignty!

THE EIGHTEENTH-CENTURY REVIVAL

The eighteenth-century evangelical revival began in the 1730s and found its centre in the English-speaking world on both sides of the

---

17 Cited A. Skevington Wood, "The Eighteenth Century Methodist Revival Reconsidered," *The Evangelical Quarterly*, 53 (1981): 135.

18 J.I. Packer, "The Spirit with the Word: The Reformational Revivalism of George Whitefield," in W.P. Stephens, ed., *The Bible, the Reformation and the Church. Essays in Honour of James Atkinson* (Journal for the Study of the New Testament Supplement Series, 105; Sheffield: Sheffield Academic Press, 1995), 180–181; M. Dorothy George, *England in Transition. Life and Work in the Eighteenth Century* (Harmondsworth: Penguin Books, 1953), 65. For an excellent overview of the state of Christianity in England at this time, see Jeffrey, "Introduction," 2–10.

19 Isaac Watts and John Guyse, "Preface" to Jonathan Edwards, *A Narrative of a Surprising Work of God,* in *Jonathan Edwards on Revival* (Edinburgh: The Banner of Truth Trust, 1965), 2–3.

Atlantic. As it ran its course, thousands were swept into the kingdom of God. In New England alone, for instance, thirty to forty thousand were converted during the three-year period from 1740 to 1742. In England, the Arminian Methodists, those evangelicals adhering to the views and beliefs of John Wesley (1703–1791) and his brother Charles (1707–1788), grew from around 22,000 in 1767 to over 88,000 by 1800. Central to the revival was the leadership of a number of gifted and Spirit-anointed preachers. In New England there was Jonathan Edwards (1703–1758), a brilliant theologian whose writings were characterized by a deep understanding of the human heart and a passion for God's glory. Even a superficial perusal of his writings reveals a mind and heart permeated with the beauty and excellence of the Triune God, and a desire to communicate this beauty and excellence to his fellow human beings.

In Great Britain, there was the Englishman George Whitefield (1714–1770), who, more than any other figure, epitomized the revival. Over the thirty-four years between his conversion in 1736 and his death, he preached around 18,000 sermons, and, in a day of laboriously slow travel, visited Scotland fifteen times, traversed the Atlantic thirteen times, and crisscrossed much of the English and Welsh countryside. A pioneer in open-air preaching, he often spoke to huge crowds of 10,000 or more. Alongside Whitefield, there were the Wesley brothers—John, an indefatigable evangelist like Whitefield, and Charles, "the supreme poet of love to Jesus" in this period of revival[20]—and the Welshmen Howel Harris (1714–1773) and Daniel Rowland (1711–1790), whose preaching and spirituality set the tone and character of the Welsh people for the next century and a half. As these men, and a host of others, opened their mouths to preach and to teach, the Spirit of God descended upon their hearers, enlightening and converting them, building them up and strengthening them, melting their hearts and setting them aflame for Christ.[21]

The chapters that follow explore key aspects of this revival—the anointed preaching, the new birth and justification, the Lord's Supper,

---

20 J.I. Packer, *God in Our Midst. Seeking and Receiving Ongoing Revival* (Ann Arbor: Servant Books, 1987), 18.

21 See a letter that Howel Harris wrote to George Whitefield in 1743, chapter 10, no. 51.

hymnody and spiritual direction—through some of its leading figures—George Whitefield, Charles Wesley, William Williams (1717–1791), William Grimshaw (1708–1763), Anne Dutton (1692–1765) and John Newton (1725–1807). Chapters 8 and 9 especially look at the lives of two Dissenters, Andrew Fuller (1754–1815) and William Carey (1761–1834), to see the way that God did indeed revive one wing of the Dissent for which Watts and Guyse prayed, namely, the Particular or Calvinistic Baptists. Suffusing this great period of revival and awakening was the unfurling of the love of God. All of these men were amazed by the love of God toward them and other rank sinners, and in this then they are fabulous guides to Christian living and to what truly matters in the Christian life. The final chapter deals primarily with a topic rather than one individual, namely, the issue of the gifts of the Spirit, one of the most divisive theological issues of the twentieth century. Our eighteenth-century forebears can help us immensely to think through this subject biblically and practically.

All of these studies are grounded upon a deep-seated conviction that the eighteenth-century is the most important Christian era along with those of the fourth and sixteenth centuries, which witnessed the hammering out of Nicene Trinitarian orthodoxy and the Reformation respectively. Our great need is for an outpouring of the Spirit that unfurls the love of God in the depth and to the extent that our eighteenth-century forebears knew. In this, then, I am fully in accord with that remarkable preacher of the twentieth century, D. Martyn Lloyd-Jones (1898–1981), who often said, "I am an eighteenth-century man."[22]

Michael A.G. Haykin
Dundas, Ontario
July 24, 2018

---

22 See, for example, Frederick and Elizabeth Catherwood, *Martyn Lloyd-Jones: The Man and His Books* (Bryntirion: Evangelical Library of Wales, 1982), 33.

2

"A flame of pure & holy fire"

George Whitefield's life & ministry and his thought about the Christian life[1]

> Happy they who have fled to Jesus Christ for refuge: they have a peace that the world cannot give. O that

---

[1] Earlier versions of portions of this chapter have appeared as "Defenders of the faith: George Whitefield and the nature of Christian perfection," *Evangelical Times*, 32, no. 10 (October 1998): 23; "Evangelical piety: grounded in justification by faith alone," *Evangelical Times*, 34, no. 1 (January 2000): 14; "Christ, our wisdom and our righteousness," *Evangelical Times*, 34, no. 2 (February 2000): 14; "'The Believer's Hollow Square': The new birth and justification by faith alone in the thought of George Whitefield," *Sovereign Grace Journal*, 2, no. 1 (2000): 4–13; "The Christian Life in the Thought of George Whitefield," *The Southern Baptist Journal of Theology*, 18, no. 2 (Summer 2014): 7–20. Used by permission.

the pleasure-taking, trifling flatterer knew what it was! He would no longer feel such an empty void, such a dreadful chasm in the heart which nothing but the presence of God can fill.
—GEORGE WHITEFIELD[2]

In 1835, Francis Alexander Cox (1783–1853) and James Hoby (1788–1871), two prominent English Baptists who were visiting fellow Baptists in the United States, made a side trip to Newburyport, Massachusetts, to view the tomb of George Whitefield. The "grand itinerant" had died on September 30, 1770, at the home of Jonathan Parsons (1705–1776), pastor of the town's First Presbyterian Church, also known as Old South. He had been interred two days later in a vault below what is now the centre aisle of this church, where, along with the coffins of Parsons and another pastor of the church, Joseph Prince (d.1791), his remains were on display all through the nineteenth century. In fact, it was not until 1932 that the coffin in which Whitefield's remains lay was covered over with a slate slab.[3]

Cox and Hoby later recalled descending with some difficulty into the subterraneous vault where Whitefield was buried. As they did so, they remembered that a "deep expectant emotions thrilled our bosoms." They sat on the two other coffins in the vault and watched as the upper half of the lid of Whitefield's coffin was opened on its hinges "to reveal the skeleton secrets of the narrow prison-house." They "contemplated and handled the skull," while they "thought of his devoted life, his blessed death, his high and happy destiny" and "whispered [their] adorations of the grace that formed him both for earth and heaven."[4] What makes this scene even more *outré* is that the skeletal remains

---

2 Letter MCXC to Lady G—H—, December 15, 1757, in *The Works of the Reverend George Whitefield, M.A.* (London: Edward and Charles Dilly, 1771), 3:225. This collection of Whitefield's literary corpus is subsequently referred to as *Works*.

3 G. Norris Foster, compiled, *First Presbyterian Church (Old South), Newburyport, Massachusetts. Historical Notes and Dates* (n.p., n.d.), 1.

4 *The Baptists in America: A Narrative of the Deputation from the Baptist Union in England to The United States and Canada* (London: T. Ward and Co., 1836), 421–422. For other similar accounts, see L. Tyerman, *The Life of the Rev. George Whitefield* (New York: Anson D. F. Randolph & Co., 1877), 2:602–603, 607.

that Cox and Hoby viewed were not intact. The main bone of Whitefield's right arm had been stolen some years earlier by another Englishman. It was not until either the late 1830s or even the 1840s that the thief's conscience brought him to the point of sending the bone back across the Atlantic in a small wooden box![5]

These accounts are a potent reminder of the fact that of all the great preachers raised up in the transatlantic evangelical revival none gripped the public mind and imagination more than George Whitefield. During his lifetime, the Congregationalist Joseph Williams (1692–1755), a merchant from Kidderminster with a keen interest in spiritual renewal, rightly termed him the "Father" of those seeking to advance the revival.[6] Henry St. John, Viscount Bolingbroke (1678–1751), who "professed himself a deist," was forced to exclaim, after hearing Whitefield preach: "the most extraordinary man of our times, the most commanding eloquence, unquenchable zeal, unquestionable piety."[7] On the other side of the Atlantic Benjamin Colman (1673–1747) and William Cooper (1694–1743) viewed Whitefield as "the wonder of the age" and were convinced that "no man more employs the pens, and fills up the conversation of people, than he does at this day."[8] Shortly after the evangelist's death Augustus Montague Toplady (1740–1778), author of the famous hymn "Rock of Ages, cleft for me," remembered him as "the apostle of the English empire."[9] And looking back from the following century, John Foster (1770–1843), the Baptist

---

5 Foster, *First Presbyterian Church (Old South)*, 1, 8. Tyerman gives the date for the bone's return as 1837 (*George Whitefield*, 2:606). Robert Philip, Whitefield's nineteenth-century biographer, knew the thief and urged him to return it. The thief sought to show Philip the bone in 1835, but the latter refused to gaze upon it. See Philip's *The Life and Times of the Reverend George Whitefield, M.A.* (London: George Virtue, 1838), 550–551.

6 "Charles Wesley in 1739 by Joseph Williams of Kidderminster," introd. Geoffrey F. Nuttall, *Proceedings of the Wesley Historical Society*, 42, no. 6 (December 1980): 182.

7 Cited Willard Connely, *The True Chesterfield: Manners—Women—Education* (London: Cassell and Co., 1939), 179.

8 "To the Reader," the Preface to Joseph Smith, *The Character, Preaching, etc. of the Reverend Mr. George Whitefield. Impartially Represented and Supported* in George Whitefield, *Fifteen Sermons Preached on Various Important Subjects* (London, 1792), 5–6.

9 "A Concise Character of the Late Rev. Mr. Whitefield," *The Works of Augustus Toplady, B.A.* (London: J. Chidley, 1837), 494.

essayist, was sure that with "the doubtful exception of Wickliffe, no man probably ever excited in this island [i.e. the British Isles] so profound, and extended, and prolonged a sensation in the public mind, by personal addresses to the understanding and conscience, on the subject of religion."[10]

"A RAY OF DIVINE LIFE": THE PATHWAY TO CONVERSION[11]

George Whitefield was the youngest son of Thomas Whitefield (1681–1716), the proprietor of the Bell Inn, at the time the finest hotel in Gloucester. George's father died when he was but two, and so he was raised by his mother Elizabeth (c.1681–1751). His school record was unremarkable, save for a noticeable talent for acting. As he later said, "During the time of my being at school, I was very fond of reading plays, and have kept from school for days together to prepare myself for acting them."[12] For a while during his teen years, when his older brother Richard took over the running of the inn, he worked as one of the servants. But his mother longed for something better for her son. Her persistence and the kindness of friends enabled him in November 1732 to enter Pembroke College, Oxford University. It was

---

10 "George Whitefield: A Critical Essay," in *George Whitefield's Journals (1737–1741)* (1905 ed.; repr. Gainesville: Scholars' Facsimiles & Reprints, 1969), 15.

11 The best biographical studies of Whitefield are Arnold Dallimore, *George Whitefield: The Life and Times of the Great Evangelist of the Eighteenth-Century Revival* (1970 and 1979 eds.; repr. Westchester: Cornerstone Books, 1979 and 1980), 2 vols., and Thomas S. Kidd, *George Whitefield: America's Spiritual Founding Father* (New Haven: Yale University Press, 2014). Dallimore has also written a one-volume account of Whitefield's life: *George Whitefield: Evangelist of the 18th-Century Revival* (London: The Wakeman Trust, 1990). For a shorter study of Whitefield, see John H. Armstrong, "George Whitefield 1714–1770," in his *Five Great Evangelists* (Fearn: Christian Focus Publications, 1997), 15–70. For two studies that are more critical and controversial in nature, see Harry S. Stout, *The Divine Dramatist: George Whitefield and the Rise of Modern Evangelicalism* (Grand Rapids: Eerdmans, 1991) and Frank Lambert, *"Pedlar in Divinity": George Whitefield and the Transatlantic Revivals, 1737–1770* (Princeton: Princeton University Press, 1994). For an insightful critique of Stout, see Eric Carlsson, "Book Reviews: Harry S. Stout, *The Divine Dramatist: George Whitefield and the Rise of Modern Evangelicalism*," *Trinity Journal*, n.s., 14, no. 2 (Fall 1993): 238–247.

12 Cited Jerome Dean Mahaffey, *The Accidental Revolutionary: George Whitefield and the Creation of America* (Waco: Baylor University Press, 2011), 3.

Richard Wagner

(1813-1883)

RICHARD WAGNER was born at Leipsic, May 22, 1813. His father was clerk to the city police court and a man of good education. During the French occupation of Leipsic he was, owing to his knowledge of French, made chief of police. He was fond of poetry and had a special love for the drama, often taking part in amateur theatricals.

Five months after Richard's birth his father died of an epidemic fever brought on by the carnage during the battle of Leipsic, October 16, 18, and 19, 1813. In 1815 his widow, whom he had left in most straitened circumstances, married Ludwig Geyer, an actor, a playwright, and a portrait painter. By inheritance from his father, by association with his stepfather, who was very fond of him, Wagner readily acquired the dramatic faculty so pronounced in his operas and music-dramas of which he is both author and composer.

At the time Wagner's mother married Geyer, he was a member of the Court Theatre at Dresden. Thither the family removed. When the boy was eight years old, he had learned to play on the pianoforte the chorus of bridesmaids from "Der Freischütz," then quite new. The day before Geyer's death, September 30, 1821, Richard was playing this piece in an adjoining room and heard Geyer say to his mother: "Do you think he might have a gift

The Complete Opera Book

for music?" Coming out of the death room Wagner's mother said to him: "Of you he wanted to make something." "From this time on," writes Wagner in his early autobiographical sketch, "I always had an idea that I was destined to amount to something in this world."

At school Wagner made quite a little reputation as a writer of verses. He was such an enthusiastic admirer of Shakespeare that at the age of fourteen he began a grand tragedy, of which he himself says that it was a jumble of *Hamlet* and *Lear*. So many people died in the course of it that their ghosts had to return in order to keep the fifth act going.

In 1833, at the age of twenty, Wagner began his career as a professional musician. His elder brother Albert was engaged as tenor, actor, and stage manager at the Würzburg theatre. A position as chorus master being offered to Richard, he accepted it, although his salary was a pittance of ten florins a month. However, the experience was valuable. He was able to profit by many useful hints from his brother, the Musikverein performed several of his compositions, and his duties were not so arduous but that he found time to write the words and music of an opera in three acts entitled "The Fairies"—first performed in June, 1888, five years after his death, at Munich. In the autumn of 1834 he was called to the conductorship of the opera at Magdeburg. There he wrote and produced an opera, "Das Liebesverbot" (Love Veto), based on Shakespeare's *Measure for Measure*. The theatre at Magdeburg was, however, on the ragged edge of bankruptcy, and during the spring of 1836 matters became so bad that it was evident the theatre must soon close. Finally only twelve days were left for the rehearsing and the performance of his opera. The result was that the production went completely to pieces, singers forgetting their lines and music, and a repetition which was announced could not

Richard Wagner

come off because of a free fight behind the scenes between two of the principal singers. Wagner describes this in the following amusing passage in his autobiographical sketch:

"All at once the husband of my prima donna (the impersonator of *Isabella*) pounced upon the second tenor, a very young and handsome fellow (the singer of my *Claudio*), against whom the injured spouse had long cherished a secret jealousy. It seemed that the prima donna's husband, who had from behind the curtains inspected with me the composition of the audience, considered that the time had now arrived when, without damage to the prospects of the theatre, he could take his revenge on his wife's lover. *Claudio* was so pounded and belaboured by him that the unhappy individual was compelled to retire to the dressing-room with his face all bleeding. *Isabella* was informed of this, and, rushing desperately toward her furious lord, received from him such a series of violent cuffs that she forthwith went into spasms. The confusion among my personnel was now quite boundless; everybody took sides with one party or the other, and everything seemed on the point of a general fight. It seemed as if this unhappy evening appeared to all of them precisely calculated for a final settling up of all sorts of fancied insults. This much was evident, that the couple who had suffered under the 'love veto' (Liebesverbot) of *Isabella's* husband, were certainly unable to appear on this occasion."

Wagner was next engaged as orchestral conductor at Königsberg, where he married the actress Wilhelmina, or Minna Planer. Later he received notice of his appointment as conductor and of the engagement of his wife and sister at the theatre at Riga, on the Russian side of the Baltic.

In Riga he began the composition of his first great suc-

The Complete Opera Book

cess, "Rienzi." He completed the libretto during the summer of 1838, and began the music in the autumn, and when his contract terminated in the spring of 1839 the first two acts were finished. In July, accompanied by his wife and a huge Newfoundland dog, he boarded a sailing vessel for London, at the port of Pilau, his intention being to go from London to Paris. "I shall never forget the voyage," he says. "It was full of disaster. Three times we nearly suffered shipwreck, and once were obliged to seek safety in a Norwegian harbour. . . . The legend of the 'Flying Dutchman' was confirmed by the sailors, and the circumstances gave it a distinct and characteristic colour in my mind." No wonder the sea is depicted so graphically in his opera "The Flying Dutchman."

He arrived in Paris in September, 1839, and remained until April 7, 1842, from his twenty-sixth to his twenty-ninth year. This Parisian sojourn was one of the bitter experiences of his life. At times he actually suffered from cold and hunger, and was obliged to do a vast amount of most uncongenial kind of hack work.

November 19, 1840, he completed the score of "Rienzi," and in December forwarded it to the director of the Royal Theatre at Dresden. While awaiting a reply, he contributed to the newspapers and did all kinds of musical drudgery for Schlesinger, the music publisher, even making arrangements for the cornet à piston. Finally word came from Dresden. "Rienzi" had aroused the enthusiasm of the chorus master, Fischer, and of the tenor Tichatschek, who saw that the title rôle was exactly suited to his robust, dramatic voice. Then there was Mme. Schroeder-Devrient for the part of *Adriano*. The opera was produced October 20, 1842, the performance beginning at six and ending just before midnight, to the enthusiastic plaudits of an immense audience. So great was the excitement that in spite of the late hour people remained awake to talk over the success.

Richard Wagner

"We all ought to have gone to bed," relates a witness, "but we did nothing of the kind." Early the next morning Wagner appeared at the theatre in order to make excisions from the score, which he thought its great length necessitated. But when he returned in the afternoon to see if they had been executed, the copyist excused himself by saying the singers had protested against any cuts. Tichatschek said: "I will have no cuts; it is too heavenly." After a while, owing to its length, the opera was divided into two evenings.

The success of "Rienzi" led the Dresden management to put "The Flying Dutchman" in rehearsal. It was brought out after somewhat hasty preparations, January 2, 1843. The opera was so different from "Rienzi," its sombre beauty contrasted so darkly with the glaring, brilliant music and scenery of the latter, that the audience failed to grasp it. In fact, after "Rienzi," it was a disappointment.

Before the end of January, 1843, not long after the success of "Rienzi," Wagner was appointed one of the Royal conductors at Dresden. He was installed February 2d. One of his first duties was to assist Berlioz at the rehearsals of the latter's concerts. Wagner's work in his new position was somewhat varied, consisting not only of conducting operas, but also music between the acts at theatrical performances and at church services. The principal operas which he rehearsed and conducted were "Euryanthe," "Freischütz," "Don Giovanni," "The Magic Flute," Gluck's "Armide," and "Iphigenia in Aulis." The last-named was revised both as regards words and music by him, and his changes are now generally accepted.

Meanwhile he worked arduously on "Tannhäuser," completing it April 13, 1844. It was produced at Dresden, October 19, 1845. At first the work proved even a greater puzzle to the public than "The Flying Dutchman" had,

The Complete Opera Book

and evoked comments which nowadays, when the opera has actually become a classic, seem ridiculous. Some people even suggested that the plot of the opera should be changed so that *Tannhäuser* should marry *Elizabeth*. The management of the Dresden theatre, which had witnessed the brilliant success of "Rienzi" and had seen "The Flying Dutchman" and "Tannhäuser" at least hold their own in spite of the most virulent opposition, looked upon his next work, "Lohengrin," as altogether too risky and put off its production indefinitely.

Thinking that political changes might put an end to the routine stagnation in musical matters, Wagner joined in the revolutionary agitation of '48 and '49. In May, 1849, the disturbances at Dresden reached such an alarming point that the Saxon Court fled. Prussian troops were dispatched to quell the riot and Wagner thought it advisable to flee. He went to Weimar, where Liszt was busy rehearsing "Tannhäuser." While attending a rehearsal of this work, May 19, news was received that orders had been issued for his arrest as a politically dangerous individual. Liszt at once procured a passport and Wagner started for Paris. In June he went to Zurich, where he found Dresden friends and where his wife joined him, being enabled to do so through the zeal of Liszt, who raised the money to defray her journey from Dresden.

Liszt brought out "Lohengrin" at Weimar, August 28, 1850. The reception of "Lohengrin" did not at first differ much from that accorded to "Tannhäuser." Yet the performance made a deep impression. The fact that the weight of Liszt's influence had been cast in its favour gave vast importance to the event, and it may be said that through this performance Wagner's cause received its first great stimulus. The so-called Wagner movement may be said to have dated from this production of "Lohengrin."

Richard Wagner

He finished the librettos of the "Nibelung" dramas in 1853. By May, 1854, the music of "Das Rheingold" was composed. The following month he began "Die Walküre" and finished all but the instrumentation during the following winter and the full score in 1856. Previous to this, in fact already in the autumn of 1854, he had sketched some of the music of "Siegfried," and in the spring of 1857 the full score of the first act and of the greater part of the second act was finished. Then, recognizing the difficulties which he would encounter in securing a performance of the "Ring," and appalled by the prospect of the battle he would be obliged to wage, he was so disheartened that he abandoned the composition of "Siegfried" at the *Waldweben* scene and turned to "Tristan." His idea at that time was that "Tristan" would be short and comparatively easy to perform. Genius that he was, he believed that because it was easy for him to write great music it would be easy for others to interpret it. A very curious, not to say laughable, incident occurred at this time. An agent of the Emperor of Brazil called and asked if Wagner would compose an opera for an Italian troupe at Rio de Janeiro, and would he conduct the work himself, all upon his own terms. The composition of "Tristan" actually was begun with a view of its being performed by Italians in Brazil!

The poem of "Tristan" was finished early in 1857, and in the winter of the same year the full score of the first act was ready to be forwarded to the engraver. The second act is dated Venice, March 2, 1859. The third is dated Lyons, August, 1859.

It is interesting to note in connection with "Tristan" that, while Wagner wrote it because he thought it would be easy to secure its performance, he subsequently found more difficulty in getting it produced than any other of his works. In September, 1859, he again went to Paris with the somewhat curious hope that he could there find opportunity to produce "Tristan" with German artists. Through the intercession of the Princess Metternich, the Emperor ordered the production of "Tannhäuser" at the Opéra. Beginning March 13, 1861, three performances were given, of which it is difficult to say whether the performance was on the stage or in the auditorium, for the uproar in the house often drowned the sounds from the stage. The members of the Jockey Club, who objected to the absence of a ballet, armed themselves with shrill whistles, on which they began to blow whenever there was the slightest hint of applause, and the result was that between the efforts of the singers to make themselved heard and of Wagner's friends to applaud, and the shrill whistling from his enemies, there was confusion worse confounded. But Wagner's friendship with Princess Metternich bore good fruit. Through her mediation, it is supposed, he received permission to return to all parts of Germany but Saxony. It was not until March, 1862, thirteen years after his banishment, that he was again allowed to enter the kingdom of his birth and first success.

His first thought now was to secure the production of "Tristan," but at Vienna, after fifty-seven rehearsals, it was put upon the shelf as impossible.

In 1863, while working upon "Die Meistersinger," at Penzing, near Vienna, he published his "Nibelung" dramas, expressing his hope that through the bounty of one of the German rulers the completion and performance of his "Ring of the Nibelung" would be made possible. But in the spring of 1864, worn out by his struggle with poverty and almost broken in spirit by his contest with public and critics, he actually determined to give up his public career, and eagerly grasped the opportunity to visit a private country seat in Switzerland. Just at this

Richard Wagner

very moment, when despair had settled upon him, the long wished for help came. King Ludwig II., of Bavaria, bade him come to Munich, where he settled in 1864. "Tristan" was produced there June 10, 1865. June 21, 1868, a model performance of "Die Meistersinger," which he had finished in 1867, was given at Munich under the direction of von Bülow, Richter acting as chorus master and Wagner supervising all the details. Wagner also worked steadily at the unfinished portion of the "Ring," completing the instrumentation of the third act of "Siegfried" in 1869 and the introduction and first act of "The Dusk of the Gods" in June, 1870.

August 25, 1870, his first wife having died January 25, 1866, after five years' separation from him, he married the divorced wife of von Bülow, Cosima Liszt. In 1869 and 1870, respectively, "The Rhinegold" and "The Valkyr" were performed at the Court Theatre in Munich.

Bayreuth having been determined upon as the place where a theatre for the special production of his "Ring" should be built, Wagner settled there in April, 1872. By November, 1874, "Dusk of the Gods" received its finishing touches, and rehearsals had already been held at Bayreuth. During the summer of 1875, under Wagner's supervision, Hans Richter held full rehearsals there, and at last, twenty-eight years after its first conception, on August 13th, 14th, 16th, and 17th, again from August 20 to 23, and from August 27 to 30, 1876, "The Ring of the Nibelung" was performed at Bayreuth with the following cast: *Wotan*, Betz; *Loge*, Vogel; *Alberich*, Hill; *Mime*, Schlosser; *Fricka*, Frau Grün; *Donner* and *Gunther*, Gura; *Erda* and *Waltraute*, Frau Jaide; *Siegmund*, Niemann; *Sieglinde*, Frl. Schefsky; *Brünnhilde*, Frau Materna; *Siegfried*, Unger; *Hagen*, Siehr; *Gutrune*, Frl. Weckerin; *Rhinedaughters;* Lilli and Marie Lehmann, and Frl. Lammert. First violin, Wilhelmj; conductor, Hans Richter.

The Complete Opera Book

The first *Rhinedaughter* was the same Lilli Lehmann who, in later years, at the Metropolitan Opera House, New York, became one of the greatest of prima donnas and, as regards the Wagnerian repertoire, set a standard for all time. Materna appeared at that house in the "Valkyr" production under Dr. Damrosch, in January, 1885, and Niemann was heard there later.

To revert to Bayreuth, "Parsifal" was produced there in July, 1882. In the autumn of that year, Wagner's health being in an unsatisfactory state, though no alarming symptoms had shown themselves, he took up his residence in Venice at the Palazzo Vendramini, on the Grand Canal. He died February 13, 1883.

In manner incidental, that is, without attention formally being called to the subject, Wagner's reform of the lyric stage is set forth in the descriptive accounts of his music-dramas which follow, and in which the leading motives are quoted in musical notation. But something directly to the point must be said here.

Once again, like Gluck a century before, Wagner opposed the assumption of superiority on the part of the interpreter—the singer—over the composer. He opposed it in manner so thorough-going that he changed the whole face of opera. A far greater tribute to Wagner's genius than the lame attempts of some German composers at imitating him, is the frank adoption of certain phases of his method by modern French and Italian composers, beginning with Verdi in "Aïda." While by no means a Wagnerian work, since it contains not a trace of the theory of the leading motive, "Aïda," through the richness of its instrumentation, the significant accompaniment of its recitative, the lack of mere *bravura* embellishment in its vocal score, and its sober reaching out for true dramatic effect in the treatment of the voices, substituting this for ostentatious brilliancy and ear-tickling fluency, plainly

Richard Wagner

shows the influence of Wagner upon the greatest of Italian composers. And what is true of "Aïda," is equally applicable to the whole school of Italian *versimo* that came after Verdi—Mascagni, Leoncavallo, Puccini.

Wagner's works are conceived and executed upon a gigantic scale. They are Shakespearian in their dimensions and in their tragic power; or, as in the "Meistersinger," in their comedy element. Each of his works is highly individual. The "Ring" dramas and "Tristan" are unmistakably Wagner. Yet how individually characteristic the music of each! That of the "Ring" is of elemental power. The "Tristan" music is molten passion. Equally characteristic and individual are his other scores.

The theory evolved by Wagner was that the lyric stage should present not a series of melodies for voice upon a mere framework of plot and versified story, but a serious work of dramatic art, the music to which should, both vocally and instrumentally, express the ever varying development of the drama. With this end in view he invented a melodious recitative which only at certain great crises in the progress of the action—such as the love-climax, the gathering at the Valkyr Rock, the "Farewell," and the "Magic Fire" scenes in "The Valkyr"; the meeting of *Siegfried* and *Brünnhilde* in "Siegfried"; the love duet and "Love Death" in "Tristan"—swells into prolonged melody. Note that I say prolonged melody. For besides these prolonged melodies, there is almost constant melody, besides marvellous orchestral colour, in the weft and woof of the recitative. This is produced by the artistic use of leading motives, every leading motive being a brief, but expressive, melody—so brief that, to one coming to Wagner without previous study or experience, the melodious quality of his recitative is not appreciated at first. After a while, however, the hearer begins to recognize certain brief, but melodious and musically

The Complete Opera Book

eloquent phrases—leading motives—as belonging to certain characters in the drama or to certain influences potent in its development, such as hate, love, jealousy, the desire for revenge, etc. Often to express a combination of circumstances, influences, passions, or personal actions, these leading motives, these brief melodious phrases, are combined with a skill that is unprecedented; or the voice may express one, while the orchestra combines with it in another.

To enable the orchestra to follow these constantly changing phases in the evolution and development of the drama, and often to give utterance to them separately, it was necessary for Wagner to have most intimate knowledge of the individual tone-quality and characteristics of every instrument in the orchestra, and this mastery of what I may call instrumental personality he possessed to a hitherto undreamed-of degree. Nor has any one since equalled him in it. The result is a choice and variety of instrumentation which in itself is almost an equivalent for dramatic action and enables the orchestra to adapt itself with unerring accuracy to the varying phases of the drama.

Consider that, when Wagner first projected his theory of the music-drama, singers were accustomed in opera to step into the limelight and, standing there, deliver themselves of set melodies, acknowledge applause and give as many encores as were called for, in fact were "it," while the real creative thing, the opera, was but secondary, and it is easy to comprehend the opposition which his works aroused among the personnel of the lyric stage; for music-drama demands a singer's absorption not only in the music but also in the action. A Wagner music-drama requires great singers, but the singers no longer absorb everything. They are part—a most important part, it is true—of a performance, in which the drama itself, the orchestra, and the stage pictures are also of great importance. A performance of a Wagner

Richard Wagner

music-drama, to be effective, must be a well-rounded, eloquent whole. The drama must be well acted from a purely dramatic point of view. It must be well sung from a purely vocal point of view. It must be well interpreted from a purely orchestral point of view. It must be well produced from a purely stage point of view. For all these elements go hand in hand. It is, of course, well known that Wagner was the author of his own librettos and showed himself a dramatist of the highest order for the lyric stage.

While his music-dramas at first aroused great opposition among operatic artists, growing familiarity with them caused these artists to change their view. The interpretation of a Wagner character was discovered to be a combined intellectual and emotional task which slowly, but surely, appealed more and more to the great singers of the lyric stage. They derived a new dignity and satisfaction from their work, especially as audiences also began to realize that, instead of mere entertainment, performances of Wagner music-dramas were experiences that both stirred the emotions to their depths and appealed to the intellect as well. To this day Lilli Lehmann is regarded by all, who had the good fortune to hear her at the Metropolitan Opera House, as the greatest prima donna and the most dignified figure in the history of the lyric stage in this country; for on the lyric stage the interpretation of the great characters in Wagnerian music-drama already had come to be regarded as equal to the interpretation of the great Shakespearian characters on the dramatic.

Wagner's genius was so supreme that, although he has been dead thirty-four years, he is still without a successor. Through the force of his own genius he appears destined to remain the sole exponent of the art form of which he was the creator. But his influence is still potent. This we discover not only in the enrichment of the orchestral accompaniment in opera, but in the banishment of sense-

The Complete Opera Book

less vocal embellishment, in the search for true dramatic expression and, in general, in the greater seriousness with which opera is taken as an art. Even the minor point of lowering the lights in the auditorium during a performance, so as to concentrate attention upon the stage, is due to him; and even the older Italian operas are now given with an attention to detail, scenic setting, and an endeavour to bring out their dramatic effects, quite unheard of before his day. He was, indeed, a reformer of the lyric stage whose influence long will be potent "all along the line."

RIENZI, DER LETZTE DER TRIBUNEN

RIENZI, THE LAST OF THE TRIBUNES

Opera in five acts. Words and music by Wagner. Produced, Dresden, October 20, 1842. London, Her Majesty's Theatre, April 16, 1869. New York, Academy of Music, 1878, with Charles R. Adams, as *Rienzi*, Pappenheim as *Adriano;* Metropolitan Opera House, February 5, 1886, with Sylva as *Rienzi*, Lehmann as *Irene*, Brandt as *Adriano*, Fischer as *Colonna*.

CHARACTERS

COLA RIENZI, Roman Tribune and Papal Notary	Tenor
IRENE, his sister	Soprano
STEFFANO COLONNA	Bass
ADRIANO, his son	Mezzo Soprano
PAOLO ORSINO	Bass
RAIMONDO, Papal Legate	Bass
BARONCELLO } Roman citizens	Tenor
CECCO DEL VECCHIO }	Bass
MESSENGER OF PEACE	Soprano

Ambassadors, Nobles, Priests, Monks, Soldiers, Messengers, and Populace in General.

Time—Middle of the Fourteenth Century. *Place*—Rome.

Orsino, a Roman patrician, attempts to abduct *Irene*, the sister of *Rienzi*, a papal notary, but is opposed at the critical moment by *Colonna*, another patrician. A fight ensues between the two factions, in the midst of which

Richard Wagner

Adriano, the son of *Colonna*, who is in love with *Irene*, appears to defend her. A crowd is attracted by the tumult, and among others *Rienzi* comes upon the scene. Enraged at the insult offered his sister, and stirred on by *Cardinal Raimondo*, he urges the people to resist the outrages of the nobles. *Adriano* is impelled by his love for *Irene* to cast his lot with her brother. The nobles are overpowered, and appear at the capitol to swear allegiance to *Rienzi*, but during the festal proceedings *Adriano* warns him that the nobles have plotted to kill him. An attempt which *Orsino* makes upon him with a dagger is frustrated by a steel breastplate which *Rienzi* wears under his robe.

The nobles are seized and condemned to death, but on *Adriano's* pleading they are spared. They, however, violate their oath of submission, and the people again under *Rienzi's* leadership rise and exterminate them, *Adriano* having pleaded in vain. In the end the people prove fickle. The popular tide turns against *Rienzi*, especially in consequence of the report that he is in league with the German emperor, and intends to restore the Roman pontiff to power. As a festive procession is escorting him to church, *Adriano* rushes upon him with a drawn dagger, being infuriated at the slaughter of his family, but the blow is averted. Instead of the "Te Deum," however, with which *Rienzi* expected to be greeted on his entrance to the church, he hears the malediction and sees the ecclesiastical dignitaries placing the ban of excommunication against him upon the doors. *Adriano* hurries to *Irene* to warn her of her brother's danger, and urges her to seek safety with him in flight. She, however, repels him, and seeks her brother, determined to die with him, if need be. She finds him at prayer in the capitol, but rejects his counsel to save herself with *Adriano*. *Rienzi* appeals to the infuriated populace which has gathered around the

The Complete Opera Book

capitol, but they do not heed him. They fire the capitol with their torches, and hurl stones at *Rienzi* and *Irene*. As *Adriano* sees his beloved one and her brother doomed to death in the flames, he throws away his sword, rushes into the capitol, and perishes with them.

The overture of "Rienzi" gives a vivid idea of the action of the opera. Soon after the beginning there is heard the broad and stately melody of *Rienzi's* prayer, and then the Rienzi Motive, a typical phrase, which is used with great effect later in the opera. It is followed in the overture by the lively melody heard in the concluding portion of the finale of the second act. These are the three most conspicuous portions of the overture, in which there are, however, numerous tumultuous passages reflecting the dramatic excitement which pervades many scenes.

The opening of the first act is full of animation, the orchestra depicting the tumult which prevails during the struggle between the nobles. *Rienzi's* brief recitative is a masterpiece of declamatory music, and his call to arms is spirited. It is followed by a trio between *Irene, Rienzi,* and *Adriano,* and this in turn by a duet for the two last-named which is full of fire. The finale opens with a double chorus for the populace and the monks in the Lateran, accompanied by the organ. Then there is a broad and energetic appeal to the people from *Rienzi,* and amid the shouts of the populace and the ringing tones of the trumpets the act closes.

The insurrection of the people against the nobles is successful, and *Rienzi,* in the second act, awaits at the capitol the patricians who are to pledge him their submission. The act opens with a broad and stately march, to which the messengers of peace enter. They sing a graceful chorus. This is followed by a chorus for the senators, and the nobles then tender their submission. There is a

Richard Wagner

terzetto, between *Adriano*, *Colonna*, and *Orsino*, in which the nobles express their contempt for the young patrician. The finale which then begins is highly spectacular. There is a march for the ambassadors, and a grand ballet, historical in character, and supposed to be symbolical of the triumphs of ancient Rome. In the midst of this occurs the assault upon *Rienzi*. *Rienzi's* pardon of the nobles is conveyed in a broadly beautiful melody, and this is succeeded by the animated passage heard in the overture. With it are mingled the chants of the monks, the shouts of the people who are opposed to the cardinal and nobles, and the tolling of bells.

The third act opens tumultuously. The people have been aroused by fresh outrages on the part of the nobles. *Rienzi's* emissaries disperse, after a furious chorus, to rouse the populace to vengeance. After they have left, *Adriano* has his great air, a number which can never fail of effect when sung with all the expression of which it is capable. The rest of the act is a grand accumulation of martial music or noise, whichever one chooses to call it, and includes the stupendous battle hymn, which is accompanied by the clashing of sword and shields, the ringing of bells, and all the tumult incidental to a riot. After *Adriano* has pleaded in vain with *Rienzi* for the nobles, and the various bands of armed citizens have dispersed, there is a duet between *Adriano* and *Irene*, in which *Adriano* takes farewell of her. The victorious populace appears and the act closes with their triumphant shouts. The fourth act is brief, and beyond the description given in the synopsis of the plot, requires no further comment.

The fifth act opens with the beautiful prayer of *Rienzi*, already familiar from the overture. There is a tender duet between *Rienzi* and *Irene*, an impassioned aria for *Rienzi*, a duet for *Irene* and *Adriano*, and then the finale, which is chiefly choral.

The Complete Opera Book

DER FLIEGENDE HOLLÄNDER

THE FLYING DUTCHMAN

Opera in three acts, words and music by Richard Wagner. Produced, Royal Opera, Dresden, January 2, 1843. London, July 23, 1870, as "L'Olandese Dannato"; October 3, 1876, by Carl Rosa, in English. New York, Academy of Music, January 26, 1877, in English, with Clara Louise Kellogg; March 12, 1877, in German; in the spring of 1883, in Italian, with Albani, Galassi, and Ravelli.

CHARACTERS

DALAND, a Norwegian sea captain.....................Bass
SENTA, his daughter................................Soprano
ERIC, a huntsman...................................Tenor
MARY, SENTA'S nurse..............................Contralto
DALAND'S Steersman.................................Tenor
THE DUTCHMAN....................................Baritone
            Sailors, Maidens, Hunters, etc.

Time—Eighteenth Century.   *Place*—A Norwegian Fishing Village.

From "Rienzi" Wagner took a great stride to "The Flying Dutchman." This is the first milestone on the road from opera to music-drama. Of his "Rienzi" the composer was in after years ashamed, writing to Liszt: "I, as an artist and man, have not the heart for the reconstruction of that, to my taste, superannuated work, which in consequence of its immoderate dimensions, I have had to remodel more than once. I have no longer the heart for it, and desire from all my soul to do something new instead." He spoke of it as a youthful error, but in "The Flying Dutchman" there is little, if anything, which could have troubled his artistic conscience.

One can hardly imagine the legend more effective dramatically and musically than it is in Wagner's libretto and score. It is a work of wild and sombre beauty, relieved only occasionally by touches of light and grace, and has all the interest attaching to a work in which for the first time a genius feels himself conscious of his greatness. If

Richard Wagner

it is not as impressive as "Tannhäuser" or "Lohengrin," nor as stupendous as the music-dramas, that is because the subject of the work is lighter. As his genius developed, his choice of subjects and his treatment of them passed through as complete an evolution as his musical theory, so that when he finally abandoned the operatic form and adopted his system of leading motives, he conceived, for the dramatic bases of his scores, dramas which it would be difficult to fancy set to any other music than that which is so characteristic in his music-dramas.

Wagner's present libretto is based upon the weirdly picturesque legend of "The Flying Dutchman"—the Wandering Jew of the ocean. A Dutch sea-captain, who, we are told, tried to double the Cape of Good Hope in the teeth of a furious gale, swore that he would accomplish his purpose even if he kept on sailing forever. The devil, hearing the oath, condemned the captain to sail the sea until Judgment Day, without hope of release, unless he should find a woman who would love him faithfully unto death. Once in every seven years he is allowed to go ashore in search of a woman who will redeem him through her faithful love.

The opera opens just as a term of seven years has elapsed. The *Dutchman's* ship comes to anchor in a bay of the coast of Norway, in which the ship of *Daland*, a Norwegian sea-captain, has sought shelter from the storm. *Daland's* home is not far from the bay, and the *Dutchman*, learning he has a daughter, asks permission to woo her, offering him in return all his treasures. *Daland* readily consents. His daughter, *Senta*, is a romantic maiden upon whom the legend of "The Flying Dutchman" has made a deep impression. As *Daland* ushers the *Dutchman* into his home *Senta* is gazing dreamily upon a picture representing the unhappy hero of the legend. The resemblance of the stranger to the face in this picture is so striking that the emotional girl is at once attracted to him, and pledges him her faith, deeming it her mission to save him. Later on, *Eric*, a young huntsman, who is in love with her, pleads his cause with her, and the *Dutchman*, overhearing them, and thinking himself again forsaken, rushes off to his vessel. *Senta* cries out that she is faithful to him, but is held back by *Eric*, *Daland*, and her friends. The *Dutchman*, who really loves *Senta*, then proclaims who he is, thinking to terrify her, and at once puts to sea. But she, undismayed by his words, and truly faithful unto death, breaks away from those who are holding her, and rushing to the edge of a cliff casts herself into the ocean, with her arms outstretched toward him. The phantom ship sinks, the sea rises high and falls back into a seething whirlpool. In the sunset glow the forms of *Senta* and the *Dutchman* are seen rising in each other's embrace from the sea and floating upward.

In "The Flying Dutchman" Wagner employs several leading motives, not, indeed, with the skill which he displays in his music-dramas, but with considerably greater freedom of treatment than in "Rienzi." There we had but one leading motive, which never varied in form. The overture, which may be said to be an eloquent and beautiful musical narrative of the whole opera, contains all these leading motives. It opens with a stormy passage, out of which there bursts the strong but sombre Motive of the Flying Dutchman himself, the dark hero of the legend. The orchestra fairly seethes and rages like the sea roaring under the lash of a terrific storm. And through all this furious orchestration there is heard again and again the motive of the *Dutchman*, as if his figure could be seen amid all the gloom and fury of the elements. There he stands, hoping for death, yet indestructible. As the excited music gradually dies away, there is heard a calm, somewhat undulating phrase which occurs in the opera when the

Richard Wagner

Dutchman's vessel puts into the quiet Norwegian harbour. Then, also, there occurs again the motive of the *Dutchman*, but this time played softly, as if the storm-driven wretch had at last found a moment's peace.

We at once recognize to whom it is due that he has found this moment of repose, for we hear like prophetic measures the strains of the beautiful ballad which is sung by *Senta* in the second act of the opera, in which she relates the legend of "The Flying Dutchman" and tells of his unhappy fate. She is the one whom he is to meet when he goes ashore. The entire ballad is not heard at this point, only the opening of the second part, which may be taken as indicating in this overture the simplicity and beauty of *Senta's* character. In fact, it would not be too much to call this opening phrase the Senta Motive. It is followed by the phrase which indicates the coming to anchor of the *Dutchman's* vessel; then we hear the Motive of the Dutchman himself, dying away with the faintest possible effect. With sudden energy the orchestra dashes into the surging ocean music, introducing this time the wild, pathetic plaint sung by the *Dutchman* in the first act of the opera. Again we hear his motive, and again the music seems to represent the surging, swirling ocean when aroused by a furious tempest. Even when we hear the measures of the sailors' chorus the orchestra continues its furious pace, making it appear as if the sailors were shouting above the storm.

Characteristic in this overture, and also throughout the opera, especially in *Senta's* ballad, is what may be called the Ocean Motive, which most graphically depicts the wild and terrible aspect of the ocean during a storm. It is varied from time to time, but never loses its characteristic force and weirdness. The overture ends with an impassioned burst of melody based upon a portion of the concluding phrases of *Senta's* ballad; phrases which we

The Complete Opera Book

hear once more at the end of the opera when she sacrifices herself in order to save her lover.

A wild and stormy scene is disclosed when the curtain rises upon the first act. The sea occupies the greater part of the scene, and stretches itself out far toward the horizon. A storm is raging. *Daland's* ship has sought shelter in a little cove formed by the cliffs. Sailors are employed in furling sails and coiling ropes. *Daland* is standing on a rock, looking about him to discover in what place they are. The orchestra, chiefly with the wild ocean music heard in the overture, depicts the raging of the storm, and above it are heard the shouts of the sailors at work: "Ho-jo-he! Hal-lo-jo!"

Daland discovers that they have missed their port by seven miles on account of the storm, and deplores his bad luck that when so near his home and his beloved child, he should have been driven out of his course. As the storm seems to be abating the sailors descend into the hold and *Daland* goes down into the cabin to rest, leaving his steersman in charge of the deck. The steersman walks the deck once or twice and then sits down near the rudder, yawning, and then rousing himself as if sleep were coming over him. As if to force himself to remain awake he intones a sailor song, an exquisite little melody, with a dash of the sea in its undulating measures. He intones the second verse, but sleep overcomes him and the phrases become more and more detached, until at last he falls asleep.

The storm begins to rage again and it grows darker. Suddenly the ship of the *Flying Dutchman*, with blood-red sails and black mast, looms up in the distance. She glides over the waves as if she did not feel the storm at all, and quickly enters the harbour over against the ship of the Norwegian; then silently and without the least noise the spectral crew furl the sails. The *Dutchman* goes on shore.

Richard Wagner

Here now occur the weird, dramatic recitative and aria: "The term is passed, and once again are ended seven long years." As the *Dutchman* leans in brooding silence against a rock in the foreground, *Daland* comes out of the cabin and observes the ship. He rouses the steersman, who begins singing again a phrase of his song, until *Daland* points out the strange vessel to him, when he springs up and hails her through a speaking trumpet. *Daland*, however, perceives the *Dutchman* and going ashore questions him. It is then that the *Dutchman*, after relating a mariner's story of ill luck and disaster, asks *Daland* to take him to his home and allow him to woo his daughter, offering him his treasures. At this point we have a graceful and pretty duet, *Daland* readily consenting that the *Dutchman* accompany him. The storm having subsided and the wind being fair, the crews of the vessels hoist sail to leave port, *Daland's* vessel disappearing just as the *Dutchman* goes on board his ship.

After an introduction in which we hear a portion of the steersman's song, and also that phrase which denotes the appearance of the *Dutchman's* vessel in the harbour, the curtain rises upon a room in *Daland's* house. On the walls are pictures of vessels, charts, and on the farther wall the portrait of a pale man with a dark beard. *Senta* leaning back in an armchair, is absorbed in dreamy contemplation of the portrait. Her old nurse, *Mary*, and her young friends are sitting in various parts of the room, spinning. Here we have that charming musical number famous all the musical world over, perhaps largely through Liszt's admirable piano arrangement of it, the "Spinning Chorus." For graceful and engaging beauty it cannot be surpassed, and may be cited as a striking instance of Wagner's gift of melody, should anybody at this late day be foolish enough to require proof of his genius in that respect. The girls tease *Senta* for gazing so dreamily at the portrait of the

The Complete Opera Book

Flying Dutchman, and finally ask her if she will not sing his ballad.

This ballad is a masterpiece of composition, vocally and intrumentally, being melodious as well as descriptive. It begins with the storm music familiar from the overture, and with the weird measures of the Flying Dutchman's Motive, which sound like a voice calling in distress across the sea.

Senta repeats the measures of this motive, and then we have the simple phrases beginning: "A ship the restless ocean sweeps." Throughout this portion of the ballad the orchestra depicts the surging and heaving of the ocean, *Senta's* voice ringing out dramatically above the accompaniment. She then tells how he can be delivered from his curse, this portion being set to the measures which were heard in the overture, *Senta* finally proclaiming, in the broadly

delivered, yet rapturous phrases with which the overture ends, that she is the woman who will save him by being faithful to him unto death. The girls about her spring up in terror and *Eric,* who has just entered the door and heard her outcry, hastens to her side. He brings news of the arrival of *Daland's* vessel, and *Mary* and the girls hasten forth to meet the sailors. *Senta* wishes to follow, but *Eric* restrains her and pleads his love for her in melodious measures. *Senta,* however, will not give him an answer at this time. He then tells her of a dream he has had, in which he saw a weird vessel from which two men, one her father, the other a ghastly-looking stranger, made their way. Her he saw going to the stranger and entreating him for his regard.

Richard Wagner

Senta, worked up to the highest pitch of excitement by *Eric's* words, now exclaims: "He seeks for me and I for him," and *Eric*, full of despair and horror, rushes away. *Senta*, after her outburst of excitement, remains again sunk in contemplation of the picture, softly repeating the measures of her romance. The door opens and the *Dutchman* and *Daland* appear. The *Dutchman* is the first to enter. *Senta* turns from the picture to him, and, uttering a loud cry of wonder, remains standing as if transfixed without removing her eyes from the *Dutchman*. *Daland*, seeing that she does not greet him, comes up to her. She seizes his hand and after a hasty greeting asks him who the stranger is. *Daland* tells her of the stranger's request, and leaves them alone. Then follows a duet for *Senta* and the *Dutchman*, with its broad, smoothly flowing melody and its many phrases of dramatic power, in which *Senta* gives herself up unreservedly to the hero of her romantic attachment, *Daland* finally entering and adding his congratulations to their betrothal. This scene closes the act.

The music of it re-echoes through the introduction of the next act and goes over into a vigorous sailors' chorus and dance. The scene shows a bay with a rocky shore. *Daland's* house is in the foreground on one side, the background is occupied by his and the *Dutchman's* ships, which lie near one another. The Norwegian ship is lighted up, and all the sailors are making merry on the deck. In strange contrast is the *Flying Dutchman's* vessel. An unnatural darkness hangs over it and the stillness of death reigns aboard. The sailors and the girls in their merrymaking call loudly toward the Dutch ship to join them, but no reply is heard from the weird vessel. Finally the sailors call louder and louder and taunt the crew of the other ship Then suddenly the sea, which has been quite calm, begins to rise. The storm wind whistles through the cordage of the strange vessel, and as dark bluish flames flare up in the rigging, the weird crew show themselves, and sing a wild chorus, which strikes terror into all the merrymakers. The girls have fled, and the Norwegian sailors quit their deck, making the sign of the cross. The crew of the Flying Dutchman observing this, disappear with shrill laughter. Over their ship comes the stillness of death. Thick darkness is spread over it and the air and the sea become calm as before.

Senta now comes with trembling steps out of the house. She is followed by *Eric*. He pleads with her and entreats her to remember his love for her, and speaks also of the encouragement which she once gave him. The *Dutchman* has entered unperceived and has been listening. *Eric* seeing him, at once recognizes the man of ghastly mien whom he saw in his vision. When the *Flying Dutchman* bids her farewell, because he deems himself abandoned, and *Senta* endeavours to follow him, *Eric* holds her and summons others to his aid. But, in spite of all resistance, *Senta* seeks to tear herself loose. Then it is that the *Flying Dutchman* proclaims who he is and puts to sea. *Senta*, however, freeing herself, rushes to a cliff overhanging the sea, and calling out,

"Praise thou thine angel for what he saith;
Here stand I faithful, yea, to death,"

casts herself into the sea. Then occurs the concluding tableau, the work ending with the portion of the ballad which brought the overture and spinning scene to a close

TANNHÄUSER

UND DER SÄNGERKRIEG AUF DEM WARTBURG

(AND THE SONG CONTEST AT THE WARTBURG)

Opera in three acts, words and music by Richard Wagner. Produced, Royal Opera, Dresden, October 19, 1845. Paris, Grand Opéra,

Von Rooy as The Flying Dutchman.

DESTINN AS ELIZABETH IN "TANNHÄUSER."

Facing p. 107]

Richard Wagner

March 13, 1861. London, Covent Garden, May 6, 1876, in Italian; Her Majesty's Theatre, February 14, 1882, in English; Drury Lane, May 23, 1882, in German, under Hans Richter. New York, Stadt Theatre, April 4, 1859, and July, 1861, conducted by Carl Bergmann; under Adolff Neuendorff's direction, 1870, and, Academy of Music, 1877; Metropolitan Opera House, opening night of German Opera, under Dr. Leopold Damrosch, November 17, 1884, with Seidl-Kraus as *Elizabeth*, Anna Slach as *Venus*, Schott as *Tannhäuser*, Adolf Robinson as *Wolfram*, Josef Kögel as the *Landgrave*.

CHARACTERS

HERMANN, Landgrave of Thuringia		*Bass*
TANNHÄUSER		*Tenor*
WOLFRAM VON ESCHENBACH		*Baritone*
WALTER VON DER VOGELWEIDE	Knights and	*Tenor*
BITEROLF	Minnesinger	*Bass*
HEINRICH DER SCHREIBER		*Tenor*
REINMAR VON ZWETER		*Bass*
ELIZABETH, niece of the Landgrave		*Soprano*
VENUS		*Soprano*
A YOUNG SHEPHERD		*Soprano*
FOUR NOBLE PAGES		*Soprano and Alto*

Nobles, Knights, Ladies, elder and younger Pilgrims, Sirens, Naiads, Nymphs, Bacchantes.

Time—Early Thirteenth Century.   *Place*—Near Eisenach.

The story of "Tannhäuser" is laid in and near the Wartburg, where, during the thirteenth century, the Landgraves of the Thuringian Valley held sway. They were lovers of art, especially of poetry and music, and at the Wartburg many peaceful contests between the famous minnesingers took place. Near this castle rises the Venusberg. According to tradition the interior of this mountain was inhabited by Holda, the Goddess of Spring, who, however, in time became identified with the Goddess of Love. Her court was filled with nymphs and sirens, and it was her greatest joy to entice into the mountain the knights of the Wartburg and hold them captive to her beauty.

The Complete Opera Book

Among those whom she has thus lured into the rosy recesses of the Venusberg is *Tannhäuser*.

In spite of her beauty, however, he is weary of her charms and longs for a glimpse of the world. He seems to have heard the tolling of bells and other earthly sounds, and these stimulate his yearning to be set free from the magic charms of the goddess.

In vain she prophesies evil to him should he return to the world. With the cry that his hope rests in the Virgin, he tears himself away from her. In one of the swiftest and most effective of scenic changes the court of *Venus* disappears and in a moment we see *Tannhäuser* prostrate before a cross in a valley upon which the Wartburg peacefully looks down. *Pilgrims* on their way to Rome pass him by and *Tannhäuser* thinks of joining them in order that at Rome he may obtain forgiveness for his crime in allowing himself to be enticed into the Venusberg. But at that moment the *Landgrave* and a number of minnesingers on their return from the chase come upon him and, recognizing him, endeavour to persuade him to return to the Wartburg with them. Their pleas, however, are vain, until one of them, *Wolfram von Eschenbach*, tells him that since he has left the Wartburg a great sadness has come over the niece of the *Landgrave, Elizabeth*. It is evident that *Tannhäuser* has been in love with her, and that it is because of her beauty and virtue that he regrets so deeply having been lured into the Vnussberg. For *Wolfram's* words stir him profoundly. To the great joy of all, he agrees to return to the Wartburg, the scene of his many triumphs as a minnesinger in the contests of song.

The *Landgrave*, feeling sure that *Tannhäuser* will win the prize at the contest of song soon to be held, offers the hand of his niece to the winner. The minnesingers sing tamely of the beauty of virtuous love, but *Tannhäuser*, suddenly remembering the seductive and magical beauties

Richard Wagner

of the Venusberg, cannot control himself, and bursts out into a reckless hymn in praise of *Venus*. Horrified at his words, the knights draw their swords and would slay him, but *Elizabeth* throws herself between him and them. Crushed and penitent, *Tannhäuser* stands behind her, and the *Landgrave*, moved by her willingness to sacrifice herself for her sinful lover, announces that he will be allowed to join a second band of pilgrims who are going to Rome and to plead with the Pope for forgiveness.

Elizabeth prayerfully awaits his return; but, as she is kneeling by the crucifix in front of the Wartburg, the *Pilgrims* pass her by and in the band she does not see her lover. Slowly and sadly she returns to the castle to die. When the *Pilgrims'* voices have died away, and *Elizabeth* has returned to the castle, leaving only *Wolfram*, who is also deeply enamoured of her, upon the scene, *Tannhäuser* appears, weary and dejected. He has sought to obtain forgiveness in vain. The Pope has cast him out forever, proclaiming that no more than that his staff can put forth leaves can he expect forgiveness. He has come back to re-enter the Venusberg. *Wolfram* seeks to restrain him, but it is not until he invokes the name of *Elizabeth* that *Tannhäuser* is saved. A cortège approaches, and, as *Tannhäuser* recognizes the form of *Elizabeth* on the bier, he sinks down on her coffin and dies. Just then the second band of pilgrims arrive, bearing *Tannhäuser's* staff, which has put forth blossoms, thus showing that his sins have been forgiven.

From "The Flying Dutchman" to "Tannhäuser," dramatically and musically, is, if anything, a greater stride than from "Rienzi" to "The Flying Dutchman." In each of his successive works Wagner demonstrates greater and deeper powers as a dramatic poet and composer. True it is that in nearly every one of them woman appears as the redeeming angel of sinful man, but the circumstances differ so that this beautiful tribute always interests us anew.

The overture of the opera has long been a favorite piece on concert programs. Like that of "The Flying Dutchman" it is the story of the whole opera told in music. It certainly is one of the most brilliant and effective pieces of orchestral music and its popularity is easily understood. It opens with the melody of the *Pilgrims'* chorus, beginning softly as if coming from a distance and gradually increasing in power until it is heard in all its grandeur. At this point it is joined by a violently agitated accompaniment on the violins. This passage evoked great criticism when it was first produced and for many years thereafter. It was thought to mar the beauty of the pilgrims' chorus. But without doing so at all it conveys additional dramatic meaning, for these agitated phrases depict the restlessness of the world as compared with the grateful tranquillity of religious faith as set forth in the melody of the *Pilgrims'* chorus.

Having reached a climax, this chorus gradually dies away, and suddenly, and with intense dramatic contrast, we have all the seductive spells of the Venusberg displayed before us—that is, musically displayed; but then the music is so wonderfully vivid, it depicts with such marvellous clearness the many-coloured alluring scene at the court of the unholy goddess, it gives vent so freely to the sinful excitement which pervades the Venusberg, that we actually seem to see what we hear. This passes over in turn to the impassioned burst of song in which *Tannhäuser* hymns Venus's praise, and immediately after we have the boisterous and vigorous music which accompanies the

Richard Wagner

threatening action of the *Landgrave* and minnesingers when they draw their swords upon *Tannhäuser* in order to take vengeance upon him for his crimes. Upon these three episodes of the drama, which so characteristically give insight into its plot and action, the overture is based, and it very naturally concludes with the *Pilgrims'* chorus which seems to voice the final forgiveness of *Tannhäuser*.

The curtain rises, disclosing all the seductive spells of the Venusberg. *Tannhäuser* lies in the arms of *Venus*, who reclines upon a flowery couch. Nymphs, sirens, and satyrs are dancing about them and in the distance are grottoes alive with amorous figures. Various mythological amours, such as that of Leda and the swan, are supposed to be in progress, but fortunately at a mitigating distance.

Much of the music familiar from the overture is heard during this scene, but it gains in effect from the distant voices of the sirens and, of course, from artistic scenery and grouping and well-executed dances of the denizens of *Venus's* court. Very dramatic, too, is the scene between *Venus* and *Tannhäuser*, when the latter sings his hymn in her praise, but at the same time proclaims that he desires to return to the world. In alluring strains she endeavours to tempt him to remain with her, but when she discovers that he is bound upon going, she vehemently warns him of the misfortunes which await him upon earth and prophe-

The Complete Opera Book

sies that he will some day return to her and penitently ask to be taken back into her realm.

Dramatic and effective as this scene is in the original score, it has gained immensely in power by the additions which Wagner made for the production of the work in Paris, in 1861. The overture does not, in this version, come to a formal close, but after the manner of Wagner's later works, the transition is made directly from it to the scene of the Venusberg. The dances have been elaborated and laid out upon a more careful allegorical basis and the music of *Venus* has been greatly strengthened from a dramatic point of view, so that now the scene in which she pleads with him to remain and afterwards warns him against the sorrows to which he will be exposed, are among the finest of Wagner's compositions, rivalling in dramatic power the ripest work in his music-dramas.

Wagner's knowledge of the stage is shown in the wonderfully dramatic effect in the change of scene from the Venusberg to the landscape in the valley of the Wartburg. One moment we have the variegated allures of the court of the Goddess of Love, with its dancing nymphs, sirens, and satyrs, its beautiful grottoes and groups; the next all this has disappeared and from the heated atmosphere of *Venus's* unholy rites we are suddenly transported to a peaceful scene whose influence upon us is deepened by the crucifix in the foreground, before which *Tannhäuser* kneels in penitence. The peacefulness of the scene is further enhanced by the appearance upon a rocky eminence to the left of a young *Shepherd* who pipes a pastoral strain, while in the background are heard the tinkling of bells, as though his sheep were there grazing upon some upland meadow. Before he has finished piping his lay the voices of the *Pilgrims* are heard in the distance, their solemn measures being interrupted by little phrases piped by the *Shepherd*. As the *Pilgrims* approach, the chorus becomes

Richard Wagner

louder, and as they pass over the stage and bow before the crucifix, their praise swells into an eloquent psalm of devotion.

Tannhäuser is deeply affected and gives way to his feelings in a lament, against which are heard the voices of the *Pilgrims* as they recede in the distance. This whole scene is one of marvellous beauty, the contrast between it and the preceding episode being enhanced by the religiously tranquil nature of what transpires and of the accompanying music. Upon this peaceful scene the notes of hunting-horns now break in, and gradually the *Landgrave* and his hunters gather about *Tannhäuser*. *Wolfram* recognizes him and tells the others who he is. They greet him in an expressive septette, and *Wolfram*, finding he is bent upon following the *Pilgrims* to Rome, asks permission of the *Landgrave* to inform him of the impression which he seems to have made upon *Elizabeth*. This he does in a melodious solo, and *Tannhäuser*, overcome by his love for *Elizabeth*, consents to return to the halls which have missed him so long. Exclamations of joy greet his decision, and the act closes with an enthusiastic *ensemble*, which is a glorious piece of concerted music, and never fails of brilliant effect when it is well executed, especially if the representative of *Tannhäuser* has a voice that can soar above the others, which, unfortunately, is not always the case. The accompanying scenic grouping should also be in keeping with the composer's instructions. The *Landgrave's* suite should gradually arrive, bearing the game which has been slain, and horses and hunting-hounds should be led on the stage. Finally, the *Landgrave* and minnesingers mount their steeds and ride away toward the castle.

The scene of the second act is laid in the singers' hall of the Wartburg. The introduction depicts *Elizabeth's* joy at *Tannhäuser's* return, and when the curtain rises she at once enters and joyfully greets the scenes of *Tannhäuser's*

The Complete Opera Book

former triumphs in broadly dramatic melodious phrases. *Wolfram* then appears, conducting *Tannhäuser* to her. *Elizabeth* seems overjoyed to see him, but then checks herself, and her maidenly modesty, which veils her transport at meeting him, again finds expression in a number of hesitating but exceedingly beautiful phrases. She asks *Tannhäuser* where he has been, but he, of course, gives misleading answers. Finally, however, he tells her she is the one who has attracted him back to the castle. Their love finds expression in a swift and rapidly flowing dramatic duet, which unfortunately is rarely given in its entirety, although as a glorious outburst of emotional music it certainly deserves to be heard in the exact form and length in which the composer wrote it.

There is then a scene of much tender feeling between the *Landgrave* and *Elizabeth*, in which the former tells her that he will offer her hand as prize to the singer whom she shall crown as winner. The first strains of the grand march are then heard. This is one of Wagner's most brilliant and effective orchestral and vocal pieces. Though in perfect march rythm, it is not intended that the guests who assembled at the Wartburg shall enter like a company of soldiers. On the contrary, they arrive in irregular detachments, stride across the floor, and make their obeisance in a perfectly natural manner. After an address by the *Landgrave*, which can hardly be called remarkably interesting, the singers draw lots to decide who among them shall begin. This prize singing is, unfortunately, not so great in musical value as the rest of the score, and, unless a person understands the words, it is decidedly long drawn out. What, however, redeems it is a gradually growing dramatic excitement as *Tannhäuser* voices his contempt for what seem to him the tame tributes paid to love by the minnesingers, an excitement which reaches its climax when, no longer able to restrain

Richard Wagner

himself, he bursts forth into his hymn in praise of the unholy charms of *Venus*.

The women cry out in horror and rush from the hall as if the very atmosphere were tainted by his presence, and the men, drawing their swords, rush upon him. This brings us to the great dramatic moment, when, with a shriek, *Elizabeth*, in spite of his betrayal of her love, throws herself protectingly before him, and thus appears a second time as his saving angel. In short and excited phrases the men pour forth their wrath at *Tannhäuser's* crime in having sojourned with *Venus*, and he, realizing its enormity, seems crushed with a consciousness of his guilt. Of wondrous beauty is the septette, "An angel has from heaven descended," which rises to a magnificent climax and is one of the finest pieces of dramatic writing in Wagner's scores, although often execrably sung and rarely receiving complete justice. The voices of young *Pilgrims* are heard in the valley. The *Landgrave* then announces the conditions upon which *Tannhäuser* can again obtain forgiveness, and *Tannhäuser* joins the pilgrims on their way to Rome.

The third act displays once more the valley of the Wartburg, the same scene as that to which the Venusberg changed in the first act. *Elizabeth*, arrayed in white, is kneeling, in deep prayer, before the crucifix. At one side, and watching her tenderly, stands *Wolfram*. After a sad recitative from *Wolfram*, the chorus of returning *Pilgrims* is heard in the distance. They sing the melody heard in the overture and in the first act; and the same effect of gradual approach is produced by a superb crescendo as they reach and cross the scene. With almost piteous anxiety and grief *Elizabeth* scans them closely as they go

The Complete Opera Book

by, to see if *Tannhäuser* be among them, and when the last one has passed and she realizes that he has not returned, she sinks again upon her knees before the crucifix and sings the prayer, "Almighty Virgin, hear my sorrow," music in which there is most beautifully combined the expression of poignant grief with trust in the will of the Almighty. As she rises and turns toward the castle, *Wolfram*, by his gesture, seems to ask her if he cannot accompany her, but she declines his offer and slowly goes her way up the mountain.

Meanwhile night has fallen upon the scene and the evening star glows softly above the castle. It is then that *Wolfram*, accompanying himself on his lyre, intones the wondrously tender and beautiful "Song to the Evening Star," confessing therein his love for the saintly *Elizabeth*.

Then *Tannhäuser*, dejected, footsore, and weary, appears and in broken accents asks *Wolfram* to show him the way back to the Venusberg. *Wolfram* bids him stay his steps and persuades him to tell him the story of his pilgrimage. In fierce, dramatic accents, *Tannhäuser* relates all that he has suffered on his way to Rome and the terrible judgment pronounced upon him by the Pope. This is a highly impressive episode, clearly foreshadowing Wagner's dramatic use of musical recitative in his later music-dramas. Only a singer of the highest rank can do justice to it.

Tannhäuser proclaims that, having lost all chance of salvation, he will once more give himself up to the delights of the Venusberg. A roseate light illumines the recesses of the mountain and the unholy company of the Venusberg again is seen, *Venus* stretching out her arms for *Tannhäuser*, to welcome him. But at last, when *Tannhäuser*

Richard Wagner

seems unable to resist *Venus'* enticing voice any longer, *Wolfram* conjures him by the memory of the sainted *Elizabeth*. Then *Venus* knows that all is lost. The light dies away and the magic charms of the Venusberg disappear. Amid tolling of bells and mournful voices a funeral procession comes down the mountain. Recognizing the features of *Elizabeth*, the dying *Tannhäuser* falls upon her corpse. The younger pilgrims arrive with the staff, which has again put forth leaves, and amid the hallelujahs of the pilgrims the opera closes.

Besides the character of *Elizabeth* that of *Wolfram* stands out for its tender, manly beauty. In love with *Elizabeth*, he is yet the means of bringing back her lover to her, and in the end saves that lover from perdition, so that they may be united in death.

LOHENGRIN

Opera in three acts, by Richard Wagner. Produced, Weimar, Germany, August 28, 1850, under the direction of Franz Liszt; London, Covent Garden, May 8, 1875; New York, Stadt Theater, in German, April 3, 1871; Academy of Music, in Italian, March 23, 1874, with Nilsson, Cary, Campanini, and Del Puente; Metropolitan Opera House, in German, November 23, 1885, with Seidl-Kraus, Brandt, Stritt, Robinson, and Fischer, American début of Anton Seidl as conductor.

Characters

HENRY THE FOWLER, King of Germany .... *Bass*
LOHENGRIN .... *Tenor*
ELSA OF BRABANT .... *Soprano*
DUKE GODFREY, her brother .... *Mute*
FREDERICK OF TELRAMUND, Count of Brabant .... *Baritone*
ORTRUD, his wife .... *Mezzo-Soprano*
THE KING'S HERALD .... *Bass*
Saxon, Thuringian, and Brabantian Counts and Nobles, Ladies of Honour, Pages, Attendants.

Time—First half of the Tenth Century.   *Scene*—Antwerp.

The Complete Opera Book

The circumstances attending the creation and first production of "Lohengrin" are most interesting.

Prior to and for more than a decade after he wrote and composed the work Wagner suffered many vicissitudes. In Paris, where he lived from hand to mouth before "Rienzi" was accepted by the Royal Opera House at Dresden, he was absolutely poverty-stricken and often at a loss how to procure the next meal.

"Rienzi" was produced at the Dresden Opera in 1842. It was brilliantly successful. "The Flying Dutchman," which followed, was less so, and "Tannhäuser" seemed even less attractive to its early audiences. Therefore it is no wonder that, although Wagner was royal conductor in Dresden, he could not succeed in having "Lohengrin" accepted there for performance. Today "Rienzi" hardly can be said to hold its own in the repertoire outside of its composer's native country. The sombre beauty of "The Flying Dutchman," though recognized by musicians and serious music lovers, has prevented its becoming popular. But "Tannhäuser," looked at so askance at first, and "Lohengrin," absolutely rejected, are standard operas and, when well given, among the most popular works of the lyric stage. Especially is this true of "Lohengrin."

This opera, at the time of its composition so novel and so strange, yet filled with beauties of orchestration and harmony that are now quoted as leading examples in books on these subjects, was composed in less than a year. The acts were finished almost, if not quite, in reversed order. For Wagner wrote the third act first, beginning it in September, 1846, and completing it March 5, 1847. The first act occupied him from May 12th to June 8th, less than a month; the second act from June 18th to August 2d. Fresh and beautiful as "Lohengrin" still sounds today, it is, in fact, a classic.

Wagner's music, however, was so little understood at

Richard Wagner

the time, that even before "Lohengrin" was produced and not a note of it had been heard, people made fun of it. A lithographer named Meser had issued Wagner's previous three scores, but the enterprise had not been a success. People said that before publishing "Rienzi," Meser had lived on the first floor. "Rienzi" had driven him to the second; "The Flying Dutchman" and "Tannhäuser" to the third; and now "Lohengrin" would drive him to the garret—a prophecy that didn't come true, because he refused to publish it.

In 1849, "Lohengrin" still not having been accepted by the Dresden Opera, Wagner, as already has been stated, took part in the May revolution, which, apparently successful for a very short time, was quickly suppressed by the military. The composer of "Lohengrin" and the future composer of the "Ring of the Nibelung," "Tristan und Isolde," "Meistersinger," and "Parsifal," is said to have made his escape from Dresden in the disguise of a coachman. Occasionally there turns up in sales as a great rarity a copy of the warrant for Wagner's arrest issued by the Dresden police. As it gives a description of him at the time when he had but recently composed "Lohengrin," I will quote it:

"Wagner is thirty-seven to thirty-eight years of age, of medium stature, has brown hair, an open forehead; eyebrows, brown; eyes, greyish blue; nose and mouth, proportioned; chin, round, and wears spectacles. Special characteristics: rapid in movements and speech. Dress: coat of dark green buckskin, trousers of black cloth, velvet vest, silk neckerchief, ordinary felt hat and boots."

Much fun has been made of the expression "chin, round, and wears spectacles." Wagner got out of Dresden on the pass of a Dr. Widmann, whom he resembled. It has been suggested that he made the resemblance still closer by discontinuing the habit of wearing spectacles on his chin.

I saw Wagner several times in Bayreuth in the summer of 1882, when I attended the first performance of "Parsifal," as correspondent by cable and letter for one of the large New York dailies. Except that his hair was grey (and that he no longer wore his spectacles on his chin) the description in the warrant still held good, especially as regards his rapidity of movement and speech, to which I may add a marked vivacity of gesture. There, too, I saw the friend, who had helped him over so many rough places in his early career, Franz Liszt, his hair white with age, but framing a face as strong and keen as an eagle's. I saw them seated at a banquet, and with them Cosima, Liszt's daughter, who was Wagner's second wife, and their son, Siegfried Wagner; Cosima the image of her father, and Siegfried a miniature replica of the composer to whom we owe "Lohengrin" and the music-dramas that followed it. The following summer one of the four was missing. I have the "Parsifal" program with mourning border signifying that the performances of the work were in memory of its creator.

In April, 1850, Wagner, then an exile in Zurich, wrote to Liszt: "Bring out my 'Lohengrin!' You are the only one to whom I would put this request; to no one but you would I entrust the production of this opera; but to you I surrender it with the fullest, most joyous confidence."

Wagner himself describes the appeal and the result, by saying that at a time when he was ill, unhappy, and in despair, his eye fell on the score of "Lohengrin" which he had almost forgotten. "A pitiful feeling overcame me that these tones would never resound from the deathly-pale paper; two words I wrote to Liszt, the answer to which was nothing else than the information that, as far as the resources of the Weimar Opera permitted, the most

Richard Wagner

elaborate preparations were being made for the production of 'Lohengrin.'"

Liszt's reply to which Wagner refers, and which gives some details regarding "the elaborate preparations," while testifying to his full comprehension of Wagner's genius and the importance of his new score as a work of art, may well cause us to smile today at the small scale on which things were done in 1850.

"Your 'Lohengrin,'" he wrote, "will be given under conditions that are most unusual and most favourable for its success. The direction will spend on this occasion almost 2000 thalers [about $1500]—a sum unprecedented at Weimar within memory of man . . . the bass clarinet has been bought," etc. Ten times fifteen hundred dollars might well be required today for a properly elaborate production of "Lohengrin," and the opera orchestra that had to send out and buy a bass clarinet would be a curiosity. But Weimar had what no other opera house could boast of—Franz Liszt as conductor.

Under his brilliant direction "Lohengrin" had at Weimar its first performance on any stage, August 28, 1850. This was the anniversary of Goethe's birth, the date of the dedication of the Weimar monument to the poet, Herder, and, by a coincidence that does not appear to have struck either Wagner or Liszt, the third anniversary of the completion of "Lohengrin." The work was performed without cuts and before an audience which included some of the leading musical and literary men of Germany. The performance made a deep impression. The circumstance that Liszt added the charm of his personality to it and that the weight of his influence had been thrown in its favour alone gave vast importance to the event. Indeed, through Liszt's production of Wagner's early operas Weimar became, as Henry T. Finck has said in *Wagner and His Works*, a sort of preliminary Bayreuth. Occa-

The Complete Opera Book

sionally special opera trains were put on for the accommodation of visitors to the Wagner performances. In January, 1853, Liszt writes to Wagner that "the public interest in 'Lohengrin' is rapidly increasing. You are already very popular at the various Weimar hotels, where it is not easy to get a room on the days when your operas are given." The Liszt production of "Lohengrin" was a turning-point in his career, the determining influence that led him to throw himself heart and soul into the composition of the "Ring of the Nibelung."

On May 15, 1861, when, through the intervention of Princess Metternich, he had been permitted to return to Germany, fourteen years after he had finished "Lohengrin" and eleven years after its production at Weimar, he himself heard it for the first time at Vienna. A tragedy of fourteen years—to create a masterpiece of the lyric stage, and be forced to wait that long to hear it!

Before proceeding to a complete descriptive account of the "Lohengrin" story and music I will give a brief summary of the plot and a similar characterization of the score.

Wagner appears to have become so saturated with the subject of his dramas that he transported himself in mind and temperament to the very time in which his scenes are laid. So vividly does he portray the mythological occurrences told in "Lohengrin" that one can almost imagine he had been an eye-witness of them. This capacity of artistic reproduction of a remote period would alone entitle him to rank as a great dramatist. But he has done much more; he has taken unpromising material, which in the original is strung out over a period of years, and, by condensing the action to two days, has converted it into a swiftly moving drama.

The story of "Lohengrin" is briefly as follows: The Hungarians have invaded Germany, and *King Henry I.*

Richard Wagner

visits Antwerp for the purpose of raising a force to combat them. He finds the country in a condition of anarchy. The dukedom is claimed by *Frederick*, who has married *Ortrud*, a daughter of the Prince of Friesland. The legitimate heir, *Godfrey*, has mysteriously disappeared, and his sister, *Elsa*, is charged by *Frederick* and *Ortrud* with having done away with him in order that she might obtain the sovereignty. The *King* summons her before him so that the cause may be tried by the ordeal of single combat between *Frederick* and a champion who may be willing to appear for *Elsa*. None of the knights will defend her cause. She then describes a champion whose form has appeared to her in a vision, and she proclaims that he shall be her champion. Her pretence is derided by *Frederick* and his followers, who think that she is out of her mind; but after a triple summons by the *Herald*, there is seen in the distance on the river, a boat drawn by a swan, and in it a knight clad in silver armour. He comes to champion *Elsa's* cause, and before the combat betroths himself to her, but makes a strict condition that she shall never question him as to his name or birthplace, for should she, he would be obliged to depart. She assents to the conditions, and the combat which ensues results in *Frederick's* ignominious defeat. Judgment of exile is pronounced on him.

Instead, however, of leaving the country he lingers in the neighbourhood of Brabant, plotting with *Ortrud* how they may compass the ruin of *Lohengrin* and *Elsa*. *Ortrud* by her entreaties moves *Elsa* to pity, and persuades her to seek a reprieve for *Frederick*, at the same time, however, using every opportunity to instil doubts in *Elsa's* mind regarding her champion, and rousing her to such a pitch of nervous curiosity that she is on the point of asking him the forbidden question. After the bridal ceremonies, and in the bridal chamber, the distrust which *Ortrud* and *Frederick* have engendered in *Elsa's* mind so overcomes her

The Complete Opera Book

faith that she vehemently puts the forbidden question to her champion. Almost at the same moment *Frederick* and four of his followers force their way into the apartment, intending to take the knight's life. A single blow of his sword, however, stretches *Frederick* lifeless, and his followers bear his corpse away. Placing *Elsa* in the charge of her ladies-in-waiting, and ordering them to take her to the presence of the *King*, he repairs thither himself.

The Brabantian hosts are gathering, and he is expected to lead them to battle, but owing to *Elsa's* question he is now obliged to disclose who he is and to take his departure. He proclaims that he is *Lohengrin*, son of Parsifal, Knight of the Holy Grail, and that he can linger no longer in Brabant, but must return to the place of his coming. The swan has once more appeared, drawing the boat down the river, and bidding *Elsa* farewell he steps into the little shell-like craft. Then *Ortrud*, with malicious glee, declares that the swan is none other than *Elsa's* brother, whom she (*Ortrud*) bewitched into this form, and that he would have been changed back again to his human shape had it not been for *Elsa's* rashness. But *Lohengrin*, through his supernatural powers, is able to undo *Ortrud's* work, and at a word from him the swan disappears and *Godfrey* stands in its place. A dove now descends, and, hovering in front of the boat, draws it away with *Lohengrin*, while *Elsa* expires in her brother's arms.

Owing to the lyric character of the story upon which "Lohengrin" is based, the opera, while not at all lacking in strong dramatic situations is characterized by a subtler and more subdued melodiousness than "Tannhäuser," is more exquisitely lyrical in fact than any Wagnerian work except "Parsifal."

There are typical themes in the score, but they are hardly handled with the varied effect that entitles them to be called leading motives. On the other hand there are

SEMBACH AS LOHENGRIN.

EMMA EAMES AS ELSA IN "LOHENGRIN."

Richard Wagner

fascinating details of orchestration. These are important because the composer has given significant clang-tints to the music that is heard in connection with the different characters in the story. He uses the brass chiefly to accompany the *King*, and, of course, the martial choruses; the plaintive, yet spiritual high wood-wind for *Elsa;* the English horn and sombre bass clarinet—the instrument that had to be bought—for *Ortrud;* the violins, especially in high harmonic positions, to indicate the Grail and its representative, for *Lohengrin* is a Knight of the Holy Grail. Even the keys employed are distinctive. The *Herald's* trumpeters blow in C and greet the *King's* arrival in that bright key. F sharp minor is the dark, threatful key that indicates *Ortrud's* appearance. The key of A, which is the purest for strings and the most ethereal in effect, on account of the greater ease of using "harmonics," announces the approach of *Lohengrin* and the subtle influence of the Grail.

Moreover Wagner was the first composer to discover that celestial effects of tone-colour are produced by the prolonged notes of the combined violins and wood-wind in the highest positions more truly than by the harp. It is the association of ideas with the Scriptures, wherein the harp frequently is mentioned, because it was the most perfected instrument of the period, that has led other composers to employ it for celestial tone-painting. But while no one appreciated the beauty of the harp more than Wagner, or has employed it with finer effect than he, his celestial tone-pictures with high-violins and wood-wind are distinctly more ecstatic than those of other composers.

The music clothes the drama most admirably. The Vospiel or Prelude immediately places the listener in the proper mood for the story which is to unfold itself, and for the score, vocal and instrumental, whose strains are to fall upon his ear.

The Prelude is based entirely upon one theme, a beau-

The Complete Opera Book

tiful one and expressive of the sanctity of the Grail, of which *Lohengrin* is one of the knights. Violins and flutes with long-drawn-out, ethereal chords open the Prelude. Then is heard on the violins, so divided as to heighten the delicacy of the effect, the Motive of the Grail, the cup in which the Saviour's blood is supposed to have been caught as it flowed from the wound in His side, while he was on the Cross. No modern book on orchestration is considered complete unless it quotes this passage from the score, which is at once the earliest and, after seventy years, still the most perfect example of the effect of celestial harmony produced on the high notes of the divided violin choir. This interesting passage in the score is as follows:

Although this is the only motive that occurs in the Prelude, the ear never wearies of it. Its effectiveness is due to the wonderful skill with which Wagner handles the theme, working it up through a superb crescendo to a magnificent climax, with all the splendours of Wagnerian orchestration, after which it dies away again to the ethereal harmonies with which it first greeted the listener.

Act I. The curtain, on rising, discloses a scene of unwonted life on the plain near the River Scheldt, where the stream winds toward Antwerp. On an elevated seat under a huge oak sits *King Henry I*. On either side are his Saxon and Thuringian nobles. Facing him with the knights of Brabant are *Count Frederick of Telramund* and his wife, *Ortrud*, daughter of the Prince of Friesland, of dark, almost forbidding beauty, and with a treacherous mingling of haughtiness and humility in her carriage

Richard Wagner

It is a strange tale the *King* has just heard fall from *Frederick of Telramund's* lips. *Henry* has assembled the Brabantians on the plain by the Scheldt in order to summon them to join his army and aid in checking the threatened invasion of Germany by the Hungarians. But he has found the Brabantians themselves torn by factional strife, some supporting, others opposing *Frederick* in his claim to the ducal succession of Brabant.

"Sire," says *Frederick*, when called upon by the *King* to explain the cause of the discord that has come upon the land, "the late Duke of Brabant upon his death-bed confided to me, his kinsman, the care of his two children, *Elsa* and her young brother *Godfrey*, with the right to claim the maid as my wife. But one day *Elsa* led the boy into the forest and returned alone. From her pale face and faltering lips I judged only too well of what had happened, and I now publicly accuse *Elsa* of having made away with her brother that she might be sole heir to Brabant and reject my right to her hand. Her hand! Horrified, I shrank from her and took a wife whom I could truly love. Now as nearest kinsman of the duke I claim this land as my own, my wife, too, being of the race that once gave a line of princes to Brabant."

So saying, he leads *Ortrud* forward, and she, lowering her dark visage, makes a deep obeisance to the *King*. To the latter but one course is open. A terrible accusation has been uttered, and an appeal must be made to the immediate judgment of God in trial by combat between *Frederick* and whoever may appear as champion for *Elsa*. Solemnly the *King* hangs his shield on the oak, the Saxons and Thuringians thrust the points of their swords into the ground, while the Brabantians lay theirs before them. The royal *Herald* steps forward. "Elsa, without delay appear!" he calls in a loud voice.

A sudden hush falls upon the scene, as a slender figure

robed in white slowly advances toward the *King*. It is *Elsa*. With her fair brow, gentle mien, and timid footsteps it seems impossible that she can be the object of *Frederick's* dire charge. But there are dark forces conspiring against her, of which none knows save her accuser and the wife he has chosen from the remoter North. In Friesland the weird rites of Odin and the ancient gods still had many secret adherents, *Ortrud* among them, and it is the hope of this heathenish woman, through the undoing of *Elsa*, and the accession of *Frederick* whom she has completely under her influence, to check the spread of the Christian faith toward the North and restore the rites of Odin in Brabant. To this end she is ready to bring all the black magic of which she secretly is mistress into play. What wonder that *Elsa*, as she encounters her malevolent gaze, lowers her eyes with a shudder!

Up to the moment of *Elsa's* entrance, the music is harsh and vigorous, reflecting *Frederick's* excitement as, incited by *Ortrud*, he brings forward his charge against *Elsa*. With her appearance a change immediately comes over the music. It is soft, gentle, and plaintive; not, however, entirely hopeless, as if the maiden, being conscious of her innocence, does not despair of her fate.

"Elsa," gently asks the King, "whom name you as your champion?" She answers as if in a trance; and it is at this point that the music of "Elsa's Dream" is heard. In the course of this, violins whisper the Grail Motive and in dreamy rapture *Elsa* sings, "I see, in splendour shining, a knight of glorious mien. His eyes rest upon me with tranquil gaze. He stands amid clouds beside a house of gold, and resting on his sword. Heaven has sent him to save me   He shall my champion be!"

The men regard each other in wonder. But a sneer curls around *Ortrud's* lips, and *Frederick* again proclaims his

Richard Wagner

readiness to prove his accusation in trial by combat for life and death.

"*Elsa*," the *King* asks once more, "whom have you chosen as your champion?"

"Him whom Heaven shall send me; and to him, whatever he shall ask of me, I freely will give, e'en though it be myself as bride!" Again there is heard the lovely, broad and flowing melody of which I have already spoken and which may be designated as the ELSA MOTIVE.

The *Herald* now stations his trumpeters at the corners of the plain and bids them blow a blast toward the four points of the compass. When the last echo has died away he calls aloud:

"He who in right of Heaven comes here to fight for *Elsa* of Brabant, let him step forth!"

The deep silence that follows is broken by *Frederick's* voice. "No one appears to repel my charge. 'Tis proven."

"My King," implores *Elsa*, whose growing agitation is watched by *Ortrud* with a malevolent smile, "my champion bides afar. He has not yet heard the summons. I pray you let it go forth once more."

Again the trumpeters blow toward the four points of the compass, again the *Herald* cries his call, again there is

The Complete Opera Book

the fateful silence. "The Heavens are silent. She is doomed," murmured the men. Then *Elsa* throws herself upon her knees and raises her eyes in prayer. Suddenly there is a commotion among the men nearest the river bank.

"A wonder!" they cry. "A swan! A swan—drawing a boat by a golden chain! In the boat stands a knight! See, it approaches! His armour is so bright it blinds our eyes! A wonder! A wonder!"

There is a rush toward the bank and a great shout of acclaim, as the swan with a graceful sweep rounds a bend in the river and brings the shell-like boat, in which stands a knight in dazzling armour and of noble mien, up to the shore. Not daring to trust her senses and turn to behold the wondrous spectacle, *Elsa* gazes in rapture heavenward, while *Ortrud* and *Telramund*, their fell intrigue suddenly halted by a marvel that surpasses their comprehension, regard each other with mingled amazement and alarm.

A strange feeling of awe overcomes the assembly, and the tumult with which the advent of the knight has been hailed dies away to breathless silence, as he extends his hand and in tender accents bids farewell to the swan, which gently inclines its head and then glides away with the boat, vanishing as it had come. There is a chorus, in which, in half-hushed voices, the crowd gives expression to the mystery of the scene. Then the men fall back and the Knight of the Swan, for a silver swan surmounts his helmet and is blazoned upon his shield, having made due obeisance to the *King*, advances to where *Elsa* stands and, resting his eyes upon her pure and radiant beauty, questions her.

"Elsa, if I become your champion and right the foul wrong that is sought to be put upon you, will you confide your future to me; will you become my bride?"

"My guardian, my defender!" she exclaims ecstatically. "All that I have, all that I am, is yours!"

Richard Wagner

"Elsa," he says slowly, as if wishing her to weigh every word, "if I champion your cause and take you to wife, there is one promise I must exact: Never must you ask me whence I come or what my name."

"I promise," she answers, serenely meeting his warning look. He repeats the warning and again she promises to observe it.

"Elsa, I love you!" he exclaims, as he clasps her in his arms. Then addressing the *King* he proclaims his readiness to defend her innocence in trial by combat.

In this scene occurs one of the significant themes of the opera, the MOTIVE OF WARNING—for it is Elsa's disregard of it and the breaking of her promise that brings her happiness to an end.

Three Saxons for the Knight and three Brabantians for *Frederick* solemnly pace off the circle within which the combatants are to fight. The *King*, drawing his sword, strikes three resounding blows with it upon his shield. At the first stroke the Knight and *Frederick* take their positions. At the second they draw their swords. At the third they advance to the encounter. *Frederick* is no coward. His willingness to meet the Knight whose coming had been so strange proves that. But his blows are skilfully warded off until the Swan Knight, finding an opening, fells him with a powerful stroke. *Frederick's* life is forfeited, but his conqueror, perchance knowing that he has been naught but a tool in the hands of a woman leagued with the powers of evil, spares it and bids his fallen foe rise. The *King* leads *Elsa* to the victor, while all hail him as her deliverer and betrothed.

The scenes here described are most stirring. Before the combat begins, the *King* intones a prayer, in which first

The Complete Opera Book

the principals and then the chorus join with noble effect, while the music of rejoicing over the Knight's victory has an irresistible onsweep.

Act II. That night in the fortress of Antwerp, the palace where abide the knights is brilliantly illuminated and sounds of revelry issue from it, and lights shine from the kemenate, where *Elsa's* maids-in-waiting are preparing her for the bridal on the morrow. But in the shadow of the walls sit two figures, a man and a woman; the man, his head bowed in despair, the woman looking vindictively toward the palace. They are *Frederick* and *Ortrud*, who have been condemned to banishment, he utterly dejected, she still trusting in the power of her heathenish gods. To her the Swan Knight's chivalrous forbearance in sparing *Frederick's* life has seemed weak instead of noble, and *Elsa* she regards as an insipid dreamer and easy victim. Not knowing that *Ortrud* still darkly schemes to ruin *Elsa* and restore him to power, *Frederick* denounces her in an outburst of rage and despair.

As another burst of revelry, another flash of light, causes *Ferederick* to bow his head in deeper gloom, *Ortrud* begins to unfold her plot to him. How long will a woman like *Elsa*—as sweet as she is beautiful, but also as weak—be able to restrain herself from asking the forbidden question? Once her suspicion aroused that the Knight is concealing from her something in his past life, growing jealousy will impel her first to seek to coax from him, then to demand of him his name and lineage. Let *Frederick* conceal himself within the minster, and when the bridal procession reaches the steps, come forth and, accusing the Knight of treachery and deceit, demand that he be compelled to disclose his name and origin. He will refuse, and thus, even before *Elsa* enters the minster, she will begin to be beset by doubts. She herself meanwhile will seek to enter the kemenate and play upon her credulousness. "She is

Richard Wagner

for me; her champion is for you. Soon the daughter of Odin will teach you all the joys of vengeance!" is *Ortrud's* sinister exclamation as she finishes.

Indeed it seems as if Fate were playing into her hand. For at that very moment *Elsa*, all clad in white, comes out upon the balcony of the kemenate and, sighing with happiness, breathes out upon the night air her rapture at the thought of what bliss the coming day has in store for her. As she lets her gaze rest on the calm night she hears a piteous voice calling her name, and looking down sees *Ortrud*, her hands raised in supplication to her. Moved by the spectacle of one but a short time before so proud and now apparently in such utter dejection, the guileless maid descends and, herself opening the door of the kemenate, hastens to *Ortrud*, raises her to her feet, and gently leads her in, while, hidden in the shadows, *Frederick of Telramund* bides his time for action. Thus within and without, mischief is plotting for the unsuspecting *Elsa*.

These episodes, following the appearance of *Elsa* upon the balcony, are known as the "Balcony Scene." It opens with the exquisite melody which *Elsa* breathes upon the zephyrs of the night in gratitude to heaven for the champion sent to her defence. Then, when in pity she has hastened down to *Ortrud*, the latter pours doubts regarding her champion into *Elsa's* mind. Who is he? Whence came he? May he not as unexpectedly depart? The whole closes with a beautiful duet, which is repeated by the orchestra, as *Ortrud* is conducted by *Elsa* into the apartment.

It is early morn. People begin to gather in the open place before the minster and, by the time the sun is high, the space is crowded with folk eager to view the bridal procession. They sing a fine and spirited chorus.

At the appointed hour four pages come out upon the balcony of the kemenate and cry out:

The Complete Opera Book

"Make way, our Lady Elsa comes!" Descending, they clear a path through the crowd to the steps of the minster. A long train of richly clad women emerges upon the balcony, slowly comes down the steps and, proceeding past the palace, winds toward the minster. At that moment a great shout, "Hail! Elsa of Brabant!" goes up, as the bride herself appears followed by her ladies-in-waiting. For the moment *Ortrud's* presence in the train is unnoticed, but as *Elsa* approaches the minster, *Frederick's* wife suddenly throws herself in her path.

"Back, Elsa!" she cries. "I am not a menial, born to follow you! Although your Knight has overthrown my husband, you cannot boast of who he is—his very name, the place whence he came, are unknown. Strong must be his motives to forbid you to question him. To what foul disgrace would he be brought were he compelled to answer!"

Fortunately the *King*, the bridegroom, and the nobles approaching from the palace, *Elsa* shrinks from *Ortrud* to her champion's side and hides her face against his breast. At that moment *Frederick of Telramund*, taking his cue from *Ortrud*, comes out upon the minster steps and repeats his wife's accusation. Then, profiting by the confusion, he slips away in the crowd. The insidious poison, however, has already begun to take effect. For even as the *King* taking the Knight on his right and *Elsa* on his left conducts them up the minster steps, the trembling bride catches sight of *Ortrud* whose hand is raised in threat and warning; and it is clinging to her champion, in love indeed but love mingled with doubt and fear, that she passes through the portal, and into the edifice.

These are crucial scenes. The procession to the minster, often known as the bridal procession, must not be confused with the "Bridal Chorus." It is familiar music, however, because at weddings it often is played softly as a musical background to the ceremony.

Richard Wagner

Act III. The wedding festivities are described in the brilliant "Introduction to Act III." This is followed in the opera by the "Bridal Chorus," which, wherever heard —on stage or in church—falls with renewed freshness and significance upon the ear. In this scene the Knight and *Elsa* are conducted to the bridal chamber in the castle. From the right enter *Elsa's* ladies-in-waiting leading the bride; from the left the *King* and nobles leading the Knight. Preceding both trains are pages bearing lights; and voices chant the bridal chorus. The *King* ceremoniously embraces the couple and then the procession makes its way out, until, as the last strains of the chorus die away, *Elsa* and her champion are for the first time alone.

It should be a moment of supreme happiness for both, and indeed, *Elsa* exclaims as her bridegroom takes her to his arms, that words cannot give expression to all its hidden sweetness. Yet, when he tenderly breathes her name, it serves only to remind her that she cannot respond by uttering his. "How sweetly sounds my name when spoken by you, while I, alas, cannot reply with yours. Surely, some day, you will tell me, all in secret, and I shall be able to whisper it when none but you is near!"

In her words the Knight perceives but too clearly the seeds of the fatal mistrust sown by *Ortrud* and *Frederick*. Gently he leaves her side and throwing open the casement, points to the moonlit landscape where the river winds its course along the plain. The same subtle magic that can conjure up this scene from the night has brought him to her, made him love her, and give unshrinking credence to her vow never to question his name or origin. Will she now wantonly destroy the wondrous spell of moonlight and love?

But still *Elsa* urges him. "Let me be flattered by your trust and confidence. Your secret will be safe in my heart. No threats, not even of death, shall tear it from my lips. Tell me who you are and whence you come!"

"Elsa!" he cries, "come to my heart. Let me feel that happiness is mine at last. Let your love and confidence compensate me for what I have left behind me. Cast dark suspicion aside. For know, I came not hither from night and grieving but from the abode of light and noble pleasures."

But his words have the very opposite effect of what he had hoped for. "Heaven help me!" exclaims *Elsa*. "What must I hear! Already you are beginning to look back with longing to the joys you have given up for me. Some day you will leave me to sorrow and regret. I have no magic spells wherewith to hold you. Ah!"—and now she cries out like one distracted and with eyes straining at distance—"See!—the swan!—I see him floating on the waters yonder! You summon him, embark!—Love—madness—whatever it may be—your name declare, your lineage and your home!"

Hardly have these mad words been spoken by her when, as she stands before her husband of a few hours, she sees something that with a sudden shock brings her to her senses. Rushing to the divan where the pages laid the Knight's sword, she seizes it and thrusts it into his hand, and he, turning to discover what peril threatens, sees *Frederick*, followed by four Brabantian nobles, burst into the room. With one stroke he lays the leader lifeless, and the others, seeing him fall, go down on their knees in token of submission. At a sign from the Knight they arise and, lifting *Frederick's* body, bear it away. Then the Knight summons *Elsa's* ladies-in-waiting and bids them prepare her in her richest garments to meet him before the *King*. "There I will make fitting answer to her questions, tell her my name, my rank, and whence I come."

Sadly he watches her being led away, while she, no longer

Richard Wagner

the happy bride, but the picture of utter dejection, turns and raises her hands to him in supplication as though she would still implore him to undo the ruin her lack of faith in him has wrought.

Some of the most beautiful as well as some of the most dramatic music of the score occurs in these scenes.

The love duet is exquisite—one of the sweetest and tenderest passages of which the lyric stage can boast. A very beautiful musical episode is that in which the Knight, pointing through the open casement to the flowery close below, softly illumined by the moon, sings to an accompaniment of what might be called musical moonbeams, "Say, dost thou breathe the incense sweet of flowers?" But when, in spite of the tender warning which he conveys to her, she begins questioning him, he turns toward her and in a passionate musical phrase begs her to trust him and abide with him in loving faith. Her dread that the memory of the delightful place from which he has come will wean him from her; the wild vision in which she imagines she sees the swan approaching to bear him away from her, and when she puts to him the forbidden questions, are details expressed with wonderful vividness in the music.

After the attack by *Frederick* and his death, there is a dramatic silence during which *Elsa* sinks on her husband's breast and faints. When I say silence I do not mean that there is a total cessation of sound, for silence can be more impressively expressed in music than by actual silence itself. It is done by Wagner in this case by long drawn-out chords followed by faint taps on the tympani. When the Knight bends down to *Elsa*, raises her, and gently places her on a couch, echoes of the love duet add to the mournfulness of the music. The scene closes with the Motive of Warning, which resounds with dread meaning.

A quick change of scene should be made at this point

The Complete Opera Book

in the performance of the opera, but as a rule the change takes so long that the third act is virtually given in two acts.

It is on the banks of the Scheldt, the very spot where he had disembarked, that the Knight elects to make reply to *Elsa's* questions. There the *King*, the nobles, and the Brabantians, whom he was to lead, are awaiting him to take command, and as their leader they hail him when he appears. This scene, "Promise of Victory," is in the form of a brilliant march and chorus, during which the Counts of Brabant, followed by their vassals, enter on horseback from various directions. In the average performance of the opera, however, much of it is sacrificed in order to shorten the representation.

The Knight answers their hail by telling them that he has come to bid them farewell, that *Elsa* has been lured to break her vow and ask the forbidden questions which he now is there to answer. From distant lands he came, from Montsalvat, where stands the temple of the Holy Grail, his father, Percival, its King, and he, *Lohengrin*, its Knight. And now, his name and lineage known, he must return, for the Grail gives strength to its knights to right wrong and protect the innocent only so long as the secret of their power remains unrevealed.

Even while he speaks the swan is seen floating down the river. Sadly *Lohengrin* bids *Elsa* farewell. Sadly all, save one, look on. For *Ortrud*, who now pushes her way through the spectators, it is a moment of triumph.

"Depart in all your glory," she calls out. "The swan that draws you away is none other than Elsa's brother Godfrey, changed by my magic into his present form. Had she kept her vow, had you been allowed to tarry, you would have freed him from my spell. The ancient gods, whom faithfully I serve, thus punish human faithlessness!"

By the river bank *Lohengrin* falls upon his knees and

[Dupont

KIRKBY LUNN AS ORTRUDE IN "LOHENGRIN."

Florence Austral as Brünnhilde.

[Vandyk

Richard Wagner

prays in silence. Suddenly a white dove descends over the boat. Rising, *Lohengrin* loosens the golden chain by which the swan is attached to the boat; the swan vanishes; in its place *Godfrey* stands upon the bank, and *Lohengrin*, entering the boat, is drawn away by the dove. At sight of the young Duke, *Ortrud* falls with a shriek, while the Brabantian nobles kneel before him as he advances and makes obeisance to the *King*. *Elsa* gazes on him in rapture until, mindful of her own sorrow, as the boat in which *Lohengrin* stands vanishes around the upper bend of the river, she cries out, "My husband! My husband!" and falls back in death in her brother's arms.

Lohengrin's narrative of his origin is beautifully set to music familiar from the Prelude; but when he proclaims his name we hear the same measures which *Elsa* sang in the second part of her dream in the first act. Very beautiful and tender is the music which he sings when he hands *Elsa* his horn, his sword, and his ring to give to her brother, should he return, and also his greeting to the swan when it comes to bear him back. The work is brought to a close with a repetition of the music of the second portion of *Elsa's* dream, followed by a superb climax with the Motive of the Grail.

Der Ring des Nibelungen

THE RING OF THE NIBELUNG

A stage-festival play for three days and a preliminary evening (Ein Bühuenfestspiel für drei Tage und einen Vorabend), words and music by Richard Wagner.

The first performance of the entire cycle of four music-dramas took place at Bayreuth, August 13, 14, 16, and 17, 1876. "Das Rheingold" had been given September 22, 1869, and "Die Walküre," June 26, 1870, at Munich.

. January 30, 1888, at the Metropolitan Opera House, New York, "Die Walküre" was given as the first performance of the "Ring"

The Complete Opera Book

in America, with the omission, however, of "Das Rheingold," the cycle therefore being incomplete, consisting only of the three music-dramas—"Die Walküre," "Siegfried," and "Götterdämmerung"; in other words the trilogy without the Vorabend, or preliminary evening.

Beginning Monday, March 4, 1889, with "Das Rheingold," the complete cycle, "Der Ring des Nibelungen," was given for the first time in America; "Die Walküre" following Tuesday, March 5; "Siegfried," Friday, March 8; "Götterdämmerung," Monday, March 11. The cycle was immediately repeated. Anton Seidl was the conductor. Among the principals were Lilli Lehmann, Max Alvary, and Emil Fischer.

Seidl conducted the production of the "Ring" in London, under the direction of Angelo Neumann, at Her Majesty's Theatre, May 5-9, 1882.

The "Ring" really is a tetralogy. Wagner, however, called it a trilogy, regarding "Das Rheingold" only as a Vorabend to the three longer music-dramas.

In the repetitions of the "Ring" in this country many distinguished artists have appeared: Lehmann, Moran-Olden, Nordica, Ternina, Fremstad, Gadski, Kurt, as *Brünnhilde;* Lehmann, Nordica, Eames, Fremstad, as *Sieglinde;* Alvary and Jean de Rezske as *Siegfried,* both in "Siegfried" and "Götterdämmerung"; Niemann and Van Dyck, as *Siegmund;* Fischer and Van Rooy as *Wotan;* Schumann-Heink and Homer as *Waltraute* and *Erda.*

INTRODUCTION

The "Ring of the Nibelung" consists of four music-dramas—"Das Rheingold" (The Rhinegold), "Die Walküre" (The Valkyr), "Siegfried," and "Götterdämmerung" (Dusk of the Gods). The "books" of these were written in inverse order. Wagner made a dramatic sketch of the Nibelung myth as early as the autumn of 1848, and between then and the autumn of 1850 he wrote the "Death of Siegfried." This subsequently became the "Dusk of the Gods." Meanwhile Wagner's ideas as to the proper treatment of the myth seem to have undergone a change. "Siegfried's Death" ended with Brünnhilde leading Siegfried to Valhalla,—dramatic, but without the deeper ethical significance of the later version, when Wagner evidently

Richard Wagner

conceived the purpose of connecting the final catastrophe of his trilogy with the "Dusk of the Gods," or end of all things, in Northern mythology, and of embodying a profound truth in the action of the music-dramas. This metaphysical significance of the work is believed to be sufficiently explained in the brief synopsis of the plot of the trilogy and in the descriptive musical and dramatic analyses below.

In the autumn of 1850 when Wagner was on the point of sketching out the music of "Siegfried's Death," he recognized that he must lead up to it with another drama, and "Young Siegfried," afterwards "Siegfried," was the result. This in turn he found incomplete, and finally decided to supplement it with the "Valkyr" and "Rhinegold."

"Das Rheingold" was produced in Munich, at the Court Theatre, September 22, 1869; "Die Walküre," on the same stage, June 20, 1870. "Siegfried" and "Dusk of the Gods" were not performed until 1876, when they were produced at Bayreuth.

Of the principal characters in the "Ring of the Nibelung," *Alberich*, the Nibelung, and *Wotan*, the chief of the gods, are symbolic of greed for wealth and power. This lust leads *Alberich* to renounce love—the most sacred of emotions—in order that he may rob the *Rhinedaughters* of the Rhinegold and forge from it the ring which is to make him all-powerful. *Wotan* by strategy obtains the ring, but instead of returning it to the *Rhinedaughters*, he gives it to the giants, *Fafner* and *Fasolt*, as ransom for *Freia*, the goddess of youth and beauty, whom he had promised to the giants as a reward for building Walhalla. *Alberich* has cursed the ring and all into whose possession it may come. The giants no sooner obtain it than they fall to quarrelling over it. *Fafner* slays *Fasolt* and then retires to a cave in the heart of a forest where, in the form of a dragon, he guards the ring and the rest of the treasure which *Wotan* wrested from *Alberich* and also gave to the giants as ransom for *Freia*. This treasure includes the Tarnhelmet, a helmet made of Rhinegold, the wearer of which can assume any guise.

Wotan having witnessed the slaying of *Fasolt*, is filled with dread lest the curse of *Alberich* be visited upon the gods. To defend *Walhalla* against the assaults of *Alberich* and the host of Nibelungs, he begets in union with *Erda*, the goddess of wisdom, the Valkyrs (chief among them *Brünnhilde*), wild maidens who course through the air on superb chargers and bear the bodies of departed heroes to Walhalla, where they revive and aid the gods in warding off the attacks of the Nibelungs. But it is also necessary that the curse-laden ring should be wrested from *Fafner* and restored through purely unselfish motives to the *Rhinedaughters*, and the curse thus lifted from the race of the gods. None of the gods can do this because their motive in doing so would not be unselfish. Hence *Wotan*, for a time, casts off his divinity, and in human disguise as Wälse, begets in union with a human woman the Wälsung twins, *Siegmund* and *Sieglinde*. *Siegmund* he hopes will be the hero who will slay *Fafner* and restore the ring to the *Rhinedaughters*. To nerve him for this task, *Wotan* surrounds the Wälsungs with numerous hardships. *Sieglinde* is forced to become the wife of her robber, *Hunding*. *Siegmund*, storm-driven, seeks shelter in *Hunding's* hut, where he and his sister, recognizing one another, flee together. *Hunding* overtakes them and *Wotan*, as *Siegmund* has been guilty of a crime against the marriage vow, is obliged, at the request of his spouse *Fricka*, the Juno of Northern mythology, to give victory to *Hunding*. *Brünnhilde*, contrary to *Wotan's* command, takes pity on *Siegmund*, and seeks to shield him against *Hunding*. For this, *Wotan* causes her to fall into a profound slumber. The hero who

Richard Wagner

will penetrate the barrier of fire with which *Wotan* has surrounded the rock upon which she slumbers can claim her as his bride.

After *Siegmund's* death *Sieglinde* gives birth to *Siegfried*, a son of their illicit union, who is reared by one of the Nibelungs, *Mime*, in the forest where *Fafner* guards the Nibelung treasure. *Mime* is seeking to weld the pieces of *Siegmund's* sword (Nothung or Needful) in order that *Siegfried* may slay *Fafner*, *Mime* hoping then to kill the youth and to possess himself of the treasure. But he cannot weld the sword. At last *Siegfried*, learning that it was his father's weapon, welds the pieces and slays *Fafner*. His lips having come in contact with his bloody fingers, he is, through the magic power of the dragon's blood, enabled to understand the language of the birds, and a little feathery songster warns him of *Mime's* treachery. *Siegfried* slays the Nibelung and is then guided to the fiery barrier around the Valkyr rock. Penetrating this, he comes upon *Brünnhilde*, and enraptured with her beauty, awakens her and claims her as his bride. She, the virgin pride of the goddess, yielding to the love of the woman, gives herself up to him. He plights his troth with the curse-laden ring which he has wrested from *Fafner*.

Siegfried goes forth in quest of adventure. On the Rhine lives the Gibichung *Gunther*, his sister *Gutrune* and their half-brother *Hagen*, none other than the son of the Nibelung *Alberich*. *Hagen*, knowing of *Siegfried's* coming, plans his destruction in order to regain the ring for the Nibelungs. Therefore, craftily concealing *Brünnhilde's* and *Siegfried's* relations from *Gunther*, he incites a longing in the latter to possess *Brünnhilde* as his bride. Carrying out a plot evolved by *Hagen*, *Gutrune* on *Siegfried's* arrival presents to him a drinking-horn filled with a love-potion. *Siegfried* drinks, is led through the effect of the potion to forget that *Brünnhilde* is his bride, and, becoming enamoured of *Gutrune*, asks her in marriage of *Gunther*. The latter consents, provided *Siegfried* will disguise himself in the Tarnhelmet as *Gunther* and lead *Brünnhilde* to him as bride. *Siegfried* readily agrees, and in the guise of *Gunther* overcomes *Brünnhilde* and delivers her to the Gibichung. But *Brünnhilde*, recognizing on *Siegfried* the ring, which her conquerer had drawn from her finger, accuses him of treachery in delivering her, his own bride, to *Gunther*. The latter, unmasked and also suspicious of *Siegfried*, conspires with *Hagen* and *Brünnhilde*, who, knowing naught of the love-potion, is roused to a frenzy of hate and jealousy by *Siegfried's* seeming treachery, to compass the young hero's death. *Hagen* slays *Siegfried* during a hunt, and then in a quarrel with *Gunther* over the ring also kills the Gibichung.

Meanwhile *Brünnhilde* has learned through the *Rhinedaughters* of the treachery of which she and *Siegfried* have been the victims. All her jealous hatred of *Siegfried* yields to her old love for him and a passionate yearning to join him in death. She draws the ring from his finger and places it on her own, then hurls a torch upon the pyre. Mounting her steed, she plunges into the flames. One of the *Rhinedaughters*, swimming in on the rising waters, seizes the curse-laden ring. *Hagen* rushes into the flooding Rhine hoping to regain it, but the other *Rhinedaughters* grasp him and draw him down into the flood. Not only the flames of the pyre, but a glow which pervades the whole horizon illumine the scene. It is Walhalla being consumed by fire. Through love—the very emotion *Alberich* renounced in order to gain wealth and power—*Brünnhilde* has caused the old order of things to pass away and a human era to dawn in place of the old mythological one of the gods.

The sum of all that has been written concerning the book of "The Ring of the Nibelung" is probably larger than the

Richard Wagner

sum of all that has been written concerning the librettos used by all other composers. What can be said of the ordinary opera libretto beyond Voltaire's remark that "what is too stupid to be spoken is sung"? But "The Ring of the Nibelung" produced vehement discussion. It was attacked and defended, praised and ridiculed, extolled and condemned. And it survived all the discussion it called forth. It is the outstanding fact in Wagner's career that he always triumphed. He threw his lance into the midst of his enemies and fought his way up to it. No matter how much opposition his music-dramas excited, they gradually found their way into the repertoire.

It was contended on many sides that a book like "The Ring of the Nibelung" could not be set to music. Certainly it could not be after the fashion of an ordinary opera. Perhaps people were so accustomed to the books of nonsense which figured as opera librettos that they thought "The Ring of the Nibelung" was so great a work that its action and climaxes were beyond the scope of musical expression. For such, Wagner has placed music on a higher level. He has shown that music makes a great drama greater.

One of the most remarkable features of Wagner's works is the author's complete absorption of the times of which he wrote. He seems to have gone back to the very period in which the scenes of his music dramas are laid and to have himself lived through the events in his plots. Hans Sachs could not have left a more faithful portrayal of life in the Nuremberg of his day than Wagner has given us in "Die Meistersinger." In "The Ring of the Nibelung" he has done more—he has absorbed an imaginary epoch; lived over the days of gods and demigods; infused life into mythological figures. "The Rhinegold," which is full of varied interest from its first note to its last, deals entirely with beings of mythology. They are presented true to

The Complete Opera Book

life—if that expression may be used in connection with beings that never lived—that is to say, they are so vividly drawn that we forget such beings never lived, and take as much interest in their doings and saying as if they were lifelike reproductions of historical characters. Was there ever a love scene more thrilling than that between *Siegmund* and *Sieglinde?* It represents the gradations of the love of two souls from its first awakening to its rapturous greeting in full self-consciousness. No one stops to think during that impassioned scene that the close relationship between *Siegmund* and *Sieglinde* would in these days have been a bar to their legal union. For all we know, in those moments when the impassioned music of that scene whirls us away in its resistless current, not a drop of related blood courses through their veins. It has been said that we could not be interested in mythological beings—that "The Ring of the Nibelung" lacked human interest. In reply, I say that wonderful as is the first act of "The Valkyr," there is nothing in it to compare in wild and lofty beauty with the last act of that music-drama—especially the scene between *Brünnhilde* and *Wotan*.

That there are faults of dramatic construction in "The Ring of the Nibelung" I admit. In what follows I have not hesitated to point them out. But there are faults of construction in Shakespeare. What would be the critical verdict if "Hamlet" were now to have its first performance in the exact form in which Shakespeare left it? With all its faults of dramatic construction "The Ring of the Nibelung" is a remarkable drama, full of life and action and logically developed, the events leading up to superb climaxes. Wagner was doubly inspired. He was both a great dramatist and a great musician.

The chief faults of dramatic construction of which Wagner was guilty in "The Ring of the Nibelung" are certain unduly prolonged scenes which are merely episodi-

Richard Wagner

cal—that is, unnecessary to the development of the plot so that they delay the action and weary the audience to a point which endangers the success of the really sublime portions of the score. In several of these scenes, there is a great amount of narrative, the story of events with which we have become familiar being retold in detail although some incidents which connect the plot of the particular music-drama with that of the preceding one are also related. But, as narrative on the stage makes little impression, and, when it is sung perhaps none at all, because it cannot be well understood, it would seem as if prefaces to the dramas could have taken the place of these narratives. Certain it is that these long drawn-out scenes did more to retard the popular recognition of Wagner's genius than the activity of hostile critics and musicians. Still, it should be remembered that these music-dramas were composed for performance under the circumstances which prevail at Bayreuth, where the performances begin in the afternoon and there are long waits between the acts, during which you can refresh yourself by a stroll or by the more mundane pleasures of the table. Then, after an hour's relaxation of the mind and of the sense of hearing, you are ready to hear another act. Under these agreeable conditions one remains sufficiently fresh to enjoy the music even of the dramatically faulty scenes.

One of the characters in "The Ring of the Nibelung," *Brünnhilde*, is Wagner's noblest creation. She takes upon herself the sins of the gods and by her expiation frees the world from the curse of lust for wealth and power. She is a perfect dramatic incarnation of the profound and beautiful metaphysical motive upon which the plot of "The Ring of the Nibelung" is based.

There now follow descriptive accounts of the stories and music of the four component parts of this work by Wagner —perhaps his greatest.

The Complete Opera Book

Das Rheingold

THE RHINEGOLD

Prologue in four scenes to the trilogy of music-dramas. "The Ring of the Nibelung," by Richard Wagner. "Das Rheingold" was produced, Munich, September 22, 1869. "The Ring of the Nibelung" was given complete for the first time in the Wagner Theatre, Bayreuth, in August, 1876. In the first American performance of "Das Rheingold," Metropolitan Opera House, New York, January 4, 1889, Fischer was *Wotan*, Alvary *Loge*, Moran-Oldern *Fricka*, and Kati Bettaque *Freia*.

CHARACTERS

WOTAN	} Gods	Baritone-Bass
DONNER		Baritone-Bass
FROH		Tenor
LOGE		Tenor
FASOLT	} Giants	Baritone-Bass
FAFNER		Bass
ALBERICH	} Nibelungs	Baritone-Bass
MIME		Tenor
FRICKA	} Goddesses	Soprano
FREIA		Soprano
ERDA		Mezzo-Soprano
WOGLINDE	} Rhine-daughters	Soprano
WELLGUNDE		Soprano
FLOSSHILDE		Mezzo-Soprano

Time—Legendary.   *Place*—The bed of the Rhine; a mountainous district near the Rhine; the subterranean caverns of Nibelheim.

In "The Rhinegold" we meet with supernatural beings of German mythology—the Rhinedaughters *Woglinde, Wellgunde,* and *Flosshilde,* whose duty it is to guard the precious Rhinegold; *Wotan,* the chief of the gods; his spouse *Fricka; Loge,* the God of Fire (the diplomat of Walhalla); *Freia,* the Goddess of Youth and Beauty; her brothers *Donner* and *Froh; Erda,* the all-wise woman; the giants *Fafner* and *Fasolt; Alberich* and *Mime* of the

Richard Wagner

race of Nibelungs, cunning, treacherous gnomes who dwell in the bowels of the earth.

The first scene of "Rhinegold" is laid in the Rhine, at the bottom of the river, where the Rhinedaughters guard the Rhinegold.

The work opens with a wonderfully descriptive Prelude, which depicts with marvellous art (marvellous because so simple) the transition from the quietude of the water-depths to the wavy life of the *Rhinedaughters*. The double basses intone E flat. Only this note is heard during four bars. Then three contra bassoons add a B flat. The chord, thus formed, sounds until the 136th bar. With the sixteenth bar there flows over this seemingly immovable triad, as the current of a river flows over its immovable bed, the **Motive of the Rhine**.

A horn intones this motive. Then one horn after another takes it up until its wave-like tones are heard on the eight horns. On the flowing accompaniment of the 'cellos the motive is carried to the wood-wind. It rises higher and higher, the other strings successively joining in the accompaniment, which now flows on in gentle undulations until the motive is heard on the high notes of the wood-wind, while the violins have joined in the accompaniment. When the theme thus seems to have stirred the waters from their depth to their surface the curtain rises.

The scene shows the bed and flowing waters of the Rhine, the light of day reaching the depths only as a greenish twilight. The current flows on over rugged rocks and through dark chasms.

The Complete Opera Book

Woglinde is circling gracefully around the central ridge of rock. To an accompaniment as wavy as the waters through which she swims, she sings:

> Weia! Waga! Woge, du Welle,
> Walle zur Wiege! Wagala weia!
> Wallala, Weiala weia!

They are sung to the **Motive of the Rhinedaughters.**

In wavy sport the *Rhinedaughters* dart from cliff to cliff. Meanwhile *Alberich* has clambered from the depths up to one of the cliffs, and watches, while standing in its shadow, the gambols of the *Rhinedaughters*. As he speaks to them there is a momentary harshness in the music, whose flowing rhythm is broken. In futile endeavours to clamber up to them, he inveighs against the "slippery slime" which causes him to lose his foothold.

Woglinde, *Wellgunde*, and *Flosshilde* in turn gambol almost within his reach, only to dart away again. He curses his own weakness in the **Motive of the Nibelungs' Servitude.**

Swimming high above him the *Rhinedaughters* incite him with gleeful cries to chase them. *Alberich* tries to ascend, but always slips and falls down. Then his gaze is attracted and held by a glow which suddenly pervades the waves above him and increases until from the highest point of the central cliff a bright, golden ray shoots through the water. Amid the shimmering accompaniment of the violins is heard on the horn the **Rhinegold Motive.**

Richard Wagner

With shouts of triumph the *Rhinedaughters* swim around the rock. Their cry "Rhinegold," is a characteristic motive. The **Rhinedaughters' Shout of Triumph** and the accompaniment to it are as follows:

As the river glitters with golden light the Rhinegold Motive rings out brilliantly on the trumpet. The Nibelung is fascinated by the sheen. The *Rhinedaughters* gossip with one another, and *Alberich* thus learns that the light is that of the Rhinegold, and that whoever shall shape a ring from this gold will become invested with great power. We hear **The Ring Motive.**

Flosshilde bids her sisters cease their prattle, lest some sinister foe should overhear them. *Wellgunde* and *Woglinde* ridicule their sister's anxiety, saying that no one would care to filch the gold, because it would give power only to him who abjures or renounces love. At this point is heard the darkly prophetic **Motive of the Renunciation of Love.**

Alberich reflects on the words of the *Rhinedaughters*. The Ring Motive occurs both in voice and orchestra in mysterious pianissimo (like an echo of *Alberich's* sinister thoughts), and is followed by the Motive of Renunciation. Then is heard the sharp, decisive rhythm of the Nibelung Motive. *Alberich* fiercely springs over to the central rock. The *Rhinedaughters* scream and dart away in different directions. *Alberich* has reached the summit of the highest cliff.

"Hark, ye floods! Love I renounce forever!" he cries, and amid the crash of the Rhinegold Motive he seizes the gold and disappears in the depths. With screams of terror the *Rhinedaughters* dive after the robber through the darkened water, guided by *Alberich's* shrill, mocking laugh.

There is a transformation. Waters and rocks sink. As they disappear, the billowy accompaniment sinks lower and lower in the orchestra. Above it rises once more the Motive of Renunciation. The Ring Motive is heard, and then, as the waves change into nebulous clouds, the billowy accompaniment rises pianissimo until, with a repetition of the Ring Motive, the action passes to the second scene. One crime has already been committed—the theft of the Rhinegold by *Alberich*. How that crime and the ring which he shapes from the gold inspire other crimes is told in the course of the following scenes of "Rhinegold." Hence the significance of the Ring Motive as a connecting link between the first and second scenes.

Scene II. Dawn illumines a castle with glittering turrets on a rocky height at the back. Through a deep valley between this and the foreground flows the Rhine.

The **Walhalla Motive** now heard is a motive of superb beauty. It greets us again and again in "Rhinegold" and frequently in the later music-dramas of the cycle. Walhalla is the abode of gods and heroes. Its motive is divinely, heroically beautiful. Though essentially broad and stately, it often assumes a tender mood, like the

Richard Wagner

chivalric gentleness which every hero feels toward woman. Thus it is here. In crescendo and decrescendo it rises and falls, as rises and falls with each breath the bosom of the beautiful *Fricka*, who slumbers at *Wotan's* side.

As *Fricka* awakens, her eyes fall on the castle. In her surprise she calls to her spouse. *Wotan* dreams on, the Ring Motive, and later the Walhalla Motive, being heard in the orchestra, for with the ring *Wotan* is planning to compensate the giants for building Walhalla, instead of rewarding them by presenting *Freia* to them as he has promised. As he opens his eyes and sees the castle you hear the Spear Motive, which is a characteristic variation of the Motive of Compact. For *Wotan* should enforce, if needful, the compacts of the gods with his spear.

Wotan sings of the glory of Walhalla. *Fricka* reminds him of his compact with the giants to deliver over to them for their work in building Walhalla, *Freia*, the Goddess of Youth and Beauty. This introduces on the 'cellos and double basses the **Motive of Compact**, a theme expressive of the binding force of law and with the inherent dignity and power of the sense of justice.

In a domestic spat between *Wotan* and *Fricka*, *Wotan* charges that she was as anxious as he to have Walhalla built. *Fricka* answers that she desired to have it erected in order to persuade him to lead a more domestic life. At *Fricka's* words,

"Halls, bright and gleaming,"

The Complete Opera Book

the **Fricka Motive** is heard, a caressing motive of much grace and beauty.

It is also prominent in *Wotan's* reply immediately following. *Wotan* tells *Fricka* that he never intended to really give up *Freia* to the giants. Chromatics, like little tongues of flame, appear in the accompaniment. They are suggestive of the Loge Motive, for with the aid of *Loge* the God of Fire, *Wotan* hopes to trick the giants and save *Freia*.

"Then save her at once!" calls *Fricka*, as *Freia* enters in hasty flight. The **Motive of Flight** is as follows:

The following is the **Freia Motive**:

With *Freia's* exclamations that the giants are pursuing her, the first suggestion of the Giant Motive appears and as these "great, hulking fellows" enter, the heavy, clumsy **Giant Motive** is heard in its entirety:

For the giants, *Fasolt*, and *Fafner*, have come to demand that *Wotan* deliver up to them *Freia*, according to his promise when they agreed to build Walhalla for him. In the ensuing scene, in which *Wotan* parleys with the *Giants*, the Giant Motive, the Walhalla Motive, the Motive of

Richard Wagner

the Compact, and the first bar of the Freia Motive figure until *Fasolt's* threatening words,

"Peace wane when you break your compact,"

when there is heard a version of the Motive of Compact characteristic enough to be distinguished as the **Motive of Compact with the Giants**:

The Walhalla, Giant, and Freia motives again are heard until *Fafner* speaks of the golden apples which grow in *Freia's* garden. These golden apples are the fruit of which the gods partake in order to enjoy eternal youth. The Motive of Eternal Youth, which now appears, is one of the loveliest in the cycle. It seems as though age could not wither it, nor custom stale its infinite variety. Its first bar is reminiscent of the Ring Motive, for there is subtle relationship between the Golden Apples of Freia and the Rhinegold. Here is the **Motive of Eternal Youth**:

It is finely combined with the Giant Motive at *Fafner's* words:

"Let her forthwith be torn from them all."

Froh and *Donner*, *Freia's* brothers, enter hastily to save their sister. *Froh* clasps her in his arms, while *Donner* confronts the giants, the Motive of Eternal Youth rings out triumphantly on the horns and wood-wind. But *Freia's* hope is short-lived. For though *Wotan* desires to keep *Freia* in Walhalla, he dare not offend the giants. At this critical moment, however, he sees his cunning adviser, *Loge*, approaching. These are *Loge's* characteristic motives:

Wotan upbraids *Loge* for not having discovered something which the giants would be willing to accept as a substitute for *Freia*. *Loge* says he has travelled the world over without finding aught that would compensate man for the renunciation of a lovely woman. This leads to *Loge's* narrative of his wanderings. With great cunning he tells *Wotan* of the theft of the Rhinegold and of the wondrous worth of a ring shaped from the gold. Thus he incites the listening giants to ask for it as a compensation for giving up *Freia*. Hence Wagner, as *Loge* begins his narrative, has blended, with a marvellous sense of musical beauty and dramatic fitness, two phrases: the Freia Motive and the accompaniment to the *Rhinedaughters'* Shout of Triumph in the first scene. This music continues until *Loge* says that he discovered but one person (*Alberich*) who was willing to renounce love. Then the Rhinegold Motive is sounded tristly in a minor key and immediately afterward is heard the Motive of Renunciation.

Loge next tells how *Alberich* stole the gold. He has already excited the curiosity of the giants, and when *Fafner* asks him what power *Alberich* will gain through the possession of the gold, he dwells upon the magical attributes of the ring shaped from Rhinegold.

Richard Wagner

Loge's diplomacy is beginning to bear results. *Fafner* tells *Fasolt* that he deems the possession of the gold more important than *Freia*. Notice here how the Freia motive, so prominent when the giants insisted on her as their compensation, is relegated to the bass and how the Rhinegold Motive breaks in upon the Motive of Eternal Youth, as *Fafner* and *Fasolt* again advance toward *Wotan*, and bid him wrest the gold from *Alberich* and give it to them as ransom for *Freia*. *Wotan* refuses, for he himself now lusts for the ring made of Rhinegold. The giants having proclaimed that they will give *Wotan* until evening to determine upon his course, seize *Freia* and drag her away. Pallor now settles upon the faces of the gods; they seem to have grown older. They are affected by the absence of *Freia*, the Goddess of Youth, whose motives are but palely reflected by the orchestra. At last *Wotan* proclaims that he will go with *Loge* to Nibelung and wrest the entire treasure of Rhinegold from *Alberich* as ransom for *Freia*.

Loge disappears down a crevice in the side of the rock. From it a sulphurous vapour at once issues. When *Wotan* has followed *Loge* into the cleft the vapour fills the stage and conceals the remaining characters. The vapours thicken to a black cloud, continually rising upward until rocky chasms are seen. These have an upward motion, so that the stage appears to be sinking deeper and deeper. With a *molto vivace* the orchestra dashes into the Motive of Flight. From various distant points ruddy gleams of light illumine the chasms, and when the Flight Motive has died away, only the increasing clangour of the smithies is heard from all directions. This is the typical **Nibelung Motive**, characteristic of Alberich's Nibelungs toiling at the anvil for him. Gradually the sounds grow fainter.

The Complete Opera Book

Then as the Ring Motive resounds like a shout of malicious triumph (expressive of *Alberich's* malignant joy at his possession of power), there is seen a subterranean cavern, apparently of illimitable depth, from which narrow shafts lead in all directions.

Scene III. *Alberich* enters from a side cleft dragging after him the shrieking *Mime*. The latter lets fall a helmet which *Alberich* at once seizes. It is the Tarnhelmet, made of Rhinegold, the wearing of which enables the wearer to become invisible or assume any shape. As *Alberich* closely examines the helmet the **Motive of the Tarnhelmet** is heard.

It is mysterious, uncanny. To test its power *Alberich* puts it on and changes into a column of vapour. He asks *Mime* if he is visible, and when *Mime* answers in the negative *Alberich* cries out shrilly, "Then feel me instead," at the same time making poor *Mime* writhe under the blows of a visible scourge. *Alberich* then departs—still in the form of a vaporous column—to announce to the *Nibelungs* that they are henceforth his slavish subjects. *Mime* cowers down with fear and pain.

Wotan and *Loge* enter from one of the upper shafts. *Mime* tells them how *Alberich* has become all-powerful through the ring and the Tarnhelmet made of the Rhinegold. Then *Alberich*, who has taken off the Tarnhelmet and hung it from his girdle, is seen in the distance, driving a crowd of *Nibelungs* before him from the caves below. They are laden with gold and silver, which he forces them to pile up in one place and so form a hoard. He suddenly perceives *Wotan* and *Loge*. After abusing *Mime* for per-

Richard Wagner

mitting strangers to enter Nibelheim, he commands the *Nibelungs* to descend again into the cavern in search of new treasure for him. They hesitate. You hear the Ring Motive. *Alberich* draws the ring from his finger, stretches it threateningly toward the *Nibelungs*, and commands them to obey their master.

They disperse in headlong flight, with *Mime*, into the cavernous recesses. *Alberich* looks with mistrust upon *Wotan* and *Loge*. *Wotan* tells him they have heard report of his wealth and power and have come to ascertain if it is true. The Nibelung points to the hoard. He boasts that the whole world will come under his sway (Ring Motive), that the gods who now laugh and love in the enjoyment of youth and beauty will become subject to him (Freia Motive); for he has abjured love (Motive of Renunciation). Hence, even the gods in Walhalla shall dread him (Walhalla Motive) and he bids them beware of the time when the night-begotten host of the Nibelungs shall rise from Nibelheim into the realm of daylight. (Rhinegold Motive followed by Walhalla Motive, for it is through the power gained by the Rhinegold that *Alberich* hopes to possess himself of Walhalla.) *Loge* cunningly flatters *Alberich*, and when the latter tells him of the Tarnhelmet, feigns disbelief of *Alberich's* statements. *Alberich*, to prove their truth, puts on the helmet and transforms himself into a huge serpent. The Serpent Motive expresses the windings and writhings of the monster. The serpent vanishes and *Alberich* reappears. When *Loge* doubts if *Alberich* can transform himself into something very small, the Nibelung changes into a toad. Now is *Loge's* chance. He calls *Wotan* to set his foot on the toad. As *Wotan* does so, *Loge* puts his hand to its head and seizes the Tarnhelmet. *Alberich* is seen writhing under *Wotan's* foot. *Loge* binds *Alberich;* both seize him, drag him to the shaft from which they descended and disappear ascending.

The Complete Opera Book

The scene changes in the reverse direction to that in which it changed when *Wotan* and *Loge* were descending to Nibelheim. The orchestra accompanies the change of scene. The Ring Motive dies away from crashing fortissimo to piano, to be succeeded by the dark Motive of Renunciation. Then is heard the clangour of the Nibelung smithies. The Giant, Walhalla, Loge, and Servitude Motives follow the last with crushing force as *Wotan* and *Loge* emerge from the cleft, dragging the pinioned *Alberich* with them. His lease of power was brief. He is again in a condition of servitude.

Scene IV. A pale mist still veils the prospect as at the end of the second scene. *Loge* and *Wotan* place *Alberich* on the ground and *Loge* dances around the pinioned Nibelung, mockingly snapping his fingers at the prisoner. *Wotan* joins *Loge* in his mockery of *Alberich*. The Nibelung asks what he must give for his freedom. "Your hoard and your glittering gold," is *Wotan's* answer. *Alberich* assents to the ransom and *Loge* frees the gnome's right hand. *Alberich* raises the ring to his lips and murmurs a secret behest. The *Nibelungs* emerge from the cleft and heap up the hoard. Then, as *Alberich* stretches out the ring toward them, they rush in terror toward the cleft, into which they disappear. *Alberich* now asks for his freedom, but *Loge* throws the Tarnhelmet on to the heap. *Wotan* demands that *Alberich* also give up the ring. At these words dismay and terror are depicted on the Nibelung's face. He had hoped to save the ring, but in vain. *Wotan* tears it from the gnome's finger. Then *Alberich*, impelled by hate and rage, curses the ring. The **Motive of the Curse:**

To it should be added the syncopated measures expres-

Richard Wagner

sive of the ever-threatening and ever-active **Nibelung's Hate**:

Amid heavy thuds of the Motive of Servitude *Alberich* vanishes in the cleft.

The mist begins to rise. It grows lighter. The Giant Motive and the Motive of Eternal Youth are heard, for the giants are approaching with *Freia*. *Donner*, *Froh*, and *Fricka* hasten to greet *Wotan*. *Fasolt* and *Fafner* enter with *Freia*. It has grown clear except that the mist still hides the distant castle. *Freia's* presence seems to have restored youth to the gods. *Fasolt* asks for the ransom for *Freia*. *Wotan* points to the hoard. With staves the giants measure off a space of the height and width of *Freia*. That space must be filled out with treasure.

Loge and *Froh* pile up the hoard, but the giants are not satisfied even when the Tarnhelmet has been added. They wish also the ring to fill out a crevice. *Wotan* turns in anger away from them. A bluish light glimmers in the rocky cleft to the right, and through it *Erda* rises. She warns *Wotan* against retaining possession of the ring. The Erda Motive bears a strong resemblance to the Rhine Motive.

The syncopated notes of the Nibelung's Malevolence, so threateningly indicative of the harm which *Alberich* is plotting, are also heard in *Erda's* warning.

Wotan, heeding her words, throws the ring up on the hoard. The giants release *Freia*, who rushes joyfully towards the gods. Here the Freia Motive, combined with the Flight Motive, now no longer agitated but joyful, rings out gleefully. Soon, however, these motives are interrupted by the Giant and Nibelung motives, and later

The Complete Opera Book

the Nibelung's Hate and Ring Motive. For *Alberich's* curse already is beginning its dread work. The giants dispute over the spoils, their dispute waxes to strife, and at last *Fafner* slays *Fasolt* and snatches the ring from the dying giant, while, as the gods gaze horror-stricken upon the scene, the Curse Motive resounds with crushing force.

Loge congratulates *Wotan* on having given up the curse-laden ring. But even *Fricka's* caresses, as she asks *Wotan* to lead her into Walhalla, cannot divert the god's mind from dark thoughts, and the Curse Motive accompanies his gloomy reflections—for the ring has passed through his hands. It was he who wrested it from *Alberich*—and its curse rests on all who have touched it.

Donner ascends to the top of a lofty rock. He gathers the mists around him until he is enveloped by a black cloud. He swings his hammer. There is a flash of lightning, a crash of thunder, and lo! the cloud vanishes. A rainbow bridge spans the valley to Walhalla, which is illumined by the setting sun.

Wotan eloquently greets Walhalla, and then, taking *Fricka* by the hand, leads the procession of the gods into the castle.

The music of this scene is of wondrous eloquence and beauty. Six harps are added to the ordinary orchestral instruments, and as the variegated bridge is seen their arpeggios shimmer like the colours of the rainbow around the broad, majestic **Rainbow Motive:**

Then the stately Walhalla Motive resounds as the gods gaze, lost in admiration, at the Walhalla. It gives way to the Ring Motive as *Wotan* speaks of the day's ills; and then as he is inspired by the idea of begetting a race of

Richard Wagner

demigods to conquer the Nibelungs, there is heard for the first time the **Sword Motive**:

The cries of the *Rhinedaughters* greet *Wotan*. They beg him to restore the ring to them. But *Wotan* must remain deaf to their entreaties. He gave the ring, which he should have restored to the *Rhinedaughters*, to the giants, as ransom for *Freia*.

The Walhalla Motive swells to a majestic climax and the gods enter the castle. Amid shimmering arpeggios the Rainbow Motive resounds. The gods have attained the height of their glory—but the Nibelung's curse is still potent, and it will bring woe upon all who have possessed or will possess the ring until it is restored to the *Rhinedaughters*. *Fasolt* was only the first victim of *Alberich's* curse.

DIE WALKÜRE

THE VALKYR

Music-drama in three acts, words and music by Richard Wagner. Produced, Munich, June 25, 1870. New York, Academy of Music, April 2, 1877, an incomplete and inadequate performance with Pappenheim as *Brünnhilde*, Pauline Canissa *Sieglinde*, A. Bischoff *Siegmund*, Felix Preusser *Wotan*, A. Blum *Hunding*, Mme. Listner *Fricka*, Frida de Gebel, *Gerhilde*, Adolf Neuendorff, conductor. The real first performance in America was conducted by Dr. Leopold Damrosch at the Metropolitan Opera House, January 30, 1885, with Materna, the original Bayreuth *Brünnhilde* in that rôle, Schott as *Siegmund*, Seidl-Kraus as *Sieglinde*, Marianne Brandt as *Fricka*, Staudigl as *Wotan*, and Koegel as *Hunding*.

CHARACTERS

SIEGMUND..................................*Tenor*
HUNDING...................................*Bass*

The Complete Opera Book

WOTAN..*Baritone-Bass*
SIEGLINDE...*Soprano*
BRÜNNHILDE..*Soprano*
FRICKA..*Mezzo-Soprano*
Valkyrs (Sopranos and Mezzo-Sopranos): Gerhilde, Ortlinde, Waltraute, Schwertleite, Helmwige, Siegrune, Grimgerde, Rossweisse.
Time—Legendary.   *Place*—Interior of Hunding's hut; a rocky height; the peak of a rocky mountain (the Brünnhilde rock).

Wotan's enjoyment of Walhalla was destined to be shortlived. Filled with dismay by the death of *Fasolt* in the combat of the giants for the accursed ring, and impelled by a dread presentiment that the force of the curse would be visited upon the gods, he descended from Walhalla to the abode of the all-wise woman, *Erda*, who bore him nine daughters. These were the Valkyrs, headed by *Brünnhilde*—the wild horsewomen of the air, who on winged steeds bore the dead heroes to Walhalla, the warriors' heaven. With the aid of the Valkyrs and the heroes they gathered to Walhalla, *Wotan* hoped to repel any assault upon his castle by the enemies of the gods.

But though the host of heroes grew to a goodly number, the terror of *Alberich's* curse still haunted the chief of gods. He might have freed himself from it had he returned the ring and helmet made of Rhinegold to the *Rhinedaughters*, from whom *Alberich* filched it; but in his desire to persuade the giants to relinquish *Freia*, whom he had promised to them as a reward for building Walhalla, he, having wrested the ring from *Alberich*, gave it to the giants instead of returning it to the *Rhinedaughters*. He saw the giants contending for the possession of the ring and saw *Fasolt* slain—the first victim of *Alberich's* curse. He knows that the giant *Fafner*, having assumed the shape of a huge serpent, now guards the Nibelung treasure, which includes the ring and the Tarnhelmet, in a cave in the heart of a

Richard Wagner

dense forest. How shall the Rhinegold be restored to the *Rhinedaughters*?

Wotan hopes that this may be consummated by a human hero who, free from the lust for power which obtains among the gods, shall, with a sword of *Wotan's* own forging, slay *Fafner*, gain possession of the Rhinegold and restore it to its rightful owners, thus righting *Wotan's* guilty act and freeing the gods from the curse. To accomplish this *Wotan*, in human guise as *Wälse*, begets, in wedlock with a human, the twins *Siegmund* and *Sieglinde*. How the curse of *Alberich* is visited upon these is related in "The Valkyr."

The dramatis personæ in "The Valkyr" are *Brünnhilde*, the valkyr, and her eight sister valkyrs; *Fricka*, *Sieglinde*, *Siegmund*, *Hunding* (the husband of *Sieglinde*), and *Wotan*. The action begins after the forced marriage of *Sieglinde* to *Hunding*. The Wälsungs are in ignorance of the divinity of their father. They know him only as *Walse*.

Act I. In the introduction to "The Rhinegold," we saw the Rhine flowing peacefully toward the sea and the innocent gambols of the *Rhinedaughters*. But "The Valkyr" opens in storm and stress. The peace and happiness of the first scene of the cycle seem to have vanished from the earth with *Alberich's* abjuration of love, his theft of the gold, and *Wotan's* equally treacherous acts.

This "Valkyr" Vorspiel is a masterly representation in tone of a storm gathering for its last infuriated onslaught. The elements are unleashed. The wind sweeps through the forest. Lightning flashes in jagged streaks across the black heavens. There is a crash of thunder and the storm has spent its force.

Two leading motives are employed in this introduction. They are the **Storm Motive** and the Donner Motive. The **Storm Motive** is as follows:

The Complete Opera Book

These themes are elemental. From them Wagner has composed storm music of convincing power.

In the early portion of this vorspiel only the string instruments are used. Gradually the instrumentation grows more powerful. With the climax we have a tremendous *ff* on the contra tuba and two tympani, followed by the crash of the Donner Motive on the wind instruments.

The storm then gradually dies away. Before it has quite passed over, the curtain rises, revealing the large hall of *Hunding's* dwelling. This hall is built around a huge ash-tree, whose trunk and branches pierce the roof, over which the foliage is supposed to spread. There are walls of rough-hewn boards, here and there hung with large plaited and woven hangings. In the right foreground is a large open hearth; back of it in a recess is the larder, separated from the hall by a woven hanging, half drawn. In the background is a large door. A few steps in the left foreground lead up to the door of an inner room. The furniture of the hall is primitive and rude. It consists chiefly of a table, bench, and stools in front of the ash-tree. Only the light of the fire on the hearth illumines the room; though occasionally its fitful gleam is slightly intensified by a distant flash of lightning from the departing storm.

The door in the background is opened from without. *Siegmund*, supporting himself with his hand on the bolt, stands in the entrance. He seems exhausted. His appearance is that of a fugitive who has reached the limit of his powers of endurance. Seeing no one in the hall, he staggers toward the hearth and sinks upon a bearskin rug before it, with the exclamation:

> Whose hearth this may be,
> Here I must rest me.

Richard Wagner

Wagner's treatment of this scene is masterly. As *Siegmund* stands in the entrance we hear the **Siegmund Motive**. This is a sad, weary strain on 'cellos and basses. It seems the wearier for the burden of an accompanying figure on the horns, beneath which it seems to stagger as *Siegmund* staggers toward the hearth. Thus the music not only reflects *Siegmund's* weary mien, but accompanies most graphically his weary gait. Perhaps Wagner's intention was more metaphysical. Maybe the burden beneath which the Siegmund Motive staggers is the curse of *Alberich*. It is through that curse that *Siegmund's* life has been one of storm and stress.

When the storm-beaten Wälsung has sunk upon the rug the Siegmund Motive is followed by the Storm Motive, *pp*—and the storm has died away. The door of the room to the left opens and a young woman—*Sieglinde*—appears. She has heard someone enter, and, thinking her husband returned, has come forth to meet him—not impelled to this by love, but by fear. For *Hunding* had, while her father and kinsmen were away on the hunt, laid waste their dwelling and abducted her and forcibly married her. Ill-fated herself, she is moved to compassion at sight of the storm-driven fugitive before the hearth, and bends over him.

Her compassionate action is accompanied by a new motive, which by Wagner's commentators has been entitled the Motive of Compassion. But it seems to me to have a further meaning as expressing the sympathy between two souls, a tie so subtle that it is at first invisible even to those whom it unites. *Siegmund* and *Sieglinde*, it will be remembered, belong to the same race; and though they are at this point of the action unknown to one another,

The Complete Opera Book

yet, as *Sieglinde* bends over the hunted, storm-beaten *Siegmund*, that subtle sympathy causes her to regard him with more solicitude than would be awakened by any other unfortunate stranger. Hence I have called this motive the **Motive of Sympathy**—taking sympathy in its double meaning of compassion and affinity of feeling:

The beauty of this brief phrase is enhanced by its unpretentiousness. It wells up from the orchestra as spontaneously as pity mingled with sympathetic sorrow wells up from the heart of a gentle woman. As it is *Siegmund* who has awakened these feelings in *Sieglinde*, the Motive of Sympathy is heard simultaneously with the Siegmund Motive.

Siegmund, suddenly raising his head, ejaculates, "Water, water!" *Sieglinde* hastily snatches up a drinking-horn and, having quickly filled it at a spring near the house, swiftly returns and hands it to *Siegmund*. As though new hope were engendered in *Siegmund's* breast by *Sieglinde's* gentle ministration, the Siegmund Motive rises higher and higher, gathering passion in its upward sweep and then, combined again with the Motive of Sympathy, sinks to an expression of heartfelt gratitude. . This passage is scored entirely for strings. Yet no composer, except Wagner, has evoked from a full orchestra sounds richer or more sensuously beautiful.

Having quaffed from the proffered cup the stranger lifts a searching gaze to her features, as if they awakened within him memories the significance of which he himself cannot fathom. She, too, is strangely affected by his gaze. How has fate interwoven their lives that these two people, a man and a woman, looking upon each other apparently for the first time, are so thrilled by a mysterious sense of affinity?

Richard Wagner

Here occurs the **Love Motive** played throughout as a violoncello solo, with accompaniment of eight violoncellos and two double basses; exquisite in tone colour and one of the most tenderly expressive phrases ever penned.

The Love Motive is the mainspring of this act. For this act tells the story of love from its inception to its consummation. Similarly in the course of this act the Love Motive rises by degrees of intensity from an expression of the first tender presentiment of affection to the very ecstasy of love.

Siegmund asks with whom he has found shelter. *Sieglinde* replies that the house is *Hunding's*, and she his wife, and requests *Siegmund* to await her husband's return.

> Weaponless am I:
> The wounded guest,
> He will surely give shelter,

is *Siegmund's* reply. With anxious celerity, *Sieglinde* asks him to show her his wounds. But, refreshed by the draught of cool spring water and with hope revived by her sympathetic presence, he gathers force and, raising himself to a sitting posture, exclaims that his wounds are but slight; his frame is still firm, and had sword and shield held half so well, he would not have fled from his foes. His strength was spent in flight through the storm, but the night that sank on his vision has yielded again to the sunshine of *Sieglinde's* presence. At these words the Motive of Sympathy rises like a sweet hope. *Sieglinde* fills the drinking-horn with mead and offers it to *Siegmund*. He asks her to take the first sip. She does so and then hands it to him. His eyes rest upon her while he drinks. As he returns the drinking-horn to her there are traces of deep emotion in his mien. He sighs and gloomily bows his head. The action at this point is most expressively accompanied by the orchestra. Specially noteworthy is an impassioned upward sweep of the Motive of Sympathy as *Siegmund* regards *Sieglinde* with traces of deep emotion in his mien.

In a voice that trembles with emotion, he says: "You have harboured one whom misfortune follows wherever he wends his footsteps. Lest through me misfortune enter this house, I will depart." With firm, determined strides he already has reached the door, when she, forgetting all in the vague memories that his presence have stirred within her, calls after him:

"Tarry! You cannot bring sorrow to the house where sorrow already reigns!"

Her words are followed by a phrase freighted as if with sorrow, the Motive of the Wälsung Race, or **Wälsung**

Motive: *Siegmund* returns to the hearth, while she, as if shamed by her outburst of feeling, allows her eyes to sink toward the ground. Leaning against the hearth, he rests his calm, steady gaze upon her, until she again raises her eyes to his, and they regard each other in long silence and with deep emotion. The woman is the first to start. She hears *Hunding* leading his horse to the stall, and soon afterward he stands upon the threshold looking darkly upon his wife and the stranger. *Hunding* is a man of great strength and stature, his eyes heavy-browed, his sinister features framed in thick black hair and beard, a sombre, threatful personality boding little good to whomever crosses his path.

With the approach of *Hunding* there is a sudden change in the character of the music. Like a premonition of *Hunding's* entrance we hear the **Hunding Motive**, *pp*.

Richard Wagner

Then as *Hunding*, armed with spear and shield, stands upon the threshold, this Hunding Motive—as dark, forbidding, and portentous of woe to the two Wälsungs as *Hunding's* sombre visage—resounds with dread power on the tubas:

Although weaponless, and *Hunding* armed with spear and shield, the fugitive meets his scrutiny without flinching, while the woman, anticipating her husband's inquiry, explains that she had discovered him lying exhausted at the hearth and given him shelter. With an assumed graciousness that makes him, if anything, more forbidding, *Hunding* orders her prepare the meal. While she does so he glances repeatedly from her to the stranger whom she has harboured, as if comparing their features and finding in them something to arouse his suspicions. "How like unto her," he mutters.

"Your name and story?" he asks, after they have seated themselves at the table in front of the ash-tree, and when the stranger hesitates, *Hunding* points to the woman's eager, inquiring look.

"Guest," she urges, little knowing the suspicions her husband harbours, "gladly would I know whence you come."

Slowly, as if oppressed by heavy memories, he begins his story, carefully, however, continuing to conceal his name, since for all he knows, *Hunding* may be one of the enemies of his race. Amid incredible hardships, surrounded by enemies against whom he and his kin constantly were obliged to defend themselves, he grew up in the forest. He and his father returned from one of their hunts to find the hut in ashes, his mother a corpse, and no trace of his twin sister. In one of the combats with their foes he became separated from his father.

The Complete Opera Book

At this point you hear the Walhalla Motive, for *Siegmund's* father was none other than *Wotan*, known to his human descendants, however, only as Wälse. In *Wotan's* narrative in the next act it will be discovered that *Wotan* purposely created these misfortunes for *Siegmund*, in order to strengthen him for his task.

Continuing his narrative *Siegmund* says that, since losing track of his father, he has wandered from place to place, ever with misfortune in his wake. That very day he has defended a maid whom her brothers wished to force into marriage. But when, in the combat that ensued, he had slain her brothers, she turned upon him and denounced him as a murderer, while the kinsmen of the slain, summoned to vengeance, attacked him from all quarters. He fought until shield and sword were shattered, then fled to find chance shelter in *Hunding's* dwelling.

The story of *Siegmund* is told in melodious recitative. It is not a melody in the old-fashioned meaning of the term, but it fairly teems with melodiousness. It will have been observed that incidents very different in kind are related by *Siegmund*. It would be impossible to treat this narrative with sufficient variety of expression in a melody. But in Wagner's melodious recitative the musical phrases reflect every incident narrated by *Siegmund*. For instance, when *Siegmund* tells how he went hunting with his father there is joyous freshness and abandon in the music, which, however, suddenly sinks to sadness as he narrates how they returned and found the Wälsung dwelling devastated by enemies. We hear also the Hunding Motive at this point, which thus indicates that whose who brought this misfortune upon the Wälsungs were none other than *Hunding* and his kinsmen. As *Siegmund* tells how, when he was separated from his father, he sought to mingle with men and women, you hear the Love Motive, while his description of his latest combat is accompanied by the

Richard Wagner

rhythm of the Hunding Motive. Those whom *Siegmund* slew were *Hunding's* kinsmen. Thus *Siegmund's* dark fate has driven him to seek shelter in the house of the very man who is the arch-enemy of his race and is bound by the laws of kinship to avenge on *Siegmund* the death of kinsmen.

As *Siegmund* concludes his narrative the Wälsung Motive is heard. Gazing with ardent longing toward *Sieglinde*, he says:

> Now know'st thou, questioning wife,
> Why "Peaceful" is not my name.

These words are sung to a lovely phrase. Then, as *Siegmund* rises and strides over to the hearth, while *Sieglinde*, pale and deeply affected by his tale, bows her head, there is heard on the horns, bassoons, violas, and 'cellos a motive expressive of the heroic fortitude of the Wälsungs in struggling against their fate. It is the **Motive of the Wälsung's Heroism,** a motive steeped in the tragedy of futile struggle against destiny.

The sombre visage at the head of the table has grown even darker and more threatening. *Hunding* arises. "I know a ruthless race to whom nothing is sacred, and hated of all," he says. "Mine were the kinsmen you slew. I, too, was summoned from my home to take blood vengeance upon the slayer. Returning, I find him here. You have been offered shelter for the night, and for the night you are safe. But to-morrow be prepared to defend yourself."

Alone, unarmed, and in the house of his enemy! And yet the same roof harbours a friend—the woman. What strange affinity has brought them together under the eye of the pitiless savage with whom she has been forced

The Complete Opera Book

into marriage? The embers on the hearth collapse. The glow that for a moment pervades the room seems to his excited senses a reflection from the eyes of the woman to whom he has been so unaccountably yet so strongly drawn. Even the spot on the old ash-tree, where he saw her glance linger before she left the room, seems to have caught its sheen. Then the embers die out. All grows dark.

The scene is eloquently set to music. *Siegmund's* gloomy thoughts are accompanied by the threatening rhythm of the Hunding Motive and the Sword Motive in a minor key, for *Siegmund* is still weaponless.

> A sword my father did promise
> . . . .
> Wälse! Wälse! Where is thy sword!

The Sword Motive rings out like a shout of triumph. As the embers of the fire collapse, there is seen in the glare, that for a moment falls upon the ash-tree, the hilt of a sword whose blade is buried in the trunk of the tree at the point upon which *Sieglinde's* look last rested. While the Motive of the Sword gently rises and falls, like the coming and going of a lovely memory, *Siegmund* apostrophizes the sheen as the reflection of *Sieglinde's* glance. And although the embers die out, and night falls upon the scene, in *Siegmund's* thoughts the memory of that pitying, loving look glimmers on.

Is it his excited fancy that makes him hear the door of the inner chamber softly open and light footsteps coming in his direction? No; for he becomes conscious of a form, her form, dimly limned upon the darkness. He springs to his feet. *Sieglinde* is by his side. She has given *Hunding* a sleeping-potion. She will point out a weapon to *Siegmund*—a sword. If he can wield it she will call him the greatest hero, for only the mightiest can wield it.

Richard Wagner

The music quickens with the subdued excitement in the breasts of the two Wälsungs. You hear the Sword Motive and above it, on horns, clarinet, and oboe, a new motive—that of the **Wälsungs' Call to Victory**:

for *Sieglinde* hopes that with the sword the stranger, who has awakened so quickly love in her breast, will overcome *Hunding*. This motive has a resistless, onward sweep. *Sieglinde*, amid the strains of the stately Walhalla Motive, followed by the Sword Motive, narrates the story of the sword. While *Hunding* and his kinsmen were feasting in honour of her forced marriage with him, an aged stranger entered the hall. The men knew him not and shrank from his fiery glance. But upon her his look rested with tender compassion. With a mighty thrust he buried a sword up to its hilt in the trunk of the ash-tree. Whoever drew it from its sheath to him it should belong. The stranger went his way. One after another the strong men tugged at the hilt—but in vain. Then she knew who the aged stranger was and for whom the sword was destined.

The Sword Motive rings out like a joyous shout, and *Sieglinde's* voice mingles with the triumphant notes of the Wälsung's Call to Victory as she turns to *Siegmund:*

> O, found I in thee
> The friend in need!

The Motive of the Wälsungs' heroism, now no longer full of tragic import, but forceful and defiant—and *Siegmund* holds *Sieglinde* in his embrace.

There is a rush of wind. The woven hangings flap and fall. As the lovers turn, a glorious sight greets their eyes. The landscape is illumined by the moon. Its silver sheen

The Complete Opera Book

flows down the hills and quivers along the meadows whose grasses tremble in the breeze. All nature seems to be throbbing in unison with the hearts of the lovers, and, turning to the woman, *Siegmund* greets her with the **Love Song:**

The Love Motive, impassioned, irresistible, sweeps through the harmonies—and Love and Spring are united. The Love Motive also pulsates through *Sieglinde's* ecstatic reply after she has given herself fully up to *Siegmund* in the Flight Motive—for before his coming her woes have fled as winter flies before the coming of spring. With *Siegmund's* exclamation:

Oh, wondrous vision!
Rapturous woman!

there rises from the orchestra like a vision of loveliness the Motive of Freia, the Venus of German mythology. In its embrace it folds this pulsating theme:

It throbs on like a love-kiss until it seemingly yields to the blandishments of this caressing phrase:

This throbbing, pulsating, caressing music is succeeded by a moment of repose. The woman again gazes searchingly into the man's features. She has seen his face before.

Richard Wagner

When? Now she remembers. It is when she has seen her own reflection in a brook! And his voice? It seems to her like an echo of her own. And his glance; has it never before rested on her? She is sure it has, and she will tell him when.

She repeats how, while *Hunding* and his kinsmen were feasting at her marriage, an aged man entered the hall and, drawing a sword thrust it to the hilt in the ash-tree. The first to draw it out, to him it should belong. One after another the men strove to loosen the sword, but in vain. Once the aged man's glance rested on her and shone with the same light as now shines in his who has come to her through night and storm. He who thrust the sword into the tree was of her own race, the Wälsungs. Who is he?

"I, too, have seen that light, but in your eyes!" exclaimed the fugitive. "I, too, am of your race. I, too, am a Wälsung, my father none other than Wälse himself."

"Was Wälse your father?" she cries ecstatically. "For you, then, this sword was thrust in the tree! Let me name you, as I recall you from far back in my childhood, *Siegmund—Siegmund—Siegmund!*"

"Yes, I am *Siegmund;* and you, too, I now know well. You are *Sieglinde*. Fate has willed that we two of our unhappy race, shall meet again and save each other or perish together."

Then, leaping upon the table, he grasps the sword-hilt which protrudes from the trunk of the ash-tree where he has seen that strange glow in the light of the dying embers. A mighty tug, and he draws it from the tree as a blade from its scabbard. Brandishing it in triumph, he leaps to the floor and, clasping *Sieglinde*, rushes forth with her into the night.

And the music? It fairly seethes with excitement. As *Siegmund* leaps upon the table, the Motive of the Wälsung's Heroism rings out as if in defiance of the enemies of the race. The Sword Motive—and he has grasped the hilt; the Motive of Compact, ominous of the fatality which hangs over the Wälsungs; the Motive of Renunciation, with its threatening import; then the Sword Motive —brilliant like the glitter of refulgent steel—and *Siegmund* has unsheathed the sword. The Wälsungs' Call to Victory, like a song of triumph; a superb upward sweep of the Sword Motive; the Love Motive, now rushing onward in the very ecstasy of passion, and *Siegmund* holds in his embrace *Sieglinde*, his bride—of the same doomed race as himself!

Act II. In the *Vorspiel* the orchestra, with an upward rush of the Sword Motive, resolved into 9-8 time, the orchestra dashes into the Motive of Flight. The Sword Motive in this 9-8 rhythm closely resembles the Motive of the Valkyr's Ride, and the Flight Motive in the version in which it appears is much like the Valkyr's Shout. The Ride and the Shout are heard in the course of the *Vorspiel*, the former with tremendous force on trumpets and trombones as the curtain rises on a wild, rocky mountain pass, at the back of which, through a natural rock-formed arch, a gorge slopes downward.

In the foreground stands *Wotan*, armed with spear, shield, and helmet. Before him is *Brünnhilde* in the superb costume of the Valkyr. The stormy spirit of the *Vorspiel* pervades the music of *Wotan's* command to *Brünnhilde* that she bridle her steed for battle and spur it to the fray to do combat for *Siegmund* against *Hunding*. *Brünnhilde* greets *Wotan's* command with the weirdly joyous **Shout of the Valkyrs**

Hojotoho! Heiaha-ha.

Walter Hyde as Siegmund in "Die Walküre."

LILLI LEHMANN AS BRUNNHILDE IN "DIE WALKURE."

Richard Wagner

It is the cry of the wild horsewomen of the air, coursing through storm-clouds, their shields flashing back the lightning, their voices mingling with the shrieks of the tempest. Weirder, wilder joy has never found expression in music. One seems to see the steeds of the air and streaks of lightning playing around their riders, and to hear the whistling of the wind.

The accompanying figure is based on the Motive of the **Ride of the Valkyrs:**

Brünnhilde, having leapt from rock to rock to the highest peak of the mountain, again faces *Wotan*, and with delightful banter calls to him that *Fricka* is approaching in her ram-drawn chariot. *Fricka* has appeared, descended from her chariot, and advances toward *Wotan*, *Brünnhilde* having meanwhile disappeared behind the mountain height.

Fricka is the protector of the marriage vow, and as such she has come in anger to demand from *Wotan* vengeance in behalf of *Hunding*. As she advances hastily toward *Wotan*, her angry, passionate demeanour is reflected by the orchestra, and this effective musical expression of *Fricka's* ire is often heard in the course of the scene. When near *Wotan* she moderates her pace, and her angry demeanour gives way to sullen dignity.

Wotan, though knowing well what has brought *Fricka* upon the scene, feigns ignorance of the cause of her agitation and asks what it is that harasses her. Her reply is preceded by the stern Hunding motive. She tells *Wotan* that she, as the protectress of the sanctity of the marriage vow, has heard *Hunding's* voice calling for vengeance upon the Wälsung twins. Her words, "His voice for vengeance

The Complete Opera Book

is raised," are set to a phrase strongly suggestive of *Alberich's curse*. It seems as though the avenging Nibelung were pursuing *Wotan's* children and thus striking a blow at *Wotan* himself through *Fricka*. The Love Motive breathes through *Wotan's* protest that *Siegmund* and *Sieglinde* only yielded to the music of the spring night. *Wotan* argues that *Siegmund* and *Sieglinde* are true lovers, and *Fricka* should smile instead of venting her wrath on them. The motive of the Love Song, the Love Motive, and the caressing phrase heard in the love scene are beautifully blended with *Wotan's* words. In strong contrast to these motives is the music in *Fricka's* outburst of wrath, introduced by the phrase reflecting her ire, which is repeated several times in the course of this episode. *Wotan* explains to her why he begat the Wälsung race and the hopes he has founded upon it. But *Fricka* mistrusts him. What can mortals accomplish that the gods, who are far mightier than mortals, cannot accomplish? *Hunding* must be avenged on *Siegmund* and *Sieglinde*. *Wotan* must withdraw his protection from *Siegmund*. Now appears a phrase which expresses *Wotan's* impotent wrath —impotent because *Fricka* brings forward the unanswerable argument that if the Wälsungs go unpunished by her, as guardian of the marriage vow, she, the Queen of the Gods, will be held up to the scorn of mankind.

Wotan would fain save the Wälsungs. But *Fricka's* argument is conclusive. He cannot protect *Siegmund* and *Sieglinde*, because their escape from punishment would bring degradation upon the queen-goddess and the whole race of the gods, and result in their immediate fall. *Wotan's* wrath rises at the thought of sacrificing his beloved children to the vengeance of *Hunding*, but he is impotent. His far-reaching plans are brought to nought. He sees the hope of having the Ring restored to the *Rhinedaughters* by the voluntary act of a hero of the Wälsung race vanish.

Richard Wagner

The curse of *Alberich* hangs over him like a dark, threatening cloud. The **Motive of Wotan's Wrath** is as follows:

Brünnhilde's joyous shouts are heard from the height. *Wotan* exclaims that he had summoned the Valkyr to do battle for *Siegmund*. In broad, stately measures, *Fricka* proclaims that her honour shall be guarded by *Brünnhilde's* shield and demands of *Wotan* an oath that in the coming combat the Wälsung shall fall. *Wotan* takes the oath and throws himself dejectedly down upon a rocky seat. *Fricka* strides toward the back. She pauses a moment with a gesture of queenly command before *Brünnhilde*, who has led her horse down the height and into a cave to the right, then departs.

In this scene we have witnessed the spectacle of a mighty god vainly struggling to avert ruin from his race. That it is due to irresistible fate and not merely to *Fricka* that *Wotan's* plans succumb, is made clear by the darkly ominous notes of Alberich's Curse, which resound as *Wotan*, wrapt in gloomy brooding, leans back against the rocky seat, and also when, in a paroxysm of despair, he gives vent to his feelings, a passage which, for overpowering intensity of expression, stands out even from among Wagner's writings. The final words of this outburst of grief:

> The saddest I among all men,

are set to this variant of the Motive of Renunciation; the meaning of this phrase having been expanded from the renunciation of love by *Alberich* to cover the renunciation of happiness which is forced upon *Wotan* by avenging fate:

The Complete Opera Book

Brünnhilde casts away shield, spear, and helmet, and sinking down at *Wotan's* feet looks up to him with affectionate anxiety. Here we see in the Valkyr the touch of tenderness, without which a truly heroic character is never complete.

Musically it is beautifully expressed by the Love Motive, which, when *Wotan*, as if awakening from a reverie, fondly strokes her hair, goes over into the Siegmund Motive. It is over the fate of his beloved Wälsungs *Wotan* has been brooding. Immediately following *Brünnhilde's* words,

> What an I were I not thy will,

is a wonderfully soft yet rich melody on four horns. It is one of those beautiful details in which Wagner's works abound.

In *Wotan's* narrative, which now follows, the chief of the gods tells *Brünnhilde* of the events which have brought this sorrow upon him, of his failure to restore the stolen gold to the *Rhinedaughters;* of his dread of *Alberich's* curse; how she and her sister Valkyrs were born to him by *Erda;* of the necessity that a hero should without aid of the gods gain the Ring and Tarnhelmet from *Fafner* and restore the Rhinegold to the *Rhinedaughters;* how he begot the Wälsungs and inured them to hardships in the hope that one of the race would free the gods from *Alberich's* curse.

The motives heard in *Wotan's* narrative will be recognized, except one, which is new. This is expressive of the stress to which the gods are subjected through *Wotan's* crime. It is first heard when *Wotan* tells of the hero who alone can regain the ring. It is the **Motive of the Gods' Stress.**

Richard Wagner

Excited by remorse and despair *Wotan* bids farewell to the glory of the gods. Then he in terrible mockery blesses the Nibelung's heir—for *Alberich* has wedded and to him has been born a son, upon whom the Nibelung depends to continue his death struggle with the gods. Terrified by this outburst of wrath, *Brünnhilde* asks what her duty shall be in the approaching combat. *Wotan* commands her to do *Fricka's* bidding and withdraw protection from *Siegmund*. In vain *Brünnhilde* pleads for the Wälsung whom she knows *Wotan* loves, and wished a victor until *Fricka* exacted a promise from him to avenge *Hunding*. But her pleading is in vain. *Wotan* is no longer the all-powerful chief of the gods—through his breach of faith he has become the slave of fate. Hence we hear, as *Wotan* rushes away, driven by chagrin, rage, and despair, chords heavy with the crushing force of fate.

Slowly and sadly *Brünnhilde* bends down for her weapons, her actions being accompanied by the Valkyr Motive. Bereft of its stormy impetuosity it is as trist as her thoughts. Lost in sad reflections, which find beautiful expression in the orchestra, she turns toward the background.

Suddenly the sadly expressive phrases are interrupted by the Motive of Flight. Looking down into the valley the Valkyr perceives *Siegmund* and *Sieglinde* approaching in hasty flight. She then disappears in the cave. With a superb crescendo the Motive of Flight reaches its climax and the two Wälsungs are seen approaching through the natural arch. For hours they have toiled forward; often *Sieglinde's* limbs have threatened to fail her, yet never have the fugitives been able to shake off the dread sound of *Hunding* winding his horn as he called upon his kinsmen to redouble their efforts to overtake the two Wälsungs. Even now, as they come up the gorge and pass under a rocky arch to the height of the divide, the pursuit can be heard. They are human quarry of the hunt. Terror has begun to unsettle *Sieglinde's* reason. When *Siegmund* bids her rest she stares wildly before her, then gazes with growing rapture into his eyes and throws her arms around his neck, only to shriek suddenly: "Away, away!" as she hears the distant horn-calls, then to grow rigid and stare vacantly before her as *Siegmund* announces to her that here he proposes to end their flight, here await *Hunding*, and test the temper of *Wälse's* sword. Then she tries to thrust him away. Let him leave her to her fate and save himself. But a moment later, although she still clings to him, she apparently is gazing into vacancy and crying out that he has deserted her. At last, utterly overcome by the strain of flight with the avenger on the trail, she faints, her hold on *Siegmund* relaxes, and she would have fallen had he not caught her form in his arms. Slowly he lets himself down on a rocky seat, drawing her with him, so that when he is seated her head rests on his lap. Tenderly he looks down upon the companion of his flight, and, while, like a mournful memory, the orchestra intones the Love Motive, he presses a kiss upon her brow—she of his own race, like him doomed to misfortune, dedicated to death, should the sword which he has unsheathed from *Hunding's* ash-tree prove traitor. As he looks up from *Sieglinde* he is startled. For there stands on the rock above them a shining apparition in flowing robes, breastplate, and helmet, and leaning upon a spear. It is *Brünnhilde*, the Valkyr, daughter of *Wotan*.

The Motive of Fate—so full of solemn import—is heard.

While her earnest look rests upon him, there is heard the **Motive of the Death-Song**, a tristly prophetic strain.

Richard Wagner

Brünnhilde advances and then, pausing again, leans with one hand on her charger's neck, and, grasping shield and spear with the other, gazes upon *Siegmund*. Then there rises from the orchestra, in strains of rich, soft, alluring beauty, an inversion of the Walhalla Motive. The Fate, Death-Song and Walhalla motives recur, and *Siegmund*, raising his eyes and meeting *Brünnhilde's* look, questions her and receives her answers. The episode is so fraught with solemnity that the shadow of death seems to have fallen upon the scene. The solemn beauty of the music impresses itself the more upon the listener, because of the agitated, agonized scene which preceded it. To the Wälsung, who meets her gaze so calmly, *Brünnhilde* speaks in solemn tones:

"Siegmund, look on me. I am she whom soon you must prepare to follow." Then she paints for him in glowing colours the joys of Walhalla, where *Wälse*, his father, is awaiting him and where he will have heroes for his companions, himself the hero of many valiant deeds. *Siegmund* listens unmoved. In reply he frames but one question: "When I enter Walhalla, will *Sieglinde* be there to greet me?"

When *Brünnhilde* answers that in Walhalla he will be attended by valkyrs and wishmaidens, but that *Sieglinde* will not be there to meet him, he scorns the delights she has held out. Let her greet *Wotan* from him, and *Wälse*, his father, too, as well as the wishmaidens. He will remain with *Sieglinde*.

Then the radiant Valkyr, moved by *Siegmund's* calm determination to sacrifice even a place among the heroes of Walhalla for the woman he loves, makes known to him the fate to which he has been doomed. *Wotan* desired

The Complete Opera Book

to give him victory over *Hunding*, and she had been summoned by the chief of the gods and commanded to hover above the combatants, and by shielding *Siegmund* from *Hunding's* thrusts, render the Wälsung's victory certain. But *Wotan's* spouse, *Fricka*, who, as the first among the goddesses, is guardian of the marriage vows, has heard *Hunding's* voice calling for vengeance, and has demanded that vengeance be his. Let *Siegmund* therefore prepare for Walhalla, but let him leave *Sieglinde* in her care. She will protect her.

"No other living being but I shall touch her," exclaims the Wälsung, as he draws his sword. "If the Wälsung sword is to be shattered on Hunding's spear, to which I am to fall a victim, it first shall bury itself in her breast and save her from a worse fate!" He poises the sword ready for the thrust above the unconscious *Sieglinde*.

"Hold!" cries *Brünnhilde*, thrilled by his heroic love. "Whatever the consequences which Wotan, in his wrath, shall visit upon me, to-day, for the first time I disobey him. Sieglinde shall live, and with her Siegmund! Yours the victory over Hunding. Now Wälsung, prepare for battle!"

Hunding's horn-calls sound nearer and nearer. *Siegmund* judges that he has ascended the other side of the gorge, intending to cross the rocky arch. Already *Brünnhilde* has gone to take her place where she knows the combatants must meet. With a last look and a last kiss for *Sieglinde*, *Siegmund* gently lays her down and begins to ascend toward the peak. Mist gathers; storm-clouds roll over the mountain; soon he is lost to sight. Slowly *Sieglinde* regains her senses. She looks for *Siegmund*. Instead of seeing him bending over her she hears *Hunding's* voice as if from among the clouds, calling him to combat; then *Siegmund's* accepting the challenge. She staggers toward the peak. Suddenly a bright light pierces the clouds. Above her

Richard Wagner

she sees the men fighting, *Brünnhilde* protecting *Siegmund* who is aiming a deadly stroke at *Hunding*.

At that moment, however, the light is diffused with a reddish glow. In it *Wotan* appears. As *Siegmund's* sword cuts the air on its errand of death, the god interposes his spear, the sword breaks in two and *Hunding* thrusts his spear into the defenceless Wälsung's breast. The second victim of *Alberich's* curse has met his fate.

With a wild shriek, *Sieglinde* falls to the ground, to be caught up by *Brünnhilde* and swung upon the Valkyr's charger, which, urged on by its mistress, now herself a fugitive from *Wotan's* anger, dashes down the defile in headlong flight for the Valkyr rock.

Act III. The third act opens with the famous " Ride of the Valkyrs," a number so familiar that detailed reference to it is scarcely necessary. The wild maidens of Walhalla coursing upon winged steeds through storm-clouds, their weapons flashing in the gleam of lightning, their weird laughter mingling with the crash of thunder, have come to hold tryst upon the Valkyr rock.

When eight of the Valkyrs have gathered upon the rocky summit of the mountain, they espy *Brünnhilde* approaching. It is with savage shouts of "Hojotoho! Heiha!" those who already have reached their savage eyrie, watch for the coming of their wild sisters. Fitful flashes of lightning herald their approach as they storm fearlessly through the wind and cloud, their weird shouts mingling with the clash of thunder. "Hojotoho! Heihe!—Hojotoho! Heiha!"

But, strange burden! Instead of a slain hero across her pommel, *Brünnhilde* bears a woman, and instead of urging her horse to the highest crag, she alights below. The Valkyrs hasten down the rock, and there the wild sisters of the air stand, curiously awaiting the approach of *Brünnhilde*.

In frantic haste the Valkyr tells her sisters what has transpired, and how *Wotan* is pursuing her to punish her

The Complete Opera Book

for her disobedience. One of the Valkyrs ascends the rock and, looking in the direction from which *Brünnhilde* has come, calls out that even now she can descry the red glow behind the storm-clouds that denotes *Wotan's* approach. Quickly *Brünnhilde* bids *Sieglinde* seek refuge in the forest beyond the Valkyr rock. The latter, who has been lost in gloomy brooding, starts at her rescuer's supplication and in strains replete with mournful beauty begs that she may be left to her fate and follow *Siegmund* in death. The glorious prophecy in which *Brünnhilde* now foretells to *Sieglinde* that she is to become the mother of *Siegfried*, is based upon the **Siegfried Motive:**

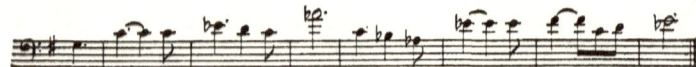

Sieglinde, in joyous frenzy, blesses *Brünnhilde* and hastens to find safety in a dense forest to the eastward, the same forest in which *Fafner*, in the form of a serpent, guards the Rhinegold treasures.

Wotan, in hot pursuit of *Brünnhilde*, reaches the mountain summit. In vain her sisters entreat him to spare her. He harshly threatens them unless they cease their entreaties, and with wild cries of fear they hastily depart.

In the ensuing scene between *Wotan* and *Brünnhilde*, in which the latter seeks to justify her action, is heard one of the most beautiful themes of the cycle.

It is the **Motive of Brünnhilde's Pleading**, which finds its loveliest expression when she addresses *Wotan* in the passage beginning:

Thou, who this love within my breast inspired.

Richard Wagner

Brünnhilde is *Wotan's* favourite daughter, but instead of the loving pride with which he always has been wont to regard her, his features are dark with anger at her disobedience of his command. He had decreed *Siegmund's* death. She has striven to give victory to the Wälsung. Throwing herself at her father's feet, she pleads that he himself had intended to save *Siegmund* and had been turned from his purpose only by *Fricka's* interference, and that he had yielded only most grudgingly to *Fricka's* insistent behest. Therefore, when she, his daughter, profoundly moved by *Siegmund's* love for *Sieglinde*, and her sympathies aroused by the sad plight of the fugitives, disregarded his command, she nevertheless acted in accordance with his real inclinations. But *Wotan* is obdurate. She has revelled in the very feelings which he was obliged, at *Fricka's* behest, to forego—admiration for *Siegmund's* heroism and sympathy for him in his misfortune. Therefore she must be punished. He will cause her to fall into a deep sleep upon the Valkyr rock, which shall become the Brünnhilde rock, and to the first man who finds her and awakens her, she, no longer a Valkyr, but a mere woman, shall fall prey.

This great scene between *Wotan* and *Brünnhilde* is introduced by an orchestral passage. The Valkyr lies in penitence at her father's feet. In the expressive orchestral measures the Motive of Wotan's Wrath mingles with that of Brünnhilde's Pleading. The motives thus form a prelude to the scene in which the Valkyr seeks to appease her father's anger, not through a specious plea, but by laying bare the promptings of a noble heart, which forced her, against the chief god's command, to intervene for *Siegmund*. The Motive of Brünnhilde's Pleading is heard in its simplest form at *Brünnhilde's* words:

> Was it so shameful what I have done,

and it may be noticed that as she proceeds the Motive of

The Complete Opera Book

Wotan's Wrath, heard in the accompaniment, grows less stern, until with her plea,

> Soften thy wrath,

it assumes a tone of regretful sorrow.

Wotan's feelings toward *Brünnhilde* have softened for the time from anger to grief that he must mete out punishment for her disobedience. In his reply excitement subsides to gloom. It would be difficult to point to other music more touchingly expressive of deep contrition than the phrase in which *Brünnhilde* pleads that *Wotan* himself taught her to love *Siegmund*. It is here that the Motive of Brünnhilde's Pleading assumes the form in the notation given above. Then we hear from *Wotan* that he had abandoned *Siegmund* to his fate, because he had lost hope in the cause of the gods and wished to end his woe in the wreck of the world. The weird terror of the Curse Motive hangs over this outburst of despair. In broad and beautiful strains *Wotan* then depicts *Brünnhilde* yielding to her emotions when she intervened for *Siegmund*.

Brünnhilde makes her last appeal. She tells her father that *Sieglinde* has found refuge in the forest, and that there she will give birth to a son, *Siegfried*,—the hero for whom the gods have been waiting to overthrow their enemies. If she must suffer for her disobedience, let *Wotan* surround her sleeping form with a fiery circle which only such a hero will dare penetrate. The Motive of Brünnhilde's Pleading and the Siegfried Motive vie with each other in giving expression to the beauty, tenderness, and majesty of this scene.

Gently the god raises her and tenderly kisses her brow; and thus bids farewell to the best beloved of his daughters. Slowly she sinks upon the rock. He closes her helmet and covers her with her shield. Then, with his spear, he invokes the god of fire. Tongues of flame leap from the

Richard Wagner

crevices of the rock. Wildly fluttering fire breaks out on all sides. The forest beyond glows like a furnace, with brighter streaks shooting and throbbing through the mass, as *Wotan*, with a last look at the sleeping form of *Brünnhilde*, vanishes beyond the fiery circle.

A majestic orchestral passage opens *Wotan's* farewell to *Brünnhilde*. In all music for bass voice this scene has no peer. Such tender, mournful beauty has never found expression in music—and this, whether we regard the vocal part or the orchestral accompaniment in which the lovely **Slumber Motive:**

As *Wotan* leads *Brünnhilde* to the rock, upon which she sinks, closes her helmet, and covers her with her shield, then invokes *Loge*, and, after gazing fondly upon the slumbering Valkyr, vanishes amid the magic flames, the Slumber Motive, the Magic Fire Motive, and the Siegfried Motive combine to place the music of the scene with the most brilliant and beautiful portion of our heritage from the great master-musician. But here, too, lurks Destiny. Towards the close of this glorious finale we hear again the ominous muttering of the Motive of Fate. *Brünnhilde* may be saved from ignominy, *Siegfried* may be born to *Sieglinde*—but the crushing weight of *Alberich's* curse still rests upon the race of the gods.

SIEGFRIED

Music-drama in three acts, by Richard Wagner. Produced, Bayreuth, August 16, 1876. London, by the Carl Rosa Company, 1898, in English. New York, Metropolitan Opera House, November 9, 1887, with Lehmann (*Brünnhilde*), Fischer (*Wotan*), Alvary (*Siegfried*), and Seidl-Kraus (*Forest bird*).

The Complete Opera Book

Characters

SIEGFRIED	*Tenor*
MIME	*Tenor*
WOTAN (disguised as the WANDERER)	*Baritone-Bass*
ALBERICH	*Baritone-Bass*
FAFNER	*Bass*
ERDA	*Contralto*
FOREST BIRD	*Soprano*
BRÜNNHILDE	*Soprano*

Time—Legendary.   *Place*—A rocky cave in the forest; deep in the forest; wild region at foot of a rocky mount; the Brünnhilde-rock.

The Nibelungs were not present in the dramatic action of "The Valkyr," though the sinister influence of *Alberich* shaped the tragedy of *Siegmund's* death. In "Siegfried" several characters of "The Rhinegold," who do not take part in "The Valkyr," reappear. These are the Nibelungs *Alberich* and *Mime;* the giant *Fafner*, who in the guise of a serpent guards the Ring, the Tarnhelmet, and the Nibelung hoard in a cavern, and *Erda*.

Siegfried has been born of *Sieglinde*, who died in giving birth to him. This scion of the Wälsung race has been reared by *Mime*, who found him in the forest by his dead mother's side. *Mime* is plotting to obtain possession of the ring and of *Fafner's* other treasures, and hopes to be aided in his designs by the lusty youth. *Wotan*, disguised as a wanderer, is watching the course of events, again hopeful that a hero of the Wälsung race will free the gods from *Alberich's* curse. Surrounded by magic fire, *Brünnhilde* still lies in deep slumber on the Brünnhilde Rock.

The *Vorspiel* of "Siegfried" is expressive of *Mime's* planning and plotting. It begins with music of a mysterious brooding character. Mingling with this is the Motive of the Hoard, familiar from "The Rhinegold." Then is heard the Nibelung Motive. After reaching a forceful climax it passes over to the Motive of the Ring.

Richard Wagner

which rises from pianissimo to a crashing climax. The ring is to be the prize of all *Mime's* plotting. He hopes to weld the pieces of *Siegmund's* sword together, and that with this sword *Siegfried* will slay *Fafner*. Then *Mime* will slay *Siegfried* and possess himself of the ring. Thus it is to serve his own ends only, that *Mime* is craftily rearing *Siegfried*.

The opening scene shows *Mime* forging a sword at a natural forge formed in a rocky cave. In a soliloquy he discloses the purpose of his labours and laments that *Siegfried* shivers every sword which has been forged for him. Could he (*Mime*) but unite the pieces of *Siegmund's* sword! At this thought the Sword Motive rings out brilliantly, and is jubilantly repeated, accompanied by a variant of the Walhalla Motive. For if the pieces of the sword were welded together, and *Siegfried* were with it to slay *Fafner*, *Mime* could surreptitiously obtain possession of the ring, slay *Siegfried*, rule over the gods in Walhalla, and circumvent *Alberich's* plans for regaining the hoard.

Mime is still at work when *Siegfried* enters, clad in a wild forest garb. Over it a silver horn is slung by a chain. The sturdy youth has captured a bear. He leads it by a bast rope, with which he gives it full play so that it can make a dash at *Mime*. As the latter flees terrified behind the forge, *Siegfried* gives vent to his high spirits in shouts of laughter. Musically his buoyant nature is expressed by a theme inspired by the fresh, joyful spirit of a wild, woodland life. It may be called, to distinguish it from the Siegfried Motive, the **Motive of Siegfried the Fearless.**

It pervades with its joyous impetuosity the ensuing scene, in which *Siegfried* has his sport with *Mime*, until tiring of it, he loosens the rope from the bear's neck and drives the animal back into the forest. In a pretty, graceful phrase *Siegfried* tells how he blew his horn, hoping it would be answered by a pleasanter companion than *Mime*. Then he examines the sword which *Mime* has been forging. The Siegfried Motive resounds as he inveighs against the weapon's weakness, then shivers it on the anvil. The orchestra, with a rush, takes up the **Motive of Siegfried the Impetuous**.

This is a theme full of youthful snap and dash. *Mime* tells *Siegfried* how he tenderly reared him from infancy. The music here is as simple and pretty as a folk-song, for *Mime's* reminiscences of *Siegfried's* infancy are set to a charming melody, as though *Mime* were recalling to *Siegfried's* memory a cradle song of those days. But *Siegfried* grows impatient. If *Mime* really tended him so kindly out of pure affection, why should *Mime* be so repulsive to him; and yet why should he, in spite of *Mime's* repulsiveness, always return to the cave? The dwarf explains that he is to *Siegfried* what the father is to the fledgling. This leads to a beautiful lyric episode. *Siegfried* says that he saw the birds mating, the deer pairing, the she-wolf nursing her cubs. Whom shall he call Mother? Who is *Mime's* wife? This episode is pervaded by the lovely **Motive of Love-Life**.

John Coates as Siegfried.

Von Rooy as Wotan in "Siegfried."

Richard Wagner

Mime endeavours to persuade *Siegfried* that he is his father and mother in one. But *Siegfried* has noticed that the young of birds and deer and wolves look like the parents. He has seen his features reflected in the brook, and knows he does not resemble the hideous *Mime*. The notes of the Love-Life Motive pervade this episode. When *Siegfried* speaks of seeing his own likeness, we also hear the Siegfried Motive. *Mime*, forced by *Siegfried* to speak the truth, tells of *Sieglinde's* death while giving birth to *Siegfried*. Throughout this scene we find reminiscences of the first act of "The Valkyr," the Wälsung Motive, the Motive of Sympathy, and the Love Motive. Finally, when *Mime* produces as evidence of the truth of his words the two pieces of *Siegmund's* sword, the Sword Motive rings out brilliantly. *Siegfried* exclaims that *Mime* must weld the pieces into a trusty weapon. Then follows *Siegfried's* "Wander Song," so full of joyous abandon. Once the sword welded, he will leave the hated *Mime* for ever. As the fish darts through the water, as the bird flies so free, he will flee from the repulsive dwarf. With joyous exclamations he runs from the cave into the forest.

The frank, boisterous nature of *Siegfried* is charmingly portrayed. His buoyant vivacity finds capital expression in the Motives of Siegfried the Fearless, Siegfried the Impetuous, and his "Wander Song," while the vein of tenderness in his character seems to run through the Love-Life Motive. His harsh treatment of *Mime* is not brutal; for *Siegfried* frankly avows his loathing for the dwarf, and we feel, knowing *Mime's* plotting against the young Wälsung, that *Siegfried's* hatred is the spontaneous aversion of a frank nature for an insidious one.

Mime has a gloomy soliloquy. It is interrupted by the entrance of *Wotan*, disguised as a wanderer. At the moment *Mime* is in despair because he cannot weld the pieces

The Complete Opera Book

of *Siegmund's* sword. When the *Wanderer* departs, he has prophesied that only he who does not know what fear is—only a fearless hero—can weld the fragments, and that through this fearless hero *Mime* shall lose his life. This prophecy is reached through a somewhat curious process which must be unintelligible to any one who has not made a study of the libretto. The *Wanderer*, seating himself, wagers his head that he can correctly answer any three questions which *Mime* may put to him. *Mime* then asks: "What is the race born in the earth's deep bowels?" The *Wanderer* answers: "The Nibelungs." *Mime'* ssecond question is: What race dwells on the earth's back? The *Wanderer* replies: "The race of giants." *Mime* finally asks: "What race dwells on cloudy heights?" The *Wanderer* answers: "The race of the gods." The *Wanderer*, having thus answered correctly *Mime's* three questions, now put three questions to *Mime:* "What is that noble race which *Wotan* ruthlessly dealt with, and yet which he deemeth most dear?" *Mime* answers correctly: "The Wälsungs." Then the *Wanderer* asks: "What sword must *Siegfried* then strike with, dealing to *Fafner* death?" *Mime* answers correctly: "With *Siegmund's* sword." "Who," asks the *Wanderer*, "can weld its fragments?" *Mime* is terrified, for he cannot answer. Then *Wotan* utters the prophecy of the fearless hero.

The scene is musically most eloquent. It is introduced by two motives, representing *Wotan* as the Wanderer. The mysterious chords of the former seem characteristic of *Wotan's* disguise.

The latter, with its plodding, heavily-tramping movement, is the motive of *Wotan's* wandering.

The third new motive found in this scene is characteristically expressive of the *Cringing Mime*.

Richard Wagner

Several motives familiar from "The Rhinegold" and "The Valkyr" are heard here. The Motive of Compact so powerfully expressive of the binding force of law, the Nibelung and Walhalla motives from "The Rhinegold," and the Wälsungs' Heroism motives from the first act of "The Valkyr," are among these.

When the *Wanderer* has vanished in the forest *Mime* sinks back on his stool in despair. Staring after *Wotan* into the sunlit forest, the shimmering rays flitting over the soft green mosses with every movement of the branches and each tremor of the leaves seem to him like flickering flames and treacherous will-o'-the-wisps. We hear the Loge Motive (*Loge* being the god of fire) familiar from "The Rhinegold" and the finale of "The Valkyr." At last *Mime* rises to his feet in terror. He seems to see *Fafner* in his serpent's guise approaching to devour him, and in a paroxysm of fear he falls with a shriek behind the anvil. Just then *Siegfried* bursts out of the thicket, and with the fresh, buoyant "Wander Song" and the Motive of Siegfried the Fearless, the weird mystery which hung over the former scene is dispelled. *Siegfried* looks about him for *Mime* until he sees the dwarf lying behind the anvil.

Laughingly the young Wälsung asks the dwarf if he has thus been welding the sword. "The sword? The sword?" repeats *Mime* confusedly, as he advances, and his mind wanders back to *Wotan's* prophecy of the fearless hero. Regaining his senses he tells *Siegfried* there is one thing he has yet to learn, namely, to be afraid; that his mother charged him (*Mime*) to teach fear to him (*Siegfried*). *Mime* asks *Siegfried* if he has never felt his heart beating when in the gloaming he heard strange sounds and saw weirdly glimmering lights in the forest. *Siegfried* replies that he never has. He knows not what fear is. If it is necessary before he goes forth in quest of adventure to learn

The Complete Opera Book

what fear is he would like to be taught. But how can *Mime* teach him?

The Magic Fire Motive and Brünnhilde's Slumber Motive familiar from Wotan's Farewell, and the Magic Fire scene in the third act of "The Valkyr" are heard here, the former depicting the weirdly glimmering lights with which *Mime* has sought to infuse dread into *Siegfried's* breast, the latter prophesying that, penetrating fearlessly the fiery circle, *Siegfried* will reach *Brünnhilde*. Then *Mime* tells *Siegfried* of *Fafner*, thinking thus to strike terror into the young Wälsung's breast. But far from it! *Siegfried* is incited by *Mime's* words to meet *Fafner* in combat. Has *Mime* welded the fragments of *Siegmund's* sword, asks *Siegfried*. The dwarf confesses his impotency. *Siegfried* seizes the fragments. He will forge his own sword. Here begins the great scene of the forging of the sword. Like a shout of victory the Motive of Siegfried the Fearless rings out and the orchestra fairly glows as *Siegfried* heaps a great mass of coal on the forge-hearth, and, fanning the heat, begins to file away at the fragments of the sword.

The roar of the fire, the sudden intensity of the fierce white heat to which the young Wälsung fans the glow—these we would respectively hear and see were the music given without scenery or action, so graphic is Wagner's score. The Sword Motive leaps like a brilliant tongue of flame over the heavy thuds of a forceful variant of the Motive of Compact, till brightly gleaming runs add to the brilliancy of the score, which reflects all the quickening, quivering effulgence of the scene. How the music flows like a fiery flood and how it hisses as *Siegfried* pours the molten contents of the crucible into a mould and then plunges the latter into water! The glowing steel lies on the anvil and *Siegfried* swings the hammer. With every stroke his joyous excitement is intensified. At last the work is done. He brandishes the sword and with one stroke

Richard Wagner

splits the anvil from top to bottom. With the crash of the Sword Motive, united with the Motive of Siegfried the Fearless, the orchestra dashes into a furious prestissimo, and *Siegfried* shouting with glee, holds aloft the sword!

Act II. The second act opens with a darkly portentous *Vorspiel*. On the very threshold of it we meet *Fafner* in his motive, which is so clearly based on the Giant Motive that there is no necessity for quoting it. Through themes which are familiar from earlier portions of the work, the *Vorspiel* rises to a crashing fortissimo.

The curtain lifts on a thick forest. At the back is the entrance to *Fafner's* cave, the lower part of which is hidden by rising ground in the middle of the stage, which slopes down toward the back. In the darkness the outlines of a figure are dimly discerned. It is the Nibelung *Alberich*, haunting the domain which hides the treasures of which he was despoiled. From the forest comes a gust of wind. A bluish light gleams from the same direction. *Wotan*, still in the guise of a Wanderer, enters.

The ensuing scene between *Alberich* and the *Wanderer* is, from a dramatic point of view, episodical. Suffice it to say that the fine self-poise of *Wotan* and the maliciously restless character of *Alberich* are superbly contrasted. When *Wotan* has departed the Nibelung slips into a rocky crevice, where he remains hidden when *Siegfried* and *Mime* enter. *Mime* endeavours to awaken dread in *Siegfried's* heart by describing *Fafner's* terrible form and powers. But *Siegfried's* courage is not weakened. On the contrary, with heroic impetuosity, he asks to be at once confronted with *Fafner*. *Mime*, well knowing that *Fafner* will soon awaken and issue from his cave to meet *Siegfried* in mortal combat, lingers on in the hope that both may fall, until the young Wälsung drives him away.

Now begins a beautiful lyric episode. *Siegfried* reclines under a linden-tree, and looks up through the branches. The

The Complete Opera Book

rustling of the trees is heard. Over the tremulous whispers of the orchestra—known from concert programs as the "Waldweben" (forest-weaving)—rises a lovely variant of the Wälsung Motive. *Siegfried* is asking himself how his mother may have looked, and this variant of the theme which was first heard in "The Valkyr," when *Sieglinde* told *Siegmund* that her home was the home of woe, rises like a memory of her image. Serenely the sweet strains of the Love-Life Motive soothe his sad thoughts. *Siegfried*, once more entranced by forest sounds, listens intently. Birds' voices greet him. A little feathery songster, whose notes mingle with the rustling leaves of the linden-tree, especially charms him.

The forest voices—the humming of insects, the piping of the birds, the amorous quiver of the branches—quicken his half-defined aspirations. Can the little singer explain his longing? He listens, but cannot catch the meaning of the song. Perhaps, if he can imitate it he may understand it. Springing to a stream hard by, he cuts a reed with his sword and quickly fashions a pipe from it. He blows on it, but it sounds shrill. He listens again to the birds. He may not be able to imitate his song on the reed, but on his silver horn he can wind a woodland tune. Putting the horn to his lips he makes the forest ring with its notes:

The notes of the horn have awakened *Fafner* who now, in the guise of a huge serpent or dragon, crawls toward *Siegfried*. Perhaps the less said about the combat between *Siegfried* and *Fafner* the better. This scene, which seems very spirited in the libretto, is ridiculous on the stage. To make it effective it should be carried out very far back —best of all out of sight—so that the magnificent music

Richard Wagner

will not be marred by the sight of an impossible monster. The music is highly dramatic. The exultant force of the Motive of Siegfried the Fearless, which rings out as *Siegfried* rushes upon *Fafner*, the crashing chord as the serpent roars when *Siegfried* buries the sword in its heart, the rearing, plunging music as the monster rears and plunges with agony —these are some of the most graphic features of the score.

Siegfried raises his fingers to his lips and licks the blood from them. Immediately after the blood has touched his lips he seems to understand the bird, which has again begun its song, while the forest voices once more weave their tremulous melody. The bird tells *Siegfried* of the ring and helmet and of the other treasures in *Fafner's* cave, and *Siegfried* enters it in quest of them. With his disappearance the forest-weaving suddenly changes to the harsh, scolding notes heard in the beginning of the Nibelheim scene in "The Rhinegold." *Mime* slinks in and timidly looks about him to make sure of *Fafner's* death. At the same time *Alberich* issues forth from the crevice in which he was concealed. This scene, in which the two Nibelungs berate each other, is capitally treated, and its humour affords a striking contrast to the preceding scenes.

As *Siegfried* comes out of the cave and brings the ring and helmet from darkness to the light of day, there are heard the Ring Motive, the Motive of the Rhinedaughters' Shout of Triumph, and the Rhinegold Motive. The forest-weaving again begins, and the birds bid the young Wälsung beware of *Mime*. The dwarf now approaches *Siegfried* with repulsive sycophancy. But under a smiling face lurks a plotting heart. *Siegfried* is enabled through the supernatural gifts with which he has become endowed to fathom the purpose of the dwarf, who unconsciously discloses his scheme to poison *Siegfried*. The young Wälsung slays *Mime*, who, as he dies, hears *Alberich's* mocking laugh. Though the Motive of Siegfried the Fearless predominates

The Complete Opera Book

at this point, we also hear the Nibelung Motive and the Motive of the Curse—indicating *Alberich's* evil intent toward *Siegfried*.

Siegfried again reclines under the linden. His soul is tremulous with an undefined longing. As he gazes in almost painful emotion up to the branches and asks if the bird can tell him where he can find a friend, his being seems stirred by awakening passion.

The music quickens with an impetuous phrase, which seems to define the first joyous thrill of passion in the youthful hero. It is the Motive of **Love's Joy**:

It is interrupted by a beautiful variant of the Motive of Love-Life, which continues until above the forest-weaving the bird again thrills him with its tale of a glorious maid who has so long slumbered upon the fire-guarded rock. With the Motive of Love's Joy coursing through the orchestra, *Siegfried* bids the feathery songster continue, and, finally, to guide him to *Brünnhilde*. In answer, the bird flutters from the linden branch, hovers over *Siegfried*, and hesitatingly flies before him until it takes a definite course toward the background. *Siegfried* follows the little singer, the Motive of Love's Joy, succeeded by that of Siegfried the Fearless, bringing the act to a close.

Act III. The third act opens with a stormy introduction in which the Motive of the Ride of the Valkyrs accompanies the Motive of the Gods' Stress, the Compact, and the Erda motives. The introduction reaches its climax with the **Motive of the Dusk of the Gods**:

Richard Wagner

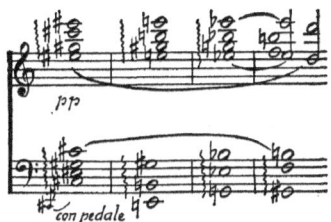

Then to the sombre, questioning phrase of the Motive of Fate, the action begins to disclose the significance of this *Vorspiel*. A wild region at the foot of a rocky mountain is seen. It is night. A fierce storm rages. In dire distress and fearful that through *Siegfried* and *Brünnhilde* the rulership of the world may pass from the gods to the human race, *Wotan* summons *Erda* from her subterranean dwelling. But *Erda* has no counsel for the storm-driven, conscience-stricken god.

The scene reaches its climax in *Wotan's* noble renunciation of the empire of the world. Weary of strife, weary of struggling against the decree of fate, he renounces his sway. Let the era of human love supplant this dynasty, sweeping away the gods and the Nibelungs in its mighty current. It is the last defiance of all-conquering fate by the ruler of a mighty race. After a powerful struggle against irresistible forces, *Wotan* comprehends that the twilight of the gods will be the dawn of a more glorious epoch. A phrase of great dignity gives force to *Wotan's* utterances. It is the **Motive of the World's Heritage:**

Siegfried enters, guided to the spot by the bird; *Wotan* checks his progress with the same spear which shivered

The Complete Opera Book

Siegmund's sword. *Siegfried* must fight his way to *Brünnhilde*. With a mighty blow the young Wälsung shatters the spear and *Wotan* disappears 'mid the crash of the Motive of Compact—for the spear with which it was the chief god's duty to enforce compacts is shattered. Meanwhile the gleam of fire has become noticeable. Fiery clouds float down from the mountain. *Siegfried* stands at the rim of the magic circle. Winding his horn he plunges into the seething flames. Around the Motive of Siegfried the Fearless and the Siegfried Motive flash the Magic Fire and Loge motives.

The flames, having flashed forth with dazzling brilliancy, gradually pale before the red glow of dawn till a rosy mist envelops the scene. When it rises, the rock and *Brünnhilde* in deep slumber under the fir-tree, as in the finale of "The Valkyr," are seen. *Siegfried* appears on the height in the background. As he gazes upon the scene there are heard the Fate and Slumber motives and then the orchestra weaves a lovely variant of the Freia Motive. This is followed by the softly caressing strains of the Fricka Motive. *Fricka* sought to make *Wotan* faithful to her by bonds of love, and hence the Fricka Motive in this scene does not reflect her personality, but rather the awakening of the love which is to thrill *Siegfried* when he has beheld *Brünnhilde's* features. As he sees *Brünnhilde's* charger slumbering in the grove we hear the Motive of the Valkyr's Ride, and when his gaze is attracted by the sheen of *Brünnhilde's* armour, the theme of Wotan's Farewell. Approaching the armed slumberer under the fir-tree, *Siegfried* raises the shield and discloses the figure of the sleeper, the face being almost hidden by the helmet.

Carefully he loosens the helmet. As he takes it off *Brünnhilde's* face is disclosed and her long curls flow down over her bosom. *Siegfried* gazes upon her enraptured. Drawing his sword he cuts the rings of mail on both sides,

Richard Wagner

gently lifts off the corselet and greaves, and *Brünnhilde*, in soft female drapery, lies before him. He starts back in wonder. Notes of impassioned import—the Motive of Love's Joy—express the feelings that well up from his heart as for the first time he beholds a woman. The fearless hero is infused with fear by a slumbering woman. The Wälsung Motive, afterwards beautifully varied with the Motive of Love's Joy, accompanies his utterances, the climax of his emotional excitement being expressed in a majestic crescendo of the Freia Motive. A sudden feeling of awe gives him at least the outward appearance of calmness. With the Motive of Fate he faces his destiny; and then, while the Freia Motive rises like a vision of loveliness, he sinks over *Brünnhilde*, and with closed eyes presses his lips to hers.

Brünnhilde awakens. *Siegfried* starts up. She rises, and with a noble gesture greets in majestic accents her return to the sight of earth. Strains of loftier eloquence than those of her greeting have never been composed. *Brünnhilde* rises from her magic slumbers in the majesty of womanhood:

With the Motive of Fate she asks who is the hero who has awakened her. The superb Siegfried Motive gives back the proud answer. In rapturous phrases they greet one another. It is the **Motive of Love's Greeting,**

which unites their voices in impassioned accents until, as if this motive no longer sufficed to express their ecstasy, it is followed by the **Motive of Love's Passion,**

which, with the Siegfried Motive, rises and falls with the heaving of *Brünnhilde's* bosom.

These motives course impetuously through this scene. Here and there we have others recalling former portions of the cycle—the Wälsung Motive, when *Brünnhilde* refers to *Siegfried's* mother, *Sieglinde;* the Motive of Brünnhilde's Pleading, when she tells him of her defiance of *Wotan's* behest; a variant of the Walhalla Motive when she speaks of herself in Walhalla; and the Motive of the World's Heritage, with which *Siegfried* claims her, this last leading over to a forceful climax of the Motive of Brünnhilde's Pleading, which is followed by a lovely, tranquil episode introduced by the **Motive of Love's Peace,**

succeeded by a motive, ardent yet tender—the **Motive of Siegfried the Protector:**

Richard Wagner

These motives accompany the action most expressively. *Brünnhilde* still hesitates to cast off for ever the supernatural characteristics of the Valkyr and give herself up entirely to *Siegfried*. The young hero's growing ecstasy finds expression in the Motive of Love's Joy. At last it awakens a responsive note of purely human passion in *Brünnhilde* and, answering the proud Siegfried Motive with the jubilant Shout of the Valkyrs and the ecstatic measures of Love's Passion, she proclaims herself his.

With a love duet—nothing puny and purring, but rapturous and proud—the music-drama comes to a close. *Siegfried*, a scion of the Wälsung race has won *Brünnhilde* for his bride, and upon her finger has placed the ring fashioned of Rhinegold by *Alberich* in the caverns of Niebelheim, the abode of the Niebelungs. Clasping her in his arms and drawing her to his breast, he has felt her splendid physical being thrill with a passion wholly responsive to his. Will the gods be saved through them, or does the curse of *Alberich* still rest on the ring worn by *Brünnhilde* as a pledge of love?

GÖTTERDÄMMERUNG

DUSK OF THE GODS

Music-drama in a prologue and three acts, words and music by Richard Wagner. Produced, Bayreuth, August 17, 1876.

New York, Metropolitan Opera House, January 25, 1888, with Lehmann (*Brünnhilde*), Seidl-Kraus (*Gutrune*), Niemann (*Siegfried*),

The Complete Opera Book

Robinson (*Gunther*), and Fischer (*Hagen*). Other performances at the Metropolitan Opera House have had, among others, Alvary and Jean de Reszke as *Siegfried* and Edouard de Reszke as *Hagen*.

CHARACTERS

SIEGFRIED	*Tenor*
GUNTHER	*Baritone*
ALBERICH	*Baritone*
HAGEN	*Bass*
BRÜNNHILDE	*Soprano*
GUTRUNE	*Soprano*
WALTRAUTE	*Mezzo-Soprano*
FIRST, SECOND, AND THIRD NORN	*Contralto, Mezzo-Soprano, and Soprano*
WOGLINDE, WELLGUNDE, AND FLOSSHILDE	*Sopranos and Mezzo-Soprano*

Vassals and Women.

Time—Legendary. *Place*—On the Brünnhilde-Rock; Gunther's castle on the Rhine; wooded district by the Rhine.

THE PROLOGUE

The first scene of the prologue is a weird conference of the three grey sisters of fate—the *Norns* who wind the skein of life. They have met on the Valkyrs' rock and their words forebode the end of the gods. At last the skein they have been winding breaks—the final catastrophe is impending.

An orchestral interlude depicts the transition from the unearthly gloom of the Norn scene to break of day, the climax being reached in a majestic burst of music as *Siegfried* and *Brünnhilde*, he in full armour, she leading her steed by the bridle, issue forth from the rocky cavern in the background. This climax owes its eloquence to three motives—that of the Ride of the Valkyrs and two new

Richard Wagner

motives, the one as lovely as the other is heroic, the **Brünnhilde Motive,**

and the **Motive of Siegfried the Hero:**

The Brünnhilde Motive expresses the strain of pure, tender womanhood in the nature of the former Valkyr, and proclaims her womanly ecstasy over wholly requited love. The motive of Siegfried the Hero is clearly developed from the motive of Siegfried the Fearless. Fearless youth has developed into heroic man. In this scene *Brünnhilde* and *Siegfried* plight their troth, and *Siegfried* having given to *Brünnhilde* the fatal ring and having received from her the steed Grane, which once bore her in her wild course through the storm-clouds, bids her farewell and sets forth in quest of further adventure. In this scene, one of Wagner's most beautiful creations, occur the two new motives already quoted, and a third—the **Motive of Brünnhilde's Love.**

A strong, deep woman's nature has given herself up to love. Her passion is as strong and deep as her nature. It is not a surface-heat passion. It is love rising from the depths of a heroic woman's soul. The grandeur of her

The Complete Opera Book

ideal of *Siegfried*, her thoughts of him as a hero winning fame, her pride in his prowess, her love for one whom she deems the bravest among men, culminate in the Motive of Brünnhilde's Love.

Siegfried disappears with the steed behind the rocks and *Brünnhilde* stands upon the cliff looking down the valley after him; his horn is heard from below and *Brünnhilde* with rapturous gesture waves him farewell. The orchestra accompanies the action with the Brünnhilde Motive, the Motive of Siegfried the Fearless, and finally with the theme of the love-duet with which "Siegfried" closed.

The curtain then falls, and between the prologue and the first act an orchestral interlude describes *Siegfried's* voyage down the Rhine to the castle of the Gibichungs where dwell *Gunther*, his sister *Gutrune*, and their half-brother *Hagen*, the son of *Alberich*. Through *Hagen* the curse hurled by *Alberich* in "The Rhinegold" at all into whose possession the ring shall come, is to be worked out to the end of its fell purpose—*Siegfried* betrayed and destroyed and the rule of the gods brought to an end by *Brünnhilde's* expiation.

In the interlude between the prologue and the first act we first hear the brilliant Motive of Siegfried the Fearless and then the gracefully flowing Motives of the Rhine, and of the Rhinedaughters' Shout of Triumph with the Motives of the Rhinegold and Ring. *Hagen's* malevolent plotting, of which we are soon to learn in the first act is foreshadowed by the sombre harmonies which suddenly pervade the music.

Act I. On the river lies the hall of the Gibichungs, where house *Gunther*, his sister *Gutrune*, and *Hagen*, their half-brother. *Gutrune* is a maiden of fair mien, *Gunther* a man of average strength and courage, *Hagen* a sinister plotter, large of stature and sombre of visage. Long

Richard Wagner

he has planned to possess himself of the ring fashioned of Rhinegold. He is aware that it was guarded by the dragon, has been taken from the hoard by *Siegfried*, and by him given to *Brünnhilde*. And now observe the subtle craft with which he prepares to compass his plans.

A descendant, through his father, *Alberich*, the Nibelung, of a race which practised the black art, he plots to make *Siegfried* forget *Brünnhilde* through a love-potion to be administered to him by *Gutrune*. Then, when under the fiery influence of the potion and all forgetful of *Brünnhilde*, *Siegfried* demands *Gutrune* to wife, the price demanded will be that he win *Brünnhilde* as bride for *Gunther*. Before *Siegfried* comes in sight, before *Gunther* and *Gutrune* so much as even know that he is nearing the hall of the Gibichungs, *Hagen* begins to lay the foundation for this seemingly impossible plot. For it is at this opportune moment *Gunther* chances to address him:

"Hark, Hagen, and let your answer be true. Do I head the race of the Gibichungs with honour?"

"Aye," replies *Hagen*, "and yet, Gunther, you remain unwived while Gutrune still lacks a husband." Then he tells *Gunther* of *Brünnhilde*—"a circle of flame surrounds the rock on which she dwells, but he who can brave that fire may win her for wife. If Siegfried does this in your stead, and brings her to you as bride, will she not be yours?" *Hagen* craftily conceals from his half-brother and from *Gutrune* the fact that *Siegfried* already has won *Brünnhilde* for himself; but having aroused in *Gunther* the desire to possess her, he forthwith unfolds his plan and reminds *Gutrune* of the magic love-potion which it is in her power to administer to *Siegfried*.

At the very beginning of this act the Hagen Motive is heard. Particularly noticeable in it are the first two sharp, decisive chords. They recur with dramatic force in the third act when *Hagen* slays *Siegfried*. The **Hagen Motive** is as follows:

This is followed by the **Gibichung Motive,** the two motives being frequently heard in the opening scene.

Added to these is the **Motive of the Love Potion** which is to cause *Siegfried* to forget *Brünnhilde*, and conceive a violent passion for *Gutrune*.

Whatever hesitation may have been in *Gutrune's* mind, because of the trick which is involved in the plot, vanishes when soon afterwards *Siegfried's* horn-call announces his approach from the river, and, as he brings his boat up to the bank, she sees this hero among men in all his youthful strength and beauty. She hastily withdraws, to carry out her part in the plot that is to bind him to her.

The three men remain to parley. *Hagen* skilfully

Edouard de Reszke as Hagen in "Götterdämmerung."

JEAN DE RESZKE AS SIEGFRIED IN "GÖTTERDÄMMERUNG."

Richard Wagner

questions *Siegfried* regarding his combat with the dragon. Has he taken nothing from the hoard?

"Only a ring, which I have left in a woman's keep," answers *Siegfried;* "and this." He points to a steel network that hangs from his girdle.

"Ha," exclaims *Hagen,* "the Tarnhelmet! I recognize it as the artful work of the Nibelungs. Place it on your head and it enables you to assume any guise." He then flings open a door and on the platform of a short flight of steps that leads up to it, stands *Gutrune,* in her hand a drinking-horn which she extends toward *Siegfried.*

"Welcome, guest, to the house of the Gibichungs. A daughter of the race extends to you this greeting." And so, while *Hagen* looks grimly on, the fair *Gutrune* offers *Siegfried* the draught that is to transform his whole nature. Courteously, but without regarding her with more than friendly interest, *Siegfried* takes the horn from her hands and drains it. As if a new element coursed through his veins, there is a sudden change in his manner. Handing the horn back to her he regards her with fiery glances, she blushingly lowering her eyes and withdrawing to the inner apartment. New in this scene is the **Gutrune Motive:**

"Gunther, your sister's name? Have you a wife?" *Siegfried* asks excitedly.

"I have set my heart on a woman," replies *Gunther,* "but may not win her. A far-off rock, fire-encircled, is her home."

The Complete Opera Book

"A far-off rock, fire encircled," repeats *Siegfried*, as if striving to remember something long forgotten; and when *Gunther* utters *Brünnhilde's* name, *Siegfried* shows by his mien and gesture that it no longer signifies aught to him. The love-potion has caused him to forget her.

"I will press through the circle of flame," he exclaims. "I will seize her and bring her to you—if you will give me Gutrune for wife."

And so the unhallowed bargain is struck and sealed with the oath of blood-brotherhood, and *Siegfried* departs with *Gunther* to capture *Brünnhilde* as bride for the Gibichung. The compact of blood-brotherhood is a most sacred one. *Siegfried* and *Gunther* each with his sword draws blood from his arm, which he allows to mingle with wine in a drinking-horn held by *Hagen;* each lays two fingers upon the horn, and then, having pledged blood-brotherhood, drinks the blood and wine. This ceremony is significantly introduced by the Motive of the Curse followed by the Motive of Compact. Phrases of *Siegfried's* and *Gunther's* pledge are set to a new motive whose forceful simplicity effectively expresses the idea of truth. It is the **Motive of the Vow.**

Abruptly following *Siegfried's* pledge:

> Thus I drink thee troth,

are those two chords of the Hagen Motive which are heard again in the third act when the Nibelung has slain *Siegfried*. It should perhaps be repeated here that *Gunther* is not aware

Richard Wagner

of the union which existed between *Brünnhilde* and *Siegfried*, *Hagen* having concealed this from his half-brother, who believes that he will receive the Valkyr in all her goddess-like virginity.

When *Siegfried* and *Gunther* have departed and *Gutrune*, having sighed her farewell after her lover, has retired, *Hagen* broods with wicked glee over the successful inauguration of his plot. During a brief orchestral interlude a dropcurtain conceals the scene which, when the curtain again rises, has changed to the Valkyr's rock, where sits *Brünnhilde*, lost in contemplation of the Ring, while the Motive of Siegfried the Protector is heard on the orchestra like a blissful memory of the love scene in "Siegfried."

Her rapturous reminiscences are interrupted by the sounds of an approaching storm and from the dark cloud there issues one of the Valkyrs, *Waltraute*, who comes to ask of *Brünnhilde* that she cast back the ring *Siegfried* has given her—the ring cursed by *Alberich*—into the Rhine, and thus lift the curse from the race of gods. But *Brünnhilde* refuses:

> More than Walhalla's welfare,
> More than the good of the gods,
> The ring I guard.

It is dusk. The magic fire rising from the valley throws a glow over the landscape. The notes of *Siegfried's* horn are heard. *Brünnhilde* joyously prepares to meet him. Suddenly she sees a stranger leap through the flames. It is *Siegfried*, but through the Tarnhelmet (the motive of which, followed by the Gunther Motive dominates the first part of the scene) he has assumed the guise of the Gibichung. In vain *Brünnhilde* seeks to defend herself with the might which the ring imparts. She is powerless against the intruder. As he tears the ring from her finger, the Motive of the Curse resounds with tragic import,

The Complete Opera Book

followed by trist echoes of the Motive of Siegfried the Protector and of the Brünnhilde Motive, the last being succeeded by the Tarnhelmet Motive expressive of the evil magic which has wrought this change in *Siegfried*. *Brünnhilde* in abject recognition of her impotence, enters the cavern. Before *Siegfried* follows her he draws his sword Nothung (Needful) and exclaims:

Now, Nothung, witness thou, that chaste my wooing is;
To keep my faith with my brother, separate me from his bride.

Phrases of the pledge of Brotherhood followed by the Brünnhilde, Gutrune, and Sword motives accompany his words. The thuds of the typical Nibelung rhythm resound, and lead to the last crashing chord of this eventful act.

Act II. The ominous Motive of the Nibelung's Malevolence introduces the second act. The curtain rises upon the exterior of the hall of the Gibichungs. To the right is the open entrance to the hall, to the left the bank of the Rhine, from which rises a rocky ascent toward the background. It is night. *Hagen*, spear in hand and shield at side, leans in sleep against a pillar of the hall. Through the weird moonlight *Alberich* appears. He urges *Hagen* to murder *Siegfried* and to seize the ring from his finger. After hearing *Hagen's* oath that he will be faithful to the hate he has inherited, *Alberich* disappears. The weirdness of the surroundings, the monotony of *Hagen's* answers, uttered seemingly in sleep, as if, even when the Nibelung slumbered, his mind remained active, imbue this scene with mystery.

A charming orchestral interlude depicts the break of day. Its serene beauty is, however, broken in upon by the **Motive of Hagen's Wicked Glee,** which I quote, as it frequently occurs in the course of succeeding events.

Richard Wagner

All night *Hagen* has watched by the bank of the river for the return of the men from the quest. It is daylight when *Siegfried* returns, tells him of his success, and bids him prepare to receive *Gunther* and *Brünnhilde*. On his finger he wears the ring—the ring made of Rhinegold, and cursed by *Alberich*—the same with which he pledged his troth to *Brünnhilde*, but which in the struggle of the night, and disguised by the Tarnhelmet as *Gunther*, he has torn from her finger—the very ring the possession of which *Hagen* craves, and for which he is plotting. *Gutrune* has joined them. *Siegfried* leads her into the hall.

Hagen, placing an ox-horn to his lips, blows a loud call toward the four points of the compass, summoning the Gibichung vassals to the festivities attending the double wedding—*Siegfried* and *Gutrune, Gunther* and *Brünnnhilde;* and when the Gibichung brings his boat up to the bank, the shore is crowded with men who greet him boisterously, while *Brünnhilde* stands there pale and with downcast eyes. But as *Siegfried* leads *Gutrune* forward to meet *Gunther* and his bride, and *Gunther* calls *Siegfried* by name, *Brünnhilde* starts, raises her eyes, stares at *Siegfried* in amazement, drops *Gunther's* hand, advances, as if by sudden impulse, a step toward the man who awakened her from her magic slumber on the rock, then recoils in horror, her eyes fixed upon him, while all look on in wonder. The Motive of Siegfried the Hero, the Sword Motive, and the Chords of the Hagen Motive emphasize with a tumultuous crash the dramatic significance of the situation. There is a sudden hush—*Brünnhilde* astounded and dumb, *Siegfried* unconscious of guilt quietly self-possessed, *Gunther, Gutrune*, and the vassals silent with amazement—it is during this moment of tension that we hear the motive which expresses the thought uppermost in *Brünnhilde*, the thought which would find expression in a burst of frenzy were not her wrath held in check by her inability to quite grasp the meaning of the situation or to fathom the depth of the treachery of which she has been the victim. This is the **Motive of Vengeance:**

"What troubles Brünnhilde?" composedly asks *Siegfried*, from whom all memory of his first meeting with the rock maiden and his love for here have been effaced by the potion. Then, observing that she sways and is about to fall, he supports her with his arm.

"Siegfried knows me not!" she whispers faintly, as she looks up into his face.

"There stands your husband," is *Siegfried's* reply, as he points to *Gunther*. The gesture discloses to *Brünnhilde's* sight the ring upon his finger, the ring he gave her, and which to her horror *Gunther*, as she supposed, had wrested from her. In the flash of its precious metal she sees the whole significance of the wretched situation in which she finds herself, and discovers the intrigue, the trick, of which she has been the victim. She knows nothing, however, of the treachery *Hagen* is plotting, or of the love-potion that has aroused in *Siegfried* an uncontrollable passion to possess *Gutrune*, has caused him to forget her, and led him to win her for *Gunther*. There at *Gutrune's* side, and about to wed her, stands the man she loves. To *Brünnhilde*, infuriated with jealousy, her pride wounded to the quick, *Siegfried* appears simply to have betrayed her to *Gunther* through infatuation for another woman.

"The ring," she cries out, "was taken from me by that man," pointing to *Gunther*. "How came it on your finger?

Richard Wagner

Or, if it is not the ring"—again she addresses *Gunther*—"where is the one you tore from my hand?"

Gunther, knowing nothing about the ring, plainly is perplexed. "Ha," cries out *Brünnhilde* in uncontrollable rage, "then it was Siegfried disguised as you and not you yourself who won it from me! Know then, Gunther, that you, too, have been betrayed by him. For this man who would wed your sister, and as part of the price bring me to you as bride, was wedded to me!"

In all but *Hagen* and *Siegfried*, *Brünnhilde's* words arouse consternation. *Hagen*, noting their effect on *Gunther*, from whom he craftily has concealed *Siegfried's* true relation to *Brünnhilde*, sees in the episode an added opportunity to mould the Gibichung to his plan to do away with *Siegfried*. The latter, through the effect of the potion, is rendered wholly unconscious of the truth of what *Brünnhilde* has said. He even has forgotten that he ever has parted with the ring, and, when the men, jealous of *Gunther's* honour, crowd about him, and *Gunther* and *Gutrune* in intense excitement wait on his reply, he calmly proclaims that he found it among the dragon's treasure and never has parted with it. To the truth of this assertion, to a denial of all *Brünnhilde* has accused him of, he announces himself ready to swear at the point of any spear which is offered for the oath, the strongest manner in which the asseveration can be made and, in the belief of the time, rendering his death certain at the point of that very spear should he swear falsely.

How eloquent the music of these exciting scenes!—Crashing chords of the Ring Motive followed by that of the Curse, as *Brünnhilde* recognizes the ring on *Siegfried's* finger, the Motive of Vengeance, the Walhalla Motive, as she invokes the gods to witness her humiliation, the touchingly pathetic Motive of Brünnhilde's Pleading, as she vainly strives to awaken fond memories in *Siegfried;* then again

The Complete Opera Book

the Motive of Vengeance, as the oath is about to be taken, the Murder Motive and the Hagen Motive at the taking of the oath, for the spear is *Hagen's;* and in *Brünnhilde's* asseveration, the Valkyr music coursing through the orchestra.

It is *Hagen* who offers his weapon for the oath. "Guardian of honour, hallowed weapon," swears *Siegfried,* "where steel can pierce me, there pierce me; where death can be dealt me, there deal it me, if ever I was wed to Brünnhilde, if ever I have wronged Gutrune's brother."

At his words, *Brünnhilde,* livid with rage, strides into the circle of men, and thrusting *Siegfried's* fingers away from the spearhead, lays her own upon it.

"Guardian of honour, hallowed weapon," she cries, "I dedicate your steel to his destruction. I bless your point that it may blight him. For broken are all his oaths, and perjured now he proves himself."

Siegfried shrugs his shoulders. To him *Brünnhilde's* imprecations are but the ravings of an overwrought brain. "Gunther, look to your lady. Give the tameless mountain maid time to rest and recover," he calls out to Gutrune's brother. "And now, men, follow us to table, and make merry at our wedding feast!" Then with a laugh and in highest spirits, he throws his arm about *Gutrune* and draws her after him into the hall, the vassals and women following them.

But *Brünnhilde, Hagen,* and *Gunther* remain behind; *Brünnhilde* half stunned at sight of the man with whom she has exchanged troth, gaily leading another to marriage, as though his vows had been mere chaff; *Gunther,* suspicious that his honour wittingly has been betrayed by *Siegfried,* and that *Brünnhilde's* words are true; *Hagen,* in whose hands *Gunther* is like clay, waiting the opportunity to prompt both *Brünnhilde* and his half-brother to vengeance.

"Coward," cries *Brünnhilde* to *Gunther,* "to hide behind

another in order to undo me! Has the race of the Gibichungs fallen so low in prowess?"

"Deceiver, and yet deceived! Betrayer, and yet myself betrayed," wails *Gunther*. "Hagen, wise one, have you no counsel?"

"No counsel," grimly answers *Hagen*, "save Siegfried's death."

"His death!"

"Aye, all these things demand his death."

"But, Gutrune, to whom I gave him, how would we stand with her if we so avenged ourselves?" For even in his injured pride *Gunther* feels that he has had a share in what *Siegfried* has done.

But *Hagen* is prepared with a plan that will free *Gunther* and himself of all accusation. "To-morrow," he suggests, "we will go on a great hunt. As Siegfried boldly rushes ahead we will fell him from the rear, and give out that he was killed by a wild boar."

"So be it," exclaims *Brünnhilde;* "let his death atone for the shame he has wrought me. He has violated his oath; he shall die!"

At that moment as they turn toward the hall, he whose death they have decreed, a wreath of oak on his brow and leading *Gutrune*, whose hair is bedecked with flowers, steps out on the threshold as though wondering at their delay and urges them to enter. *Gunther*, taking *Brünnhilde* by the hand, follows him in. *Hagen* alone remains behind, and with a look of grim triumph watches them as they disappear within. And so, although the valley of the Rhine re-echoes with glad sounds, it is the Murder Motive that brings the act to a close.

Act III. How picturesque the *mise-en-scène* of this act —a clearing in the forest primeval near a spot where the bank of the Rhine slopes toward the river. On the shore, above the stream, stands *Siegfried*. Baffled in the pursuit of game, he is looking for *Gunther*, *Hagen*, and his other comrades of the hunt, in order to join them.

One of the loveliest scenes of the trilogy now ensues. The *Rhinedaughters* swim up to the bank and, circling gracefully in the current of the river, endeavour to coax from him the ring of Rhinegold. It is an episode full of whimsical badinage and, if anything, more charming even than the opening of "Rhinegold."

Siegfried refuses to give up the ring. The *Rhinedaughters* swim off leaving him to his fate.

Here is the principal theme of their song in this scene:

Distant hunting-horns are heard. *Gunther, Hagen,* and their attendants gradually assemble and encamp themselves. *Hagen* fills a drinking-horn and hands it to *Siegfried* whom he persuades to relate the story of his life. This *Siegfried* does in a wonderfully picturesque, musical, and dramatic story in which motives, often heard before, charm us anew.

In the course of his narrative he refreshes himself by a draught from the drinking-horn into which meanwhile *Hagen* has pressed the juice of an herb. Through this the effect of the love-potion is so far counteracted that tender memories of *Brünnhilde* well up within him and he tells with artless enthusiasm how he penetrated the circle of flame about the Valkyr, found *Brünnhilde* slumbering there awoke her with his kiss, and won her. *Gunther* springs up aghast at this revelation. Now he knows that *Brünnhilde's* accusation is true.

Richard Wagner

Two ravens fly overhead. As *Siegfried* turns to look after them the Motive of the Curse resounds and *Hagen* plunges his spear into the young hero's back. *Gunther* and the vassals throw themselves upon *Hagen*. The Siegfried Motive, cut short with a crashing chord, the two murderous chords of the Hagen Motive forming the bass—and *Siegfried*, who with a last effort has heaved his shield aloft to hurl it at *Hagen*, lets it fall, and, collapsing, drops upon it. So overpowered are the witnesses—even *Gunther*—by the suddenness and enormity of the crime that, after a few disjointed exclamations, they gather, bowed with grief, around *Siegfried*. *Hagen*, with stony indifference turns away and disappears over the height.

With the fall of the last scion of the Wälsung race we hear a new motive, simple yet indescribably fraught with sorrow, the **Death Motive.**

Siegfried, supported by two men, rises to a sitting posture, and with a strange rapture gleaming in his glance, intones his death-song. It is an ecstatic greeting to *Brünnhilde*. "Brünnhilde!" he exclaims, "thy wakener comes to wake thee with his kiss." The ethereal harmonies of the Motive of Brünnhilde's Awakening, the Motive of Fate, the Siegfried Motive swelling into the Motive of Love's Greeting and dying away through the Motive of Love's Passion to Siegfried's last whispered accents—"Brünnhilde beckons to me"—in the Motive of Fate—and *Siegfried* sinks back in death.

The Complete Opera Book

Full of pathos though this episode be, it but brings us to the threshold of a scene of such overwhelming power that it may without exaggeration be singled out as the supreme musico-dramatic climax of all that Wagner wrought, indeed of all music. *Siegfried's* last ecstatic greeting to his Valkyr bride has made us realize the blackness of the treachery which tore the young hero and *Brünnhilde* asunder and led to his death; and now as we are bowed down with a grief too deep for utterance—like the grief with which a nation gathers at the grave of its noblest hero—Wagner voices for us, in music of overwhelmingly tragic power, feelings which are beyond expression in human speech. This is not a "funeral march," as it is often absurdly called—it is the awful mystery of death itself expressed in music.

Motionless with grief the men gather around *Siegfried's* corpse. Night falls. The moon casts a pale, sad light over the scene. At the silent bidding of *Gunther* the vassals raise the body and bear it in solemn procession over the rocky height. Meanwhile with majestic solemnity the orchestra voices the funeral oration of the "world's greatest hero." One by one, but tragically interrupted by the Motive of Death, we hear the motives which tell the story of the Wälsung's futile struggle with destiny—the Wälsung Motive, the Motive of the Wälsung's Heroism, the Motive of Sympathy, and the Love Motive, the Sword Motive, the Siegfried Motive, and the Motive of Siegfried the Hero, around which the Death Motive swirls and crashes like a black, death-dealing, all-wrecking flood, forming an overwhelmingly powerful climax that dies away into the Brünnhilde Motive with which, as with a heart-broken sigh, the heroic dirge is brought to a close.

Meanwhile the scene has changed to the Hall of the Gibichungs as in the first act. *Gutrune* is listening through the

Richard Wagner

night for some sound which may announce the return of the hunt.

Men and women bearing torches precede in great agitation the funeral train. *Hagen* grimly announces to *Gutrune* that *Siegfried* is dead. Wild with grief she overwhelms *Gunther* with violent accusations. He points to *Hagen* whose sole reply is to demand the ring as spoil. *Gunther* refuses. *Hagen* draws his sword and after a brief combat slays *Gunther*. He is about to snatch the ring from *Siegfried's* finger, when the corpse's hand suddenly raises itself threateningly, and all—even *Hagen*—fall back in consternation.

Brünnhilde advances solemnly from the back. While watching on the bank of the Rhine she has learned from the *Rhinedaughters* the treachery of which she and *Siegfried* have been the victims. Her mien is ennobled by a look of tragic exaltation. To her the grief of *Gutrune* is but the whining of a child. When the latter realizes that it was *Brünnhilde* whom she caused *Siegfried* to forget through the love-potion, she falls fainting over *Gunther's* body. *Hagen* leaning on his spear is lost in gloomy brooding.

Brünnhilde turns solemnly to the men and women and bids them erect a funeral pyre. The orchestral harmonies shimmer with the Magic Fire Motive through which courses the Motive of the Ride of the Valkyrs. Then, her countenance transfigured by love, she gazes upon her dead hero and apostrophizes his memory in the Motive of Love's Greeting. From him she looks upward and in the Walhalla Motive and the Motive of Brünnhilde's Pleading passionately inveighs against the injustice of the gods. The Curse Motive is followed by a wonderfully beautiful combination of the Walhalla Motive and the Motive of the Gods' Stress at Brünnhilde's words:

<blockquote>Rest thee! Rest thee! O, God!</blockquote>

The Complete Opera Book

For with the fading away of Walhalla, and the inauguration of the reign of human love in place of that of lust and greed—a change to be wrought by the approaching expiation of *Brünnhilde* for the crimes which began with the wresting of the Rhinegold from the *Rhinedaughters*—*Wotan's* stress will be at an end. *Brünnhilde* having told in the graceful, rippling Rhine music how she learned of *Hagen's* treachery through the *Rhinedaughters*, places upon her finger the ring. Then turning toward the pyre upon which *Siegfried's* body rests, she snatches a huge firebrand from one of the men, and flings it upon the pyre, which kindles brightly. As the moment of her immolation approaches the Motive of Expiation begins to dominate the scene.

Brünnhilde mounts her Valkyr charger, Grane, who oft bore her through the clouds, while lightning flashed and thunder reverberated. With one leap the steed bears her into the blazing pyre.

The Rhine overflows. Borne on the flood, the *Rhinedaughters* swim to the pyre and draw, from *Brünnhilde's* finger, the ring. *Hagen*, seeing the object of all his plotting in their possession, plunges after them. Two of them encircle him with their arms and draw him down with them into the flood. The third holds up the ring in triumph.

In the heavens is perceived a deep glow. It is Götterdämmerung—the dusk of the gods. An epoch has come to a close. Valhalla is in flames. Once more its stately motive resounds, only to crumble, like a ruin, before the onsweeping power of the motive of expiation. The Siegfried Motive with a crash in the orchestra; once more then the Motive of Expiation. The sordid empire of the gods has passed away. A new era, that of human love, has dawned through the expiation of *Brünnhilde*. As in "The Flying Dutchman" and "Tannhäuser," it is through woman that comes redemption.

Richard Wagner

TRISTAN UND ISOLDE

TRISTAN AND ISOLDE

Music-drama in three acts, words and music by Richard Wagner, who calls the work, "eine Handlung" (an action). Produced, under the direction of Hans von Bülow, Munich, June 10, 1865. First London production, June 20, 1882. Produced, December 1, 1886, with Anton Seidl as conductor, at the Metropolitan Opera House, New York, with Niemann (*Tristan*), Fischer (*King Marke*), Lehmann (*Isolde*), Robinson (*Kurwenal*), von Milde (*Melot*), Brandt (*Brangäne*), Kemlitz (a *Shepherd*), Alvary (a *Sailor*), Sänger (a *Helmsman*). Jean de Reszke is accounted the greatest *Tristan* heard at the Metropolitan. Nordica, Ternina, Fremstad, and Gadski are other *Isoldes*, who have been heard at that house. Edouard de Reszke sang *King Marke*, and Bispham *Kurwenal*.

CHARACTERS

TRISTAN, a Cornish knight, nephew to KING MARKE.....*Tenor*
KING MARKE, of Cornwall.......................*Bass*
ISOLDE, an Irish princess.........................*Soprano*
KURWENAL, one of TRISTAN's retainers...............*Baritone*
MELOT, a courtier................................*Baritone*
BRANGÄNE, ISOLDE's attendant....................*Mezzo-Soprano*
A SHEPHERD......................................*Tenor*
A SAILOR..*Tenor*
A HELMSMAN ....*Baritone*
Sailors, Knights, Esquires, and Men-at-Arms.
Time—Legendary. *Place*—A ship at sea; outside *King Marke's* palace, Cornwall; the platform at Kareol, *Tristan's* castle.

Wagner was obliged to remodel the "Tristan" legend thoroughly before it became available for a modern drama. He has shorn it of all unnecessary incidents and worked over the main episodes into a concise, vigorous, swiftly moving drama, admirably adapted for the stage. He shows keen dramatic insight in the manner in which he adapts the love-potion of the legends to his purpose. In the legends the love of Tristan and Isolde is merely "chemical" —entirely the result of the love-philtre. Wagner, however,

The Complete Opera Book

presents them from the outset as enamoured of one another, so that the potion simply quickens a passion already active.

To the courtesy of G. Schirmer, Inc., publishers of my *Wagner's Music Dramas Analysed*, I am indebted, as I have already stated elsewhere, for permission to use material from that book. I have there placed a brief summary of the story of "Tristan and Isolde" before the descriptive account of the "book" and music, and, accordingly do so here.

In the Wagnerian version the plot is briefly as follows: *Tristan*, having lost his parents in infancy, has been reared at the court of his uncle, *Marke*, King of Cornwall. He has slain in combat Morold, an Irish knight, who had come to Cornwall, to collect the tribute that country had been paying to Ireland. Morold was affianced to his cousin *Isolde*, daughter of the Irish king. *Tristan*, having been dangerously wounded in the combat, places himself, without disclosing his identity, under the care of Morold's affianced, *Isolde*, who comes of a race skilled in magic arts. She discerns who he is; but, although she is aware that she is harbouring the slayer of her affianced, she spares him and carefully tends him, for she has conceived a deep passion for him. *Tristan* also becomes enamoured of her, but both deem their love unrequited. Soon after *Tristan's* return to Cornwall, he is dispatched to Ireland by *Marke*, that he may win *Isolde* as Queen for the Cornish king.

The music-drama opens on board the vessel in which *Tristan* bears *Isolde* to Cornwall. Deeming her love for *Tristan* unrequited she determines to end her sorrow by quaffing a death-potion; and *Tristan*, feeling that the woman he loves is about to be wedded to another, readily consents to share it with her. But *Brangäne*, *Isolde's* companion, substitutes a love-potion for the death-draught. This rouses their love to resistless passion. Not long after they reach Cornwall, they are surprised in the castle

NORDICA AS ISOLDE.

JOHN COATES AS TRISTAN.

Richard Wagner

garden by the *King* and his suite, and *Tristan* is severely wounded by *Melot*, one of *Marke's* knights. *Kurwenal*, *Tristan's* faithful retainer, bears him to his native place, Kareol. Hither *Isolde* follows him, arriving in time to fold him in her arms as he expires. She breathes her last over his corpse.

THE VORSPIEL

All who have made a study of opera, and do not regard it merely as a form of amusement, are agreed that the score of "Tristan and Isolde" is the greatest setting of a love-story for the lyric stage. In fact to call it a love-story seems a slight. It is a tale of tragic passion, culminating in death, unfolded in the surge and palpitation of immortal music.

This passion smouldered in the heart of the man and woman of this epic of love. It could not burst into clear flame because over it lay the pall of duty—a knight's to his king, a wife's to her husband. They elected to die; drank, as they thought, a death potion. Instead it was a magic love-philtre, craftily substituted by the woman's confidante. Then love, no longer, vague and hesitating, but roused by sorcerous means to the highest rapture, found expression in the complete abandonment of the lovers to their ecstasy —and their fate.

What precedes the draught of the potion in the drama, is narrative, explanatory and prefatorial. Once *Tristan* and *Isolde* have shared the goblet, passion is unleashed. The goal is death.

The magic love-philtre is the excitant in this story of rapture and gloom. The *Vorspiel* therefore opens most fittingly with a motive which expresses the incipient effect of the potion upon *Tristan* and *Isolde*. It clearly can be divided into two parts, one descending, the other ascend-

The Complete Opera Book

ing chromatically. The potion overcomes the restraining influence of duty in two beings and leaves them at the mercy of their passions. The first part, with its descending chromatics, is pervaded by a certain trist mood, as if *Tristan* were still vaguely forewarned by his conscience of the impending tragedy. The second soars ecstatically upward. It is the woman yielding unquestioningly to the rapture of requited love. Therefore, while the phrase may be called the Motive of the Love-Potion, or, as Wolzogen calls it, of Yearning, it seems best to divide it into the **Tristan and Isolde Motives** (A and B).

The two motives having been twice repeated, there is a fermate. Then the Isolde Motive alone is heard, so that the attention of the hearer is fixed upon it. For in this tragedy, as in that of Eden, it is the woman who takes the first decisive step. After another fermate, the last two notes of the Isolde Motive are twice repeated, dying away to *pp*. Then a variation of the Isolde Motive leads

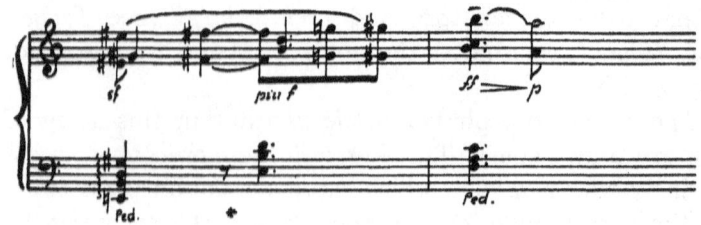

with an impassioned upward sweep into another version,

Richard Wagner

full of sensuous yearning, and distinct enough to form a new motive, the **Motive of the Love Glance.**

This occurs again and again in the course of the *Vorspiel*. Though readily recognized, it is sufficiently varied with each repetition never to allow the emotional excitement to subside. In fact, the *Vorspiel* gathers impetus as it proceeds, until, with an inversion of the Love Glance Motive, borne to a higher and higher level of exaltation by upward rushing runs, it reaches its climax in a paroxysm

of love, to die away with repetitions of the Tristan, the Isolde, and the Love Glance motives.

In the themes it employs this prelude tells, in music, the story of the love of *Tristan* and *Isolde*. We have the motives of the hero and heroine of the drama, and the Motive of the Love Glance. When as is the case in concerts, the finale of the work, "Isolde's Love-Death," is linked to the *Vorspiel*, we are entrusted with the beginning and the end of the music-drama, forming an eloquent epitome of the tragic story.

Act I. Wagner wisely refrains from actually placing before us on the stage, the events that transpired in Ireland before *Tristan* was despatched thither to bring *Isolde* as a bride to *King Marke*. The events, which led to the two meetings between *Tristan* and *Isolde*, are told in *Isolde's* narrative, which forms an important part of the first act. This act opens aboard the vessel in which *Tristan* is conveying *Isolde* to Cornwall.

The Complete Opera Book

The opening scene shows *Isolde* reclining on a couch, her face hid in soft pillows, in a tent-like apartment on the forward deck of a vessel. It is hung with rich tapestries, which hide the rest of the ship from view. *Brangäne* has partially drawn aside one of the hangings and is gazing out upon the sea. From above, as though from the rigging, is heard the voice of a young *Sailor* singing a farewell song to his "Irish maid." It has a wild charm and is a capital example of Wagner's skill in giving local colouring to his music. The words, "Frisch weht der Wind der Heimath zu" (The wind blows freshly toward our home) are sung to a phrase which occurs frequently in the course of this scene. It represents most graphically the heaving of the sea and may be appropriately termed the Ocean Motive. It undulates gracefully through *Brangäne's* reply to *Isolde's* question as to the vessel's course, surges wildly around *Isolde's* outburst of impotent anger when she learns that Cornwall's shore is not far distant, and breaks itself in savage fury against her despairing wrath as she invokes the elements to destroy the ship and all upon it. **Ocean Motive.**

It is her hopeless passion for *Tristan* which has prostrated *Isolde*, for the Motive of the Love Glance accompanies her first exclamation as she starts up excitedly.

Isolde calls upon *Brangäne* to throw aside the hangings, that she may have air. *Brangäne* obeys. The deck of the ship,

Richard Wagner

and, beyond it, the ocean, are disclosed. Around the mainmast sailors are busy splicing ropes. Beyond them, on the after deck, are knights and esquires. A little aside from them stands *Tristan*, gazing out upon the sea. At his feet reclines *Kurwenal*, his esquire. The young sailor's voice is again heard. *Isolde* beholds *Tristan*. Her wrath at the thought that he whom she loves is bearing her as bride to another vents itself in a vengeful phrase. She invokes death upon him. This phrase is the **Motive of Death**.

The Motive of the Love Glance is heard—and gives away *Isolde's* secret—as she asks *Brangäne* in what estimation she holds *Tristan*. It develops into a triumphant strain as *Brangäne* sings his praises. *Isolde* then bids her command *Tristan* to come into her presence. This command is given with the Motive of Death, for it is their mutual death *Isolde* wishes to compass. As *Brangäne* goes to do her mistress's bidding, a graceful variation of the Ocean Motive is heard, the bass marking the rhythmic motions of the sailors at the ropes. *Tristan* refuses to leave the helm and when *Brangäne* repeats *Isolde's* command, *Kurwenal* answers in deft measures in praise of *Tristan*. Knights, esquires, and sailors repeat the refrain. The boisterous measures—"Hail to our brave Tristan!"—form the **Tristan Call**.

The Complete Opera Book

Isolde's wrath at *Kurwenal's* taunts find vent in a narrative in which she tells *Brangäne* that once a wounded knight calling himself Tantris landed on Ireland's shore to seek her healing art. Into a niche in his sword she fitted a sword splinter she had found imbedded in the head of Morold, which had been sent to her in mockery after he had been slain in a combat with the Cornish foe. She brandished the sword over the knight, whom thus by his weapon she knew to be *Tristan*, her betrothed's slayer. But *Tristan's* glance fell upon her. Under its spell she was powerless. She nursed him back to health, and he vowed eternal gratitude as he left her. The chief theme of this narrative is derived from the Tristan Motive.

What of the boat, so bare, so frail,
That drifted to our shore?
What of the sorely stricken man feebly extended there?
Isolde's art he humbly sought;
With balsam, herbs, and healing salves,
From wounds that laid him low,
She nursed him back to strength.

Exquisite is the transition of the phrase "His eyes in mine were gazing," to the Isolde and Love Glance motives. The passage beginning: "Who silently his life had spared," is followed by the Tristan Call, *Isolde* seeming to compare sarcastically what she considers his betrayal of her with his fame as a hero. Her outburst of wrath as she inveighs against his treachery in now bearing her as bride to *King Marke*, carries the narrative to a superb

Richard Wagner

climax. *Brangäne* seeks to comfort *Isolde*, but the latter, looking fixedly before her, confides, almost involuntarily, her love for *Tristan*.

It is clear, even from this brief description, with what constantly varying expression the narrative of *Isolde* is treated. Wrath, desire for vengeance, rapturous memories that cannot be dissembled, finally a confession of love to *Brangäne*—such are the emotions that surge to the surface.

They lead *Brangäne* to exclaim: "Where lives the man who would not love you?" Then she weirdly whispers of the love-potion and takes a phial from a golden salver. The motives of the Love Glance and of the Love-Potion accompany her words and action. But *Isolde* seizes another phial, which she holds up triumphantly. It is the death-potion. Here is heard an ominous phrase of three notes—the **Motive of Fate**.

A forceful orchestral climax, in which the demons of despairing wrath seem unleashed, is followed by the cries of the sailors greeting the sight of the land, where she is to be married to *King Marke*. *Isolde* hears them with growing terror. *Kurwenal* brusquely calls to her and *Brangäne* to prepare soon to go ashore. *Isolde* orders *Kurwenal* that he command *Tristan* to come into her presence; then bids *Brangäne* prepare the death-potion. The Death Motive accompanies her final commands to *Kurwenal* and *Brangäne*, and the Fate Motive also drones threatfully through the weird measures. But *Brangäne* artfully substitutes the love-potion for the death-draught.

Kurwenal announces *Tristan's* approach. *Isolde*, seeking to control her agitation, strides to the couch, and, supporting herself by it, gazes fixedly at the entrance where

The Complete Opera Book

Tristan remains standing. The motive which announces his appearance is full of tragic defiance, as if *Tristan* felt that he stood upon the threshold of death, yet was ready to meet his fate unflinchingly. It alternates effectively with the Fate Motive, and is used most dramatically throughout the succeeding scene between *Tristan* and *Isolde*. Sombrely impressive is the passage when he bids *Isolde* slay him with the sword she once held over him.

> If so thou didst love thy lord,
> Lift once again this sword,
> Thrust with it, nor refrain,
> Lest the weapon fall again.

Shouts of the sailors announce the proximity of land. In a variant of her narrative theme *Isolde* mockingly anticipates *Tristan's* praise of her as he leads her into *King Marke's* presence. At the same time she hands him the goblet which contains, as she thinks, the death-potion and invites him to quaff it. Again the shouts of the sailors are heard, and *Tristan*, seizing the goblet, raises it to his lips with the ecstasy of one from whose soul a great sorrow is about to be lifted. When he has half emptied it, *Isolde* wrests it from him and drains it.

The tremor that passes over *Isolde* loosens her grasp upon the goblet. It falls from her hand. She faces *Tristan*.

Is the weird light in their eyes the last upflare of passion before the final darkness? What does the music answer as it enfolds them in its wondrous harmonies? The Isolde Motive;—then what? Not the glassy stare of death; the Love Glance, like a swift shaft of light penetrating the gloom. The spell is broken. *Isolde* sinks into *Tristan's* embrace.

Voices! They hear them not. Sailors are shouting

Richard Wagner

with joy that the voyage is over. Upon the lovers all sounds are lost, save their own short, quick interchange of phrases, in which the rapture of their passion, at last uncovered, finds speech. Music surges about them. But for *Brangäne* they would be lost. It is she who parts them, as the hangings are thrust aside.

Knights, esquires, sailors crowd the deck. From a rocky height *King Marke's* castle looks down upon the ship, now riding at anchor in the harbour. Peace and joy everywhere save in the lovers' breasts! *Isolde* faints in *Tristan's* arms. Yet it is a triumphant climax of the Isolde Motive that is heard above the jubilation of the ship-folk, as the act comes to a close.

Act II. This act also has an introduction, which together with the first scene between *Isolde* and *Brangäne*, constitutes a wonderful mood picture in music. Even Wagner's bitterest critic, Edward Hanslick, of Vienna, was forced to compare it with the loveliest creations of Schubert, in which that composer steeps the senses in dreams of night and love.

And so, this introduction of the second act opens with a motive of peculiar significance. During the love scene in the previous act, *Tristan* and *Isolde* have inveighed against the day which jealously keeps them apart. They may meet only under the veil of darkness. Even then their joy is embittered by the thought that the blissful night will soon be succeeded by day. With them, therefore, the day stands for all that is inimical, night for all that is friendly. This simile is elaborated with considerable metaphysical subtlety, the lovers even reproaching the day with *Tristan's* willingness to lead *Isolde* to *King Marke*, *Tristan* charging that in the broad light of the jealous day his duty to win *Isolde* for his king stood forth so clearly as to overpower the passion for her which he had nurtured during the silent watches of the night. The phrase, there-

The Complete Opera Book

fore, which begins the act as with an agonized cry is the **Day Motive.**

The Day Motive is followed by a phrase whose eager, restless measures graphically reflect the impatience with which *Isolde* awaits the coming of *Tristan*—the **Motive of Impatience.**

Over this there hovers a dulcet, seductive strain, the **Motive of the Love Call,** which is developed into the rapturous measures of the **Motive of Ecstasy.**

When the curtain rises, the scene it discloses is the palace garden, into which *Isolde's* apartments open. It is a

Richard Wagner

summer night, balmy and with a moon. The *King* and his suite have departed on a hunt. With them is *Melot*, a knight who professes devotion to *Tristan*, but whom *Brangäne* suspects.

Brangäne stands upon the steps leading to *Isolde's* apartment. She is looking down a bosky *allée* in the direction taken by the hunt. This silently gliding, uncanny creature, the servitor of sin in others, is uneasy. She fears the hunt is but a trap; and that its quarry is not the wild deer, but her mistress and the knight, who conveyed her for bride to *King Marke*.

Meanwhile against the open door of *Isolde's* apartment is a burning torch. Its flare through the night is to be the signal to *Tristan* that all is well, and that *Isolde* waits.

The first episode of the act is one of those exquisite tone paintings in the creation of which Wagner is supreme. The notes of the hunting-horns become more distant. *Isolde* enters from her apartment into the garden. She asks *Brangäne* if she cannot now signal for *Tristan*. *Brangäne* answers that the hunt is still within hearing. *Isolde* chides her—is it not some lovely, prattling rill she hears? The music is deliciously idyllic—conjuring up a dream-picture of a sylvan spring night bathed in liquescent moonlight. *Brangäne* warns *Isolde* against *Melot;* but *Isolde* laughs at her fears. In vain *Brangäne* entreats her mistress not to signal for *Tristan*. The seductive measures of the Love Call and of the Motive of Ecstasy tell throughout this scene of the yearning in *Isolde's* breast. When *Brangäne* informs *Isolde* that she substituted the love-potion for the death-draught, *Isolde* scorns the suggestion that her guilty love for *Tristan* is the result of her quaffing the potion. This simply intensified the passion already in her breast. She proclaims this in the rapturous phrases of the Isolde Motive; and then, when she declares her fate to be in the hands of the

The Complete Opera Book

goddess of love, there are heard the tender accents of the **Love Motive.**

In vain *Brangäne* warns once more against possible treachery from *Melot*. The Love Motive rises with ever increasing passion until *Isolde's* emotional exaltation finds expression in the Motive of Ecstasy as she bids *Brangäne* hie to the lookout, and proclaims that she will give *Tristan* the signal by extinguishing the torch, though in doing so she were to extinguish the light of her life. The Motive of the Love Call ringing out triumphantly accompanies her action, and dies away into the Motive of Impatience as she gazes down a bosky avenue through which she seems to expect *Tristan* to come to her. Then the Motive of Ecstasy and *Isolde's* rapturous gesture tell that she has discerned her lover; and, as this Motive reaches a fiercely impassioned climax, *Tristan* and *Isolde* rush into each other's arms.

The music fairly seethes with passion as the lovers greet one another, the Love Motive and the Motive of Ecstasy vying in the excitement of this rapturous meeting. Then begins the exchange of phrases in which the lovers pour forth their love for one another. This is the scene dominated by the Motive of the Day, which, however, as the day sinks into the soft night, is softened into the **Night Motive,** which soothes the senses with its ravishing caress.

Richard Wagner

This motive throbs through the rapturous harmonies of the duet: "Oh, sink upon us, Night of Love," and there is nothing in the realms of music or poetry to compare in suggestiveness with these caressing, pulsating phrases.

The duet is broken in upon by *Brangäne's* voice warning the lovers that night will soon be over. The *arpeggios* accompanying her warning are like the first grey streaks of dawn. But the lovers heed her not. In a smooth, soft melody—the **Motive of Love's Peace**—whose sensuous grace is simply entrancing, they whisper their love.

It is at such a moment, enveloped by night and love, that death should have come to them; and, indeed, it is for such a love-death they yearn. Hence we have here, over a quivering accompaniment, the **Motive of the Love-Death,**

Once more *Brangäne* calls. Once more *Tristan* and *Isolde* heed her not.

> Night will shield us for aye!

Thus exclaims *Isolde* in defiance of the approach of dawn, while the Motive of ecstasy, introduced by a rapturous mordent, soars ever higher.

The Complete Opera Book

A cry from *Brangäne, Kurwenal* rushing upon the scene calling to *Tristan* to save himself—and the lovers' ravishing dream is ended. Surrounded by the *King* and his suite, with the treacherous *Melot*, they gradually awaken to the terror of the situation. Almost automatically *Isolde* hides her head among the flowers, and *Tristan* spreads out his cloak to conceal her from view while phrases reminiscent of the love scene rise like mournful memories.

Now follows a soliloquy for the *King*, whose sword instead should have leapt from its scabbard and buried itself in *Tristan's* breast. For it seems inexplicable that the monarch, who should have slain the betrayer of his honour, indulges instead in a philosophical discourse, ending:

> The unexplained,
> Unpenetrated
> Cause of all these woes,
> Who will to us disclose?

Tristan turns to *Isolde*. Will she follow him to the bleak land of his birth? Her reply is that his home shall be her's. Then *Melot* draws his sword. *Tristan* rushes upon him, but as *Melot* thrusts, allows his guard to fall and receives the blade. *Isolde* throws herself on her wounded lover's breast.

Act III. The introduction to this act opens with a variation of the Isolde Motive, sadly prophetic of the desolation which broods over the scene to be disclosed when the curtain rises. On its third repetition it is continued in a long-drawn-out ascending phrase, which seems to represent musically the broad waste of ocean upon which *Tristan's* castle looks down from its craggy height.

The whole passage appears to represent *Tristan* hopelessly yearning for *Isolde*, letting his fancy travel back over the watery waste to the last night of love, and then giving himself up wholly to his grief.

The curtain rises upon the desolate grounds of Kareoi,

JEAN DE RESZKE AS TRISTAN.

Ternina as Isolde.

Richard Wagner

between the outer walls of *Tristan's* castle and the main structure, which stands upon a rocky eminence overlooking the sea. *Tristan* is stretched, apparently lifeless, under a huge linden-tree. Over him, in deep sorrow, bends the faithful *Kurwenal*. A *Shepherd* is heard piping a strain, whose plaintive notes harmonize most beautifully with the despairing desolation and sadness of the scene. It is the **Lay of Sorrow,** and by it, the *Shepherd* who scans the sea, conveys to *Kurwenal* information that the ship he has dispatched to Cornwall to bear *Isolde* to Kareol has not yet hove in sight.

The Lay of Sorrow is a strain of mournful beauty, with the simplicity and indescribable charm of a folk-song. Its plaintive notes cling like ivy to the grey and crumbling ruins of love and joy.

The *Shepherd* peers over the wall and asks if *Tristan* has shown any signs of life. *Kurwenal* gloomily replies in the negative. The *Shepherd* departs to continue his lookout, piping the sad refrain. *Tristan* slowly opens his eyes. "The old refrain; why wakes it me? Where am I?" he murmurs. *Kurwenal* is beside himself with joy at these signs of returning life. His replies to *Tristan's* feeble and wandering questions are mostly couched in a motive which beautifully expresses the sterling nature of this faithful retainer, one of the noblest characters Wagner has drawn.

The Complete Opera Book

When *Tristan* loses himself in sad memories of *Isolde*, *Kurwenal* seeks to comfort him with the news that he has sent a trusty man to Cornwall to bear *Isolde* to him that she may heal the wound inflicted by *Melot* as she once healed that dealt *Tristan* by Morold. In *Tristan's* jubilant reply, during which he draws *Kurwenal* to his breast, the Isolde Motive assumes a form in which it becomes a theme of joy.

But it is soon succeeded by the **Motive of Anguish,**

when *Tristan* raves of his yearning for *Isolde*. "The ship! the ship!" he exclaims. "Kurwenal, can you not see it?" The Lay of Sorrow, piped by the *Shepherd*, gives the sad answer. It pervades his sad reverie until, when his mind wanders back to *Isolde's* tender nursing of his wound in Ireland, the theme of Isolde's Narrative is heard again. Finally his excitement grows upon him, and in a paroxysm of anguish bordering on insanity he even curses love.

Tristan sinks back apparently lifeless. But no—as *Kurwenal* bends over him and the Isolde Motive is breathed by the orchestra; he again whispers of *Isolde*. In ravishing beauty the Motive of Love's Peace caressingly follows his vision as he seems to see *Isolde* gliding toward him o'er the waves. With ever-growing excitement he orders *Kurwenal* to the lookout to watch the ship's coming. What he sees so clearly cannot *Kurwenal* also see? Suddenly the music changes in character. The ship is in sight, for the *Shepherd* is heard piping a joyous lay. It pervades the music of

Richard Wagner

Tristan's excited questions and *Kurwenal's* answers as to the vessel's movements. The faithful retainer rushes down toward the shore to meet *Isolde* and lead her to *Tristan*. The latter, his strength sapped by his wound, his mind inflamed to insanity by his passionate yearning, struggles to rise. He raises himself a little. The Motive of Love's Peace, no longer tranquil, but with frenzied rapidity, accompanies his actions as, in his delirium, he tears the bandage from his wounds and rises from his couch.

Isolde's voice! Into her arms, outstretched to receive him, staggers *Tristan*. Gently she lets him down upon his couch, where he has lain in the anguish of expectancy.

"Tristan!"

"Isolde!" he answers in broken accents. This last look resting rapturously upon her, while in mournful beauty the Love-Glance Motive rises from the orchestra, he expires.

In all music there is no scene more deeply shaken with sorrow.

Tumultuous sounds are heard. A second ship has arrived. *Marke* and his suite have landed. *Tristan's* men, thinking the *King* has come in pursuit of *Isolde*, attack the new-comers, *Kurwenal* and his men are overpowered, and *Kurwenal*, having avenged *Tristan* by slaying *Melot*, sinks, himself mortally wounded, dying by *Tristan's* side. He reaches out for his dead master's hand, and his last words are: "Tristan, chide me not that faithfully I follow you."

When *Brangäne* rushes in and hurriedly announces that she has informed the *King* of the love-potion, and that he comes bringing forgiveness, *Isolde* heeds her not. As the Love-Death Motive rises softly over the orchestra and slowly swells into the impassioned Motive of Ecstasy, to reach its climax with a stupendous crash of instrumental forces, she gazes with growing transport upon her dead

The Complete Opera Book

lover, until, with rapture in her last glance, she sinks upon his corpse and expires.

In the Wagnerian version of the legend this love-death for which *Tristan* and *Isolde* prayed and in which they are united, is more than a mere farewell together to life. It is tinged with Oriental philosophy, and symbolizes the taking up into and the absorption of by nature of all that is spiritual, and hence immortal, in lives rendered beautiful by love.

DIE MEISTERSINGER VON NÜRNBERG

THE MASTERSINGERS OF NUREMURG

Opera in three acts, words and music by Richard Wagner. Produced, Munich, June 21, 1868, under direction of Hans von Bülow. London, Drury Lane, May 30, 1882, under Hans Richter; Covent Garden, July 13, 1889, in Italian; Manchester, in English, by the Carl Rosa Company, April 16, 1896. New York, Metropolitan Opera House, January 4, 1886, with Fischer (*Hans Sachs*), Seidl-Kraus (*Eva*), Marianne Brandt (*Magdalena*), Stritt (*Walther*), Kemlitz (*Beckmesser*); Conductor, Seidl. *Sachs* has also been sung by Edouard de Reszke, Van Rooy, and Whitehill; *Walther* by Jean de Reszke; *Eva* by Eames, Gadski, and Hempel; *Beckmesser* by Goritz; *Magdalena* by Schumann-Heink and Homer.

CHARACTERS

HANS SACHS, Cobbler............	⎫	............*Bass*
VEIT POGNER, Goldsmith...........		............*Bass*
KUNZ VOGELGESANG, Furrier.......		............*Tenor*
CONRAD NACHTIGALL, Buckle-Maker		............*Bass*
SIXTUS BECKMESSER, Town Clerk...		............*Bass*
FRITZ KOTHNER, Baker............	⎬ Mastersingers	............*Bass*
BALTHAZAR ZORN, Pewterer........		............*Tenor*
ULRICH EISLINGER, Grocer.........		............*Tenor*
AUGUST MOSER, Tailor............		............*Tenor*
HERMANN ORTEL, Soap-boiler.......		............*Bass*
HANS SCHWARZ, Stocking-Weaver....		............*Bass*
HANS FOLZ, Coppersmith..........	⎭	............*Bass*
WALTHER VON STOLZING, a young Franconian knight...........		*Tenor*

Richard Wagner

DAVID, apprentice to HANS SACHS.................... ....*Tenor*
A NIGHT WATCHMAN..*Bass*
EVA, daughter of POGNER..............................*Soprano*
MAGDALENA, EVA'S nurse.........................*Mezzo-Soprano*
    Burghers of the Guilds, Journeymen, 'Prentices, Girls, and Populace.
Time—Middle of the Sixteenth Century.   *Place*—Nuremburg.

Wagner's music-dramas are all unmistakably Wagner, yet they are wonderfully varied. The style of the music in each adapts itself plastically to the character of the story. Can one, for instance, imagine the music of "Tristan" wedded to the story of "The Mastersingers," or *vice versa?* A tragic passion, inflamed by the arts of sorcery inspired the former. The latter is a thoroughly human tale set to thoroughly human music. Indeed, while "Tristan" and "The Ring of the Nibelung" are tragic, and "Parsifal" is deeply religious, "The Mastersingers" is a comic work, even bordering in one scene on farce. Like Shakespeare, Wagner was equally at home in tragedy and comedy.

    Walther von Stolzing is in love with *Eva.* Her father having promised her to the singer to whom at the coming midsummer festival the *Mastersingers* shall adjudge the prize, it becomes necessary for *Walther* to seek admission to their art union. He is, however, rejected, his song violating the rules to which the Mastersingers slavishly adhere. *Beckmesser* is also instrumental in securing *Walther's* rejection. The town clerk is the "marker" of the union. His duty is to mark all violations of the rules against a candidate. *Beckmesser*, being a suitor for *Eva's* hand, naturally makes the most of every chance to put down a mark against *Walther.*

    Sachs alone among the *Mastersingers* has recognized the beauty of *Walther's* song. Its very freedom from rule and rote charms him, and he discovers in the young knight's untrammelled genius the power which, if properly directed, will lead art from the beaten path of tradition toward a new and loftier ideal.

After *Walther's* failure before the Mastersingers the impetuous young knight persuades *Eva* to elope with him. But at night as they are preparing to escape, *Beckmesser* comes upon the scene to serenade *Eva*. *Sachs*, whose house is opposite *Pogner's*, has meanwhile brought his work bench out into the street and insists on "marking" what he considers *Beckmesser's* mistakes by bringing his hammer down upon his last with a resounding whack. The louder *Beckmesser* sings the louder *Sachs* whacks. Finally the neighbours are aroused. *David*, who is in love with *Magdalena* and thinks *Beckmesser* is serenading her, falls upon him with a cudgel. The whole neighbourhood turns out and a general *mêlée* ensues, during which *Sachs* separates *Eva* and *Walther* and draws the latter into his home.

The following morning *Walther* sings to *Sachs* a song which has come to him in a dream, *Sachs* transcribing the words and passing friendly criticism upon them and the music. The midsummer festival is to take place that afternoon, and through a ruse *Sachs* manages to get *Walther's* poem into *Beckmesser's* possession, who, thinking the words are by the popular cobbler-poet, feels sure he will be the chosen master. *Eva*, coming into the workshop to have her shoes fitted, finds *Walther*, and the lovers depart with *Sachs*, *David*, and *Magdalena* for the festival. Here *Beckmesser*, as *Sachs* had anticipated, makes a wretched failure, as he has utterly missed the spirit of the poem, and *Walther*, being called upon by *Sachs* to reveal its beauty in music, sings his prize song, winning at once the approbation of the *Mastersingers* and the populace. He is received into their art union and at the same time wins *Eva* as his bride.

The Mastersingers were of burgher extraction. They flourished in Germany, chiefly in the imperial cities, during

Richard Wagner

the fourteenth, fifteenth, and sixteenth centuries. They did much to generate and preserve a love of art among the middle classes. Their musical competitions were judged according to a code of rules which distinguished by particular names thirty-two faults to be avoided. Scriptural or devotional subjects were usually selected and the judges or Merker (Markers) were, in Nuremburg, four in number, the first comparing the words with the Biblical text, the second criticizing the prosody, the third the rhymes, and the fourth the tune. He who had the fewest marks against him received the prize.

Hans Sachs, the most famous of the Mastersingers, born November 5, 1494, died January, 1576, in Nuremburg, is said to have been the author of some six thousand poems. He was a cobbler by trade—

> Hans Sachs was a shoe-
> Maker and poet too.

A monument was erected to him in the city of his birth in 1874.

"The Mastersingers" is a simple, human love story, simply told, with many touches of humour to enliven it, and its interest enhanced by highly picturesque, historical surroundings. As a drama it conveys also a perfect picture of the life and customs of Nuremburg of the time in which the story plays. Wagner must have made careful historical researches, but his book lore is not thrust upon us. The work is so spontaneous that the method and manner of its art are lost sight of in admiration of the result. Hans Sachs himself could not have left a more faithful portrait of life in Nuremburg in the middle of the sixteenth century.

"The Mastersingers" has a peculiarly Wagnerian interest. It is Wagner's protest against the narrow-minded critics and the prejudiced public who so long refused him recognition. Edward Hanslick, the bitterest of Wagner's critics, regarded the libretto as a personal insult to himself. Being present by invitation at a private reading of the libretto, which Wagner gave in Vienna, Hanslick rose abruptly and left after the first act. *Walther von Stolzing* is the incarnation of new aspirations in art; the champion of a new art ideal, and continually chafing under the restraints imposed by traditional rules and methods. *Hans Sachs* is a conservative. But, while preserving what is best in art traditions, he is able to recognize the beautiful in what is new. He represents enlightened public opinion. *Beckmesser* and the other *Mastersingers* are the embodiment of rank prejudice—the critics. *Walther's* triumph is also Wagner's. Few of Wagner's dramatic creations equal in life-like interest the character of *Sachs*. It is drawn with a strong, firm hand, and filled in with many delicate touches.

The *Vorspiel* gives a complete musical epitome of the story. It is full of life and action—pompous, impassioned, and jocose in turn, and without a suggestion of the overwrought or morbid. Its sentiment and its fun are purely human. In its technical construction it has long been recognized as a masterpiece.

In the sense that it precedes the rise of the curtain, this orchestral composition is a *Vorspiel*, or prelude. As a work, however, it is a full-fledged overture, rich in thematic material. These themes are Leading Motives heard many times, and in wonderful variety in the three acts of "The Mastersingers." To a great extent an analysis of this overture forecasts the work itself. Accordingly, again through the courtesy of G. Schirmer Inc., I avail myself of my *Wagner's Music-Dramas Analysed*, in the account of the *Vorspiel* and of the action and music that follow it.

The pompous **Motive of the Mastersingers** opens the *Vorspiel*. This theme gives capital musical expression to the characteristics of these dignitaries; eminently worthy but self-sufficient citizens who are slow to receive new

Von Rooy as Hans Sachs in "Die Meistersinger."

ARTHUR JORDAN AS WALTHER IN "DIE MEISTERSINGER."

Richard Wagner

impressions and do not take kindly to innovations. Our term of old fogy describes them imperfectly, as it does not allow for their many excellent qualities. They are slow to act, but if they are once aroused their ponderous influence bears down all opposition. At first an obstacle to genuine reform, they are in the end the force which pushes it to success. Thus there is in the Motive of the Mastersingers a certain ponderous dignity which well emphasizes the idea of conservative power.

In great contrast to this is the **Lyric Motive,** which seems to express the striving after a poetic ideal untrammelled by old-fashioned restrictions, such as the rules of the *Mastersingers* impose.

But, the sturdy conservative forces are still unwilling to be persuaded of the worth of this new ideal. Hence the Lyric Motive is suddenly checked by the sonorous measures of the **Mastersingers' March.**

In this the majesty of law and order finds expression. It is followed by a phrase of noble breadth and beauty, obviously developed from portions of the Motive of the Mastersingers, and so typical of the goodwill which should exist among the members of a fraternity that it may be called the **Motive of the Art Brotherhood.**

It reaches an eloquent climax in the **Motive of the Ideal.**

Opposed, however, to this guild of conservative masters is the restless spirit of progress. Hence, though stately the strains of the Mastersingers' March and of the Guild Motive, soon yield to a theme full of emotional energy and much like the Lyric Motive. *Walther* is the champion of this new ideal—not, however, from a purely artistic impulse, but rather through his love for *Eva*. Being ignorant of the rules and rote of the *Mastersingers* he sings, when he presents himself for admission to the fraternity, measures which soar untrammelled into realms of beauty beyond the imagination of the masters. But it was his love for *Eva* which impelled him to seek admission to the brotherhood, and love inspired his song. He is therefore a reformer only by accident; it is not his love of art, but his passion for *Eva*, which really brings about through his prize song a great musical reform. This is one of Wagner's finest dramatic touches—the love story is the mainspring of the action, the moral is pointed only incidentally Hence all the motives in which the restless striving after a new ideal, or the struggles of a new art form to break through the barriers of conservative prejudice, find expression, are so many love motives, *Eva* being the incarnation of *Walther's* ideal. Therefore the motive which breaks in upon the

Richard Wagner

Mastersingers' March and Guild Motive with such emotional energy expresses *Walther's* desire to possess *Eva*, more than his yearning for a new ideal in art. So I call it the **Motive of Longing.**

A portion of "Walther's Prize Song," like a swiftly

whispered declaration of love, leads to a variation of one of the most beautiful themes of the work—the **Motive of Spring.**

And now Wagner has a fling at the old fogyism which was so long an obstacle to his success. He holds the masters up to ridicule in a delightfully humorous passage which parodies the Mastersingers' and Art Brotherhood motives, while the Spring Motive vainly strives to assert itself. In the bass, the following quotation is the **Motive of Ridicule,** the treble being a variant of the Art Brotherhood Motive.

The Complete Opera Book

When it is considered that the opposition Wagner encountered from prejudiced critics, not to mention a prejudiced public, was the bane of his career, it seems wonderful that he should have been content to protest against it with this pleasant raillery instead of with bitter invective. The passage is followed by the Motive of the Mastersingers, which in turn leads to an imposing combination of phrases. We hear the portion of the Prize Song already quoted—the Motive of the Mastersingers as bass—and in the middle voices portions of the Mastersingers' March; a little later the Motive of the Art Brotherhood and the Motive of Ridicule are added, this grand massing of orchestral forces reaching a powerful climax, with the Motive of the Ideal, while the Motive of the Mastersingers brings the *Vorspiel* to a fitting close. In this noble passage, in which the "Prize Song" soars above the various themes typical of the masters, the new ideal seems to be borne to its triumph upon the shoulders of the conservative forces which, won over at last, have espoused its cause with all their sturdy energy.

This concluding passage in the *Vorspiel* thus brings out with great eloquence the inner significance of "Die Meistersinger." In whatever the great author and composer of this work wrote for the stage, there always was an ethical meaning back of the words and music. Thus we draw our conclusion of the meaning of "Die Meistersinger" story from the wonderful combination of leading motives in the peroration of its *Vorspiel*.

In his fine book, *The Orchestra and Orchestral Music*, W. J. Henderson relates this anecdote:

"A professional musician was engaged in a discussion of Wagner in the corridor of the Metropolitan Opera House, while inside the orchestra was playing the 'Meistersinger' overture.

"'It is a pity,' said this wise man, in a condescending

Richard Wagner

manner, 'but Wagner knows absolutely nothing about counterpoint.'

"At that instant the orchestra was singing five different melodies at once; and, as Anton Seidl was the conductor, they were all audible."

In a rare book by J. C. Wagenseil, printed in Nuremburg in 1697, are given four "Prize Master Tones." Two of these Wagner has reproduced in modern garb, the former in the Mastersingers' March, the latter in the Motive of the Art Brotherhood.

Act I. The scene of this act is laid in the Church of St. Catherine, Nuremburg. The congregation is singing the final chorale of the service. Among the worshippers are *Eva* and her maid, *Magdalena*. *Walther* stands aside, and, by means of nods and gestures, communicates with *Eva*. This mimic conversation is expressively accompanied by interludes between the verses of the chorale, interludes expressively based on the Lyric, Spring, and Prize Song motives, and contrasting charmingly with the strains of the chorale.

The service over, the Motive of Spring, with an impetuous upward rush, seems to express the lovers' joy that the restraint is removed, and the Lyric Motive resounds exultingly as the congregation departs, leaving *Eva*, *Magdalena*, and *Walther* behind.

Eva, in order to gain a few words with *Walther*, sends *Magdalena* back to the pew to look for a kerchief and hymn-book, she has purposely left there. *Magdalena* urges *Eva* to return home, but just then *David* appears in the background and begins putting things to rights for the meeting of the *Mastersingers*. *Magdalena* is therefore

The Complete Opera Book

only too glad to linger. The Mastersinger and Guild motives, which naturally accompany *David's* activity, contrast soberly with the ardent phrases of the lovers. *Magdalena* explains to *Walther* that *Eva* is already affianced, though she herself does not know to whom. Her father wishes her to marry the singer to whom at the coming contest the *Mastersingers* shall award the prize; and, while she shall be at liberty to decline him, she may marry none but a master. *Eva* exclaims: "I will choose no one but my knight!" Very pretty and gay is the theme heard when *David* joins the group—the **Apprentice Motive.**

How capitally this motive expresses the light-heartedness of gay young people, in this case the youthful apprentices, among whom *David* was as gay and bouyant as any. Every melodious phrase—every motive—employed by Wagner appears to express exactly the character, circumstance, thing, or feeling, to which he applies it. The opening episodes of "Die Meistersinger" have a charm all their own.

The scene closes with a beautiful little terzet, after *Magdalena* has ordered *David*, under penalty of her displeasure, to instruct the knight in the art rules of the *Mastersingers*.

When the 'prentices enter, they proceed to erect the marker's platform, but stop at times to annoy the somewhat self-sufficient *David*, while he is endeavouring to instruct *Walther* in the rules of the *Mastersingers*. The merry Apprentice Motive runs through the scene and brings it to a close as the 'prentices sing and dance around the marker's box, suddenly, however, breaking off, for the *Mastersingers* appear.

Richard Wagner

There is a roll-call and then the fine passage for bass voice, in which *Pogner* offers *Eva's* hand in marriage to the winner of the coming song contest—with the proviso that *Eva* adds her consent. The passage is known on concert programmes as "Pogner's Address."

Walther is introduced by *Pogner*. The Knight Motive:

Beckmesser, jealous, and determined that *Walther* shall fail, enters the marker's box.

Kothner now begins reading off the rules of singing established by the masters, which is a capital take-off on old-fashioned forms of composition and never fails to raise a hearty laugh if delivered with considerable pomposity and unction. Unwillingly enough *Walther* takes his seat in the candidate's chair. *Beckmesser* shouts from the marker's box: "Now begin!" After a brilliant chord, followed by a superb ascending run on the violins, *Walther*, in ringing tones, enforced by a broad and noble chord, repeats *Beckmesser's* words. But such a change has come over the music that it seems as if that upward rushing run had swept away all restraint of ancient rule and rote, just as the spring wind whirling through the forest tears up the spread of dry, dead leaves, thus giving air and sun to the yearning mosses and flowers. In *Walther's* song the Spring Motive forms an ever-surging, swelling accompaniment, finally joining in the vocal melody and bearing it higher and higher to an impassioned climax. In his song, however, *Walther* is interrupted by the scratching made by *Beck-*

The Complete Opera Book

messer as he chalks the singer's violations of the rules on the slate, and *Walther*, who is singing of love and spring, changes his theme to winter, which, lingering behind a thorny hedge, is plotting how it can mar the joy of the vernal season. The knight then rises from the chair and sings a second stanza with defiant enthusiasm. As he concludes it *Beckmesser* tears open the curtains which concealed him in the marker's box, and exhibits his board completely covered with chalk marks. *Walther* protests, but the masters, with the exception of *Sachs* and *Pogner*, refuse to listen further, and deride his singing. We have here the **Motive of Derision.**

Sachs protests that, while he found the knight's art method new, he did not find it formless. The **Sachs Motive** is here introduced.

The Sachs Motive betokens the genial nature of this sturdy, yet gentle man—the master spirit of the drama. He combines the force of a conservative character with the

Richard Wagner

tolerance of a progressive one, and is thus the incarnation of the idea which Wagner is working out in this drama, in which the union of a proper degree of conservative caution with progressive energy produces a new ideal in art. To *Sachs's* innuendo that *Beckmessers'* marking hardly could be considered just, as he is a candidate for *Eva's* hand, *Beckmesser*, by way of reply, chides *Sachs* for having delayed so long in finishing a pair of shoes for him, and as *Sachs* makes a humorously apologetic answer, the Cobbler Motive is heard.

The sturdy burgher calls to *Walther* to finish his song in spite of the masters. And now a finale of masterful construction begins. In short, excited phrases the masters chaff and deride *Walther*. His song, however, soars above all the hubbub. The a'prentices see their opportunity in the confusion, and joining hands they dance around the marker's box, singing as they do so. We now have combined with astounding skill *Walther's* song, the a'prentices' chorus, and the exclamations of the masters. The latter finally shout their verdict: "Rejected and outsung!" The knight, with a proud gesture of contempt, leaves the church. The a'prentices put the seats and benches back in their proper places, and in doing so greatly obstruct the masters as they crowd toward the doors. *Sachs*, who has lingered behind, gazes thoughtfully at the singer's empty chair, then, with a humorous gesture of discouragement, turns away.

Act II. The scene of this act represents a street in Nuremburg crossing the stage and intersected in the middle by a narrow, winding alley. There are thus two corner houses—on the right corner of the alley *Pogner's*, on the left *Sachs's*. Before the former is a linden-tree, before the latter an elder. It is a lovely summer evening.

The opening scene is a merry one. *David* and the a'prentices are closing shop. After a brisk introduction

The Complete Opera Book

based on the Midsummer Festival Motive the 'prentices quiz *David* on his love affair with *Magdalena*. The latter appears with a basket of dainties for her lover, but on learning that the knight has been rejected, she snatches the basket away from *David* and hurries back to the house. The 'prentices now mockingly congratulate *David* on his successful wooing. *David* loses his temper and shows fight, but *Sachs*, coming upon the scene, sends the 'prentices on their way and then enters his workshop with *David*. The music of this episode, especially the 'prentices' chorus, is bright and graceful.

Pogner and *Eva*, returning from an evening stroll, now come down the alley. Before retiring into the house the father questions the daughter as to her feelings concerning the duty she is to perform at the Mastersinging on the morrow. Her replies are discreetly evasive. The music beautifully reflects the affectionate relations between *Pogner* and *Eva*. When *Pogner*, his daughter seated beside him under the linden-tree, speaks of the morrow's festival and *Eva's* part in it in awarding the prize to the master of her choice before the assembled burghers of Nuremburg, the stately **Nuremburg Motive** is ushered in.

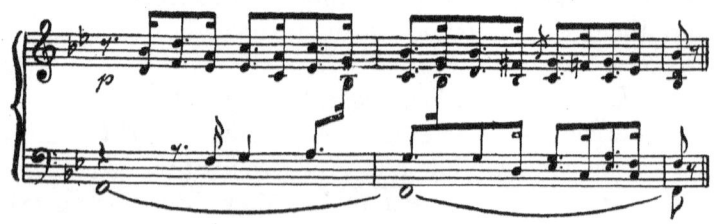

Magdalena appears at the door and signals to *Eva*. The latter persuades her father that it is too cool to remain outdoors and, as they enter the house, *Eva* learns from

Richard Wagner

Magdalena of *Walther's* failure before the masters. *Magdalena* advises her to seek counsel with *Sachs* after supper.

The Cobbler Motive shows us *Sachs* and *David* in the former's workshop. When the master has dismissed his 'prentice till morning, he yields to his poetic love of the balmy midsummer night and, laying down his work, leans over the half-door of his shop as if lost in reverie. The Cobbler Motive dies away to *pp*, and then there is wafted from over the orchestra like the sweet scent of the blooming elder the Spring Motive, while tender notes on the horn blossom beneath a nebulous veil of tremolo violins into memories of *Walther's* song. Its measures run through *Sachs's* head until, angered at the stupid conservatism of his associates, he resumes his work to the brusque measures of the Cobbler's Motive. As his ill humour yields again to the beauties of the night, this motive yields once more to that of spring, which, with reminiscences of *Walther's* first song before the masters, imbues this masterful monologue with poetic beauty of the highest order. The last words in praise of *Walther* ("The bird who sang to-day," etc.) are sung to a broad and expressive melody.

Eva now comes out into the street and, shyly approaching the shop, stands at the door unnoticed by *Sachs* until she speaks to him. The theme which pervades this scene seems to breathe forth the very spirit of lovely maidenhood which springs from the union of romantic aspirations, feminine reserve, and rare physical graces. It is the **Eva Motive,** which, with the delicate touch of a master, Wagner so varies that it follows the many subtle dramatic suggestions of the scene. The Eva Motive, in its original form, is as follows:

The Complete Opera Book

When at *Eva's* first words *Sachs* looks up, there is this elegant variation of the Eva Motive:

Then the scene being now fully ushered in, we have the Eva Motive itself. *Eva* leads the talk up to the morrow's festival, and when *Sachs* mentions *Beckmesser* as her chief wooer, roguishly hints, with evident reference to *Sachs* himself, that she might prefer a hearty widower to a bachelor of such disagreeable characteristics as the marker. There are sufficient indications that the sturdy master is not indifferent to *Eva's* charms, but, whole-souled, genuine friend that he is, his one idea is to further the love affair between his fair neighbour and *Walther*. The music of this passage is very suggestive. The melodic leading of the upper voice in the accompaniment, when *Eva* asks: "Could not a widower hope to win me?" is identical with a variation of the Isolde Motive in "Tristan and Isolde," while the Eva Motive, shyly *pp*, seems to indicate the artfulness of *Eva's* question. The reminiscence from "Tristan" can hardly be regarded as accidental, for *Sachs* afterwards boasts that he does not care to share the fate of poor King Marke. *Eva* now endeavours to glean particulars of *Walther's* experience in the morning, and we have the Motive of Envy, the Knight Motive, and the Motive of Ridicule. *Eva* does not appreciate the fine satire in *Sachs's* severe strictures on *Walther's* singing—he re-echoes not his own views, but those of the other masters, for whom, not for the knight, his strictures are really intended—and she leaves him in anger. This shows *Sachs* which way the

Richard Wagner

wind blows, and he forthwith resolves to do all in his power to bring *Eva's* and *Walther's* love affair to a successful conclusion. While *Eva* is engaged with *Magdalena*, who has come out to call her, he busies himself in closing the upper half of his shop door so far that only a gleam of light is visible, he himself being completely hidden. *Eva* learns from *Magdalena* of *Beckmesser's* intended serenade, and it is agreed that the maid shall personate *Eva* at the window.

Steps are heard coming down the alley. *Eva* recognizes *Walther* and flies to his arms, *Magdalena* discreetly hurrying into the house. The ensuing ardent scene between *Eva* and *Walther* brings familiar motives. The knight's excitement is comically broken in upon by the *Night Watchman's* cow-horn, and, as *Eva* lays her hand soothingly upon his arm and counsels that they retreat within the shadow of the linden-tree, there steals over the orchestra, like the fragrance of the summer night, a delicate variant of the Eva Motive —The Summer Night Motive.

Eva vanishes into the house to prepare to elope with *Walther*. The *Night Watchman* now goes up the stage intoning a mediæval chant. Coming in the midst of the beautiful modern music of "The Mastersingers," its effect is most quaint.

As *Eva* reappears and she and the knight are about to make their escape, *Sachs*, to prevent this precipitate and foolish step, throws open his shutters and allows his lamp to shed a streak of brilliant light across the street.

The lovers hesitate; and now *Beckmesser* sneaks in after the *Night Watchman* and, leaning against *Sachs's* house, begins to tune his lute, the peculiar twang of which, contrasted with the rich orchestration, sounds irresistibly ridiculous.

Meanwhile, *Eva* and *Walther* have once more retreated into the shade of the linden-tree, and *Sachs*, who has placed his work bench in front of his door, begins hammering at the last and intones a song which is one of the rough diamonds of musical invention, for it is purposely brusque and rough, just such a song as a hearty, happy artisan might sing over his work. It is aptly introduced by the Cobbler Motive. *Beckmesser*, greatly disturbed lest his serenade be ruined, entreats *Sachs* to cease singing. The latter agrees, but with the proviso that he shall "mark" each of *Beckmesser's* mistakes with a hammer stroke. As if to bring out as sharply as possible the ridiculous character of the serenade, the orchestra breathes forth once more the summer night's music before *Beckmesser* begins his song, and this is set to a parody of the Lyric Motive. Wagner, with keen satire, seems to want to show how a beautiful melody may become absurd through old-fogy methods. *Beckmesser* has hardly begun before *Sachs's* hammer comes down on the last with a resounding whack, which makes the town clerk fairly jump with anger. He resumes, but soon is rudely interrupted again by a blow of *Sachs's* hammer. The whacks come faster and faster. *Beckmesser*, in order to make himself heard above them, sings louder and louder. Some of the neighbours are awakened by the noise and coming to their windows bid *Beckmesser* hold his peace. *David*, stung by jealousy as he sees *Magdalena* listening to the serenade, leaps from his room and falls upon the town clerk with a cudgel. The neighbours, male and female, run out into the street and a general *mêlée* ensues, the masters, who hurry upon the scene, seeking to restore quiet, while the 'prentices vent their high spirits by doing all in their power to add to the hubbub. All is now noise and disorder, pandemonium

Richard Wagner

seeming to have been let loose upon the dignified old town.

Musically this tumult finds expression in a fugue whose chief theme is the **Cudgel Motive**.

From beneath the hubbub of voices—those of the 'prentices and journeymen, delighted to take part in the shindy, of the women who are terrified at it, and of the masters who strive to stop it, is heard the theme of *Beckmesser's* song, the real cause of the row. This is another of those many instances in which Wagner vividly expresses in his music the significance of what transpires on the stage.

Sachs finally succeeds in shoving the 'prentices and journeymen out of the way. The street is cleared, but not before the cobbler-poet has pushed *Eva*, who was about to elope with *Walther*, into her father's arms and drawn *Walther* after him into his shop.

The street is quiet. And now, the rumpus subsided and all concerned in it gone, the *Night Watchman* appears, rubs his eyes and chants his mediæval call. The street is flooded with moonlight. The *Watchman* with his clumsy halberd lunges at his own shadow, then goes up the alley.

We have had hubbub, we have had humour, and now we have a musical ending elvish, roguish, and yet exquisite in sentiment. The effect is produced by the Cudgel Motive played with the utmost delicacy on the flute, while the theme of *Beckmesser's* serenade merrily runs after itself on clarinet and bassoon, and the muted violins softly breathe the Midsummer Festival Motive.

The Complete Opera Book

Act III. During this act the tender strain in *Sachs's* sturdy character is brought out in bold relief. Hence the prelude develops what may be called three Sachs themes, two of them expressive of his twofold nature as poet and cobbler, the third standing for the love which his fellow-burghers bear him.

The prelude opens with the Wahn Motive or Motive of Poetic Illusion. This reflects the deep thought and poetic aspirations of *Sachs* the poet. It is followed by the theme of the beautiful chorus, sung later in the act, in praise of *Sachs:* "Awake! draws nigh the break of day." This theme, among the three heard in the prelude, points to *Sachs's* popularity. The third consists of portions of the cobbler's song in the second act. This prelude has long been considered one of Wagner's masterpieces. The themes are treated with the utmost delicacy, so that we recognize through them both the tender, poetic side of *Sachs's* nature and his good-humoured brusqueness. **The Motive of Poetic Illusion** is deeply reflective, and it might be preferable to name it the Motive of Poetic Thought, were it not that it is better to preserve the significance of the term Wahn Motive, which there is ample reason to believe originated with Wagner himself. The prelude is, in fact, a subtle analysis of character expressed in music.

How peaceful the scene on which the curtain rises. *Sachs* is sitting in an arm-chair in his sunny workshop, reading in a large folio. The Illusion Motive has not yet died away in the prelude, so that it seems to reflect the thoughts awakened in *Sachs* by what he is reading. *David*, dressed for the festival, enters just as the prelude ends.

Richard Wagner

There is a scene full of charming *bonhomie* between *Sachs* and his 'prentice, which is followed, when the latter has withdrawn, by *Sachs's* monologue: "Wahn! Wahn! Ueberall Wahn!" (Illusion, everywhere illusion.)

While the Illusion Motive seems to weave a poetic atmosphere about him, *Sachs*, buried in thought, rests his head upon his arm over the folio. The Illusion Motive is followed by the Spring Motive, which in turn yields to the Nuremburg Motive as *Sachs* sings the praises of the stately old town. At his reference to the tumult of the night before there are in the score corresponding allusions to the music of that episode. "A glowworm could not find its mate," he sings, referring to *Walther* and *Eva*. The Midsummer Festival, Lyric, and Nuremburg motives in union foreshadow the triumph of true art through love on Nuremburg soil, and thus bring the monologue to a stately conclusion.

Walther now enters from the chamber, which opens upon a gallery, and, descending into the workshop, is heartily greeted by *Sachs* with the Sachs Motive, which dominates the immediately ensuing scene. Very beautiful is the theme in which *Sachs* protests against *Walther's* derision of the masters; for they are, in spite of their many old-fogyish notions, the conservators of much that is true and beautiful in art.

Walther tells *Sachs* of a song which came to him in a dream during the night, and sings two stanzas of this "Prize Song," *Sachs* making friendly critical comments as he writes down the words. The Nuremburg Motive in sonorous and festive instrumentation closes this melodious episode.

When *Sachs* and *Walther* have retired *Beckmesser* is seen peeping into the shop. Observing that it is empty he enters hastily. He is ridiculously overdressed for the approaching festival, limps, and occasionally rubs his muscles as if he were still stiff and sore from his drubbing. By chance his glance falls on the manuscript of the "Prize Song" in *Sachs's* handwriting on the table, when he breaks forth in wrathful exclamations, thinking now that he has in the popular master a rival for *Eva's* hand. Hearing the chamber door opening he hastily grabs the manuscript and thrusts it into his pocket. *Sachs* enters. Observing that the manuscript is no longer on the table, he realizes that *Beckmesser* has stolen it, and conceives the idea of allowing him to keep it, knowing that the marker will fail most wretchedly in attempting to give musical expression to *Walther's* inspiration.

The scene places *Sachs* in a new light. A fascinating trait of his character is the dash of scapegrace with which it is seasoned. Hence, when he thinks of allowing *Beckmesser* to use the poem the Sachs Motive takes on a somewhat facetious, roguish grace. There now ensues a charming dialogue between *Sachs* and *Eva*, who enters when *Beckmesser* has departed. This is accompanied by a transformation of the Eva Motive, which now reflects her shyness and hesitancy in taking *Sachs* into her confidence.

With it is joined the Cobbler Motive when *Eva* places her foot upon the stool while *Sachs* tries on the shoes she is to wear at the festival. When, with a cry of joy, she recognizes her lover as he appears upon the gallery, and remains motionless, gazing upon him as if spellbound, the lovely Summer Night Motive enhances the beauty of the tableau. While *Sachs* cobbles and chats away, pretending not to observe the lovers, the Motive of Maidenly Reserve passes through many modulations until there is heard a phrase from "Tristan and Isolde" (the Isolde Motive), an allusion which is explained below. The Lyric Motive introduces the third stanza of *Walther's* "Prize Song," with which he now greets *Eva*, while she, overcome with joy at seeing her lover, sinks upon *Sachs's* breast. The

Richard Wagner

Illusion Motive rhapsodizes the praises of the generous cobbler-poet, who seeks relief from his emotions in bantering remarks, until *Eva* glorifies him in a noble burst of love and gratitude in a melody derived from the Isolde Motive.

It is after this that *Sachs*, alluding to his own love of *Eva*, exclaims that he will have none of King Marke's triste experience; and the use of the King Marke Motive at this point shows that the previous echoes of the Isolde Motive were premeditated rather than accidental.

Magdalena and *David* now enter, and *Sachs* gives to *Walther's* "Prize Song" its musical baptism, utilizing chiefly the first and second lines of the chorale which opens the first act. *David* then kneels down and, according to the custom of the day, receives from *Sachs* a box on the ear in token that he is advanced from 'prentice to journeyman. Then follows the beautiful quintet, in which the "Prize Song," as a thematic germ, puts forth its loveliest blossoms. This is but one of many instances in which Wagner proved that when the dramatic situation called for it he could conceive and develop a melody of most exquisite fibre.

After the quintet the orchestra resumes the Nuremburg Motive and all depart for the festival. The stage is now shut off by a curtain behind which the scene is changed from *Sachs's* workshop to the meadow on the banks of the Pegnitz, near Nuremburg. After a tumultuous orchestral interlude, which portrays by means of motives already familiar, with the addition of the fanfare of the town musicians, the noise and bustle incidental to preparations for a great festival, the curtain rises upon a lively scene. Boats decked out in flags and bunting and full of festively clad members of the various guilds and their wives and children are constantly arriving. To the right is a platform decorated with the flags of the guilds which have already gathered. People are making merry under tents and

The Complete Opera Book

awnings where refreshments are served. The 'prentices are having a jolly time of it heralding and marshalling the guilds who disperse and mingle with the merrymakers after the standard bearers have planted their banners near the platform.

Soon after the curtain rises the cobblers arrive, and as they march down the meadow, conducted by the 'prentices, they sing in honour of St. Crispin, their patron saint, a chorus, based on the Cobbler Motive, to which a melody in popular style is added. The town watchmen, with trumpets and drums, the town pipers, lute makers, etc., and then the journeymen, with comical sounding toy instruments, march past, and are succeeded by the tailors, who sing a humorous chorus, telling how Nuremburg was saved from its ancient enemies by a tailor, who sewed a goatskin around him and pranced around on the town walls, to the terror of the hostile army, which took him for the devil. The bleating of a goat is capitally imitated in this chorus.

With the last chord of the tailors' chorus the bakers strike up their song and are greeted in turn by cobblers and tailors with their respective refrains. A boatful of young peasant girls in gay costumes now arrives, and the 'prentices make a rush for the bank. A charming dance in waltz time is struck up. The 'prentices with the girls dance down toward the journeymen, but as soon as these try to get hold of the girls, the 'prentices veer off with them in another direction. This veering should be timed to fall at the beginning of those periods of the dance to which Wagner has given, instead of eight measures, seven and nine, in order by this irregularity to emphasize the ruse of the 'prentices.

The dance is interrupted by the arrival of the masters, the 'prentices falling in to receive, the others making room for the procession. The *Mastersingers* advance to the stately strains of the Mastersinger Motive, which, when

[Hana

ROBERT RADFORD AS POGNER IN "DIE MEISTERSINGER."

Kirkby Lunn as Kundry in "Parsifal."

Richard Wagner

Kothner appears bearing their standard with the figure of King David playing on his harp, goes over into the sturdy measures of the Mastersingers' March. *Sachs* rises and advances. At sight of him the populace intone the noblest of all choruses: "Awake! draws nigh the break of day," the words of which are a poem by the real Hans Sachs.

At its conclusion the populace break into shouts in praise of *Sachs*, who modestly yet most feelingly gives them thanks. When *Beckmesser* is led to the little mound of turf upon which the singer is obliged to stand, we have the humorous variation of the Mastersinger Motive from the Prelude. *Beckmesser's* attempt to sing *Walther's* poem ends, as Sachs had anticipated, in utter failure. The town clerk's effort is received with jeers. Before he rushes away, infuriated but utterly discomfited, he proclaims that *Sachs* is the author of the song they have derided. The cobbler-poet declares to the people that it is not by him; that it is a beautiful poem if sung to the proper melody and that he will show them the author of the poem, who will in song disclose its beauties. He then introduces *Walther*. The knight easily succeeds in winning over people and masters, who repeat the closing melody of his "Prize Song" in token of their joyous appreciation of his new and wondrous art. *Pogner* advances to decorate *Walther* with the insignia of the Mastersingers' Guild.

In more ways than one the "Prize Song" is a mainstay of "Die Meistersinger." It has been heard in the previous scene of the third act, not only when *Walther* rehearses it for

The Complete Opera Book

Sachs, but also in the quintet. Moreover, versions of it occur in the overture and indeed, throughout the work, adding greatly to the romantic sentiment of the score. For "Die Meistersinger" is a comedy of romance.

In measures easily recognized from the Prelude, to which the Nuremburg Motive is added, *Sachs* now praises the masters and explains their noble purpose as conservators of art. *Eva* takes the wreath with which *Walther* has been crowned, and with it crowns *Sachs*, who has meanwhile decorated the knight with the insignia. *Pogner* kneels, as if in homage, before *Sachs*, the masters point to the cobbler as to their chief, and *Walther* and *Eva* remain on either side of him, leaning gratefully upon his shoulders. The chorus repeats *Sachs's* final admonition to the closing measures of the Prelude.

PARSIFAL

Stage Dedication Festival Play (Bühnenweihfestspiel) in three acts, words and music by Richard Wagner. Produced Bayreuth, July 26, 1882. Save in concert form, the work was not given elsewhere until December 24, 1903, when it was produced at the Metropolitan Opera House at that time under the direction of Heinrich Conried.

At the Bayreuth performances there were alternating casts. Winckelmann was the *Parsifal* of the *première*, Gudehus of the second performance, Jäger of the third. The alternating *Kundrys* were Materna, Marianne Brandt, and Malten; *Gurnemanz* Scaria and Siehr; *Amfortas* Reichmann; *Klingsor*, Hill and Fuchs. Hermann Levi conducted.

In the New York cast Ternina was *Kundry*, Burgstaller *Parsifal*, Van Rooy *Amfortas*, Blass *Gurnemanz*, Goritz *Klingsor*, Journet *Titurel*, Miss Moran and Miss Braendle the first and second, Harden and Bayer the third and fourth *Esquires*, Bayer and Mühlmann two *Knights* of the Grail, Homer a *Voice*.

CHARACTERS

AMFORTAS, son of TITUREL, ruler of the Kingdom of the Grail
Baritone-Bass
TITUREL, former ruler..*Bass*
GURNEMANZ, a veteran Knight of the Grail....................*Bass*
KLINGSOR, a magician...*Bass*
PARSIFAL..*Tenor*

Richard Wagner

KUNDRY..Soprano
FIRST AND SECOND KNIGHTS......................Tenor and Bass
FOUR ESQUIRES............................Sopranos and Tenors
SIX OF KLINGSOR'S FLOWER MAIDENS.....................Sopranos
    Brotherhood of the Knights of the Grail; Youths and Boys;
    Flower Maidens (two choruses of sopranos and altos).
Time—The Middle Ages. *Place*—Spain, near and in the Castle of the
                  Holy Grail; in Klingsor's enchanted castle and in the garden of his castle.

"Parsifal" is a familiar name to those who have heard "Lohengrin." Lohengrin, it will be remembered, tells Elsa that he is Parsifal's son and one of the knights of the Holy Grail. The name is written Percival in "Lohengrin," as well as in Tennyson's "Idyls of the King." Now, however, Wagner returns to the quainter and more "Teutonic" form of spelling. "Parsifal" deals with an earlier period in the history of the Grail knighthood than "Lohengrin." But there is a resemblance between the Grail music in "Parsifal" and the "Lohengrin" music—a resemblance not in melody, nor even in outline, but merely in the purity and spirituality that breathes through both.

Three legends supplied Wagner with the principal characters in this music-drama. They were "Percival le Galois; or Contes de Grail," by Chrétien de Troyes (1190); "Parsifal," by Wolfram von Eschenbach, and a manuscript of the fourteenth century called by scholars the "Mabinogion." As usual, Wagner has not held himself strictly to any one of these, but has combined them all, and revivified them through the alchemy of his own genius.

Into the keeping of *Titurel* and his band of Christian knights has been given the Holy Grail, the vessel from which the Saviour drank when He instituted the Last Supper. Into their hands, too, has been placed, as a weapon of defence against the ungodly, the Sacred Spear, the arm with which the Roman soldier wounded the Saviour's side.

The Complete Opera Book

The better to guard these sanctified relics *Titurel,* as King of the Grail knighthood, has reared a castle, Montsalvat, which, from its forest-clad height, facing Arabian Spain, forms a bulwark of Christendom against the pagan world and especially against *Klingsor,* a sorcerer and an enemy of the good. Yet time and again this *Klingsor,* whose stronghold is near-by, has succeeded in enticing champions of the Grail into his magic garden, with its lure of flower-maidens and its archenchantress *Kundry,* a rarely beautiful woman, and in making them his servitors against their one-time brothers-in-arms.

Even *Amfortas Titurel's* son, to whom *Titurel,* grown old in service and honour, has confided his reign and wardship, has not escaped the thrall of *Klingsor's* sorcery. Eager to begin his reign by destroying *Klingsor's* power at one stroke, he penetrated into the garden to attack and slay him. But he failed to reckon with human frailty. Yielding to the snare so skilfully laid by the sorcerer and forgetting, at the feet of the enchantress, *Kundry,* the mission upon which he had sallied forth, he allowed the Sacred Spear to drop from his hand. It was seized by the evil-doer he had come to destroy, and he himself was grievously wounded with it before the knights who rushed to his rescue could bear him off.

This wound no skill has sufficed to heal. It is sapping *Amfortas's* strength. Indecision, gloom, have come over the once valiant brotherhood. Only the touch of the Sacred Spear that made the wound will avail to close it, but there is only one who can regain it from *Klingsor.* For to *Amfortas,* prostrate in supplication for a sign, a mystic voice from the sanctuary of the Grail replied:

> By pity guided,
> The guileless fool;
> Wait for him,
> My chosen tool.

This prophecy the knights construe to signify that their king's salvation can be wrought only by youth so "guile

Richard Wagner

less," so wholly ignorant of sin, that, instead of succumbing to the temptations of *Klingsor's* magic garden, he will become, through resisting them, cognizant of *Amfortas's* guilt, and, stirred by pity for him, make his redemption the mission of his life, regain the Spear and heal him with it. And so the Grail warders are waiting, waiting for the coming of the "guileless fool."

The working out of this prophecy forms the absorbing subject of the story of "Parsifal." The plot is allegorical. *Parsifal* is the personification of Christianity, *Klingsor* of Paganism, and the triumph of *Parsifal* over *Klingsor* is the triumph of Christianity over Paganism.

The character of *Kundry* is one of Wagner's most striking creations. She is a sort of female Ahasuerus—a wandering Jewess. In the Mabinogion manuscript she is no other than Herodias, condemned to wander for ever because she laughed at the head of John the Baptist. Here Wagner makes another change. According to him she is condemned for laughing in the face of the Saviour as he was bearing the cross. She seeks forgiveness by serving the Grail knights as messenger on her swift horse, but ever and anon she is driven by the curse hanging over her back to *Klingsor*, who changes her to a beautiful woman and places her in his garden to lure the Knights of the Grail. She can be freed only by one who resists her temptations. Finally she is freed by *Parsifal* and is baptized. In her character of Grail messenger she has much in common with the wild messengers of Walhalla, the Valkyrs. Indeed, in the Edda Saga, her name appears in the first part of the compound Gundryggja, which denotes the office of the Valkyrs.

THE VORSPIEL

The *Vorspiel* to "Parsifal" is based on three of the most deeply religious motives in the entire work. It opens with the **Motive of the Sacrament,** over which, when it is repeated, *arpeggios* hover, as in the religious paintings of old masters angel forms float above the figure of virgin or saint.

Through this motive we gain insight into the office of the Knights of the Grail, who from time to time strengthen themselves for their spiritual duties by partaking of the communion, on which occasions the Grail itself is uncovered. This motive leads to the **Grail Motive,** effectively swelling to forte and then dying away in ethereal harmonies, like the soft light with which the Grail illumines the hall in which the knights gather to worship.

The trumpets then announce the **Motive of Faith,** severe but sturdy—portraying superbly the immutability of faith.

The Grail Motive is heard again and then the Motive of Faith is repeated, its severity exquisitely softened, so that it conveys a sense of peace which "passeth all understanding."

Richard Wagner

The rest of the *Vorspiel* is agitated. That portion of the Motive of the Sacrament which appears later as the Spear Motive here assumes through a slight change a deeply sad character, and becomes typical throughout the work of the sorrow wrought by *Amfortas's* crime. I call it the **Elegiac Motive.**

Thus the *Vorspiel* depicts both the religious duties which play so prominent a part in the drama, and unhappiness which *Amfortas's* sinful forgetfulness of these duties has brought upon himself and his knights.

Act I. One of the sturdiest of the knights, the aged *Gurnemanz*, grey of head and beard, watches near the outskirts of the forest. One dawn finds him seated under a majestic tree. Two young *Esquires* lie in slumber at his feet. Far off, from the direction of the castle, sounds a solemn reveille.

"Hey! Ho!" *Gurnemanz* calls with brusque humour to the *Esquires*. "Not forest, but sleep warders I deem you!" The youths leap to their feet; then, hearing the solemn reveille, kneel in prayer. The Motive of Peace echoes their devotional thoughts. A wondrous peace seems to rest upon the scene. But the transgression of the *King* ever breaks the tranquil spell. For soon two *Knights* come in the van of the train that thus early bears the *King* from a bed of suffering to the forest lake near-by, in whose waters he would bathe his wound. They pause to parley with *Gurnemanz*, but are interrupted by outcries from the youths and sounds of rushing through air.

"Mark the wild horsewoman!"—"The mane of the devil's mare flies madly!"—"Aye, 'tis Kundry!"—"She has swung herself off," cry the *Esquires* as they watch the

The Complete Opera Book

approach of the strange creature that now rushes in—a woman clad in coarse, wild garb girdled high with a snakeskin, her thick black hair tumbling about her shoulders, her features swarthy, her dark eyes now flashing, now fixed and glassy. Precipitately she thrusts a small crystal flask into *Gurnemanz's* hand.

"Balsam—for the king!" There is a savagery in her manner that seems designed to ward off thanks, when *Gurnemanz* asks her whence she has brought the flask, and she replies: "From farther away than your thought can travel. If it fail, Arabia bears naught else that can ease his pain. Ask no further. I am weary."

Throwing herself upon the ground and resting her face on her hands, she watches the *King* borne in, replies to his thanks for the balsam with a wild, mocking laugh, and follows him with her eyes as they bear him on his litter toward the lake, while *Gurnemanz* and four *Esquires* remain behind.

Kundry's rapid approach on her wild horse is accompanied by a furious gallop in the orchestra. Then, as she

rushes upon the stage, the **Kundry Motive**—a headlong descent of the string instruments through four octaves—is heard.

Kundry's action in seeking balsam for the *King's* wound gives us insight into the two contradictory natures repre-

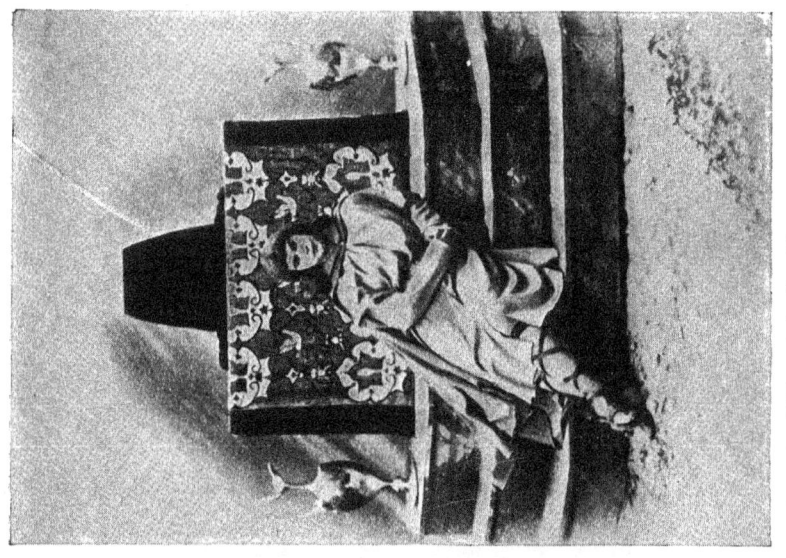

Photographs of the First Performance of "Parsifal," 1882.
The Grail Bearer.

Photographs of First Performance of "Parsifal," Beyreuth, 1882.
Winckelmann and Materna as Parsifal and Kundry. Scaria as Gurnemanz.

Richard Wagner

sented by her character. For here is the woman who has brought all his suffering upon *Amfortas* striving to ease it when she is free from the evil sway of *Klingsor*. She is at times the faithful messenger of the Grail; at times the evil genius of its defenders.

When *Amfortas* is borne in upon a litter there is heard the **Motive of Amfortas's Suffering,** expressive of his physical and mental agony. It has a peculiar heavy, dragging rhythm, as if his wound slowly were sapping his life.

A beautiful idyl is played by the orchestra when the knights bear *Amfortas* to the forest lake.

One of the youths, who has remained with *Gurnemanz*, noting that *Kundry* still lies where she had flung herself upon the ground, calls out scornfully, "Why do you lie there like a savage beast?"

"Are not even the beasts here sacred?" she retorts, but harshly, and not as if pleading for sufferance. The other *Esquires* would have joined in harassing her had not *Gurnemanz* stayed them.

The Complete Opera Book

"Never has she done you harm. She serves the Grail, and only when she remains long away, none knows in what distant lands, does harm come to us." Then, turning to where she lies, he asks: "Where were you wandering when our leader lost the Sacred Spear? Why were you not here to help us then?"

"I never help!" is her sullen retort, although a tremor, as if caused by a pang of bitter reproach, passes over her frame.

"If she wants to serve the Grail, why not send her to recover the Sacred Spear!" exclaims one of the *Esquires* sarcastically; and the youths doubtless would have resumed their nagging of *Kundry*, had not mention of the holy weapon caused *Gurnemanz* to give voice to memories of the events that have led to its capture by *Klingsor*. Then, yielding to the pressing of the youths who gather at his feet beneath the tree, he tells them of *Klingsor*—how the sorcerer has sued for admission to the Grail brotherhood, which was denied him by *Titurel*, how in revenge he has sought its destruction and now, through possession of the Sacred Spear, hopes to compass it.

Prominent with other motives already heard, is a new one, the Klingsor Motive:

During this recital *Kundry* still lies upon the ground, a sullen, forbidding looking creature. At the point when *Gurnemanz* tells of the sorcerer's magic garden and of the enchantress who has lured *Amfortas* to his downfall, she turns in quick, angry unrest, as if she would away, but is held to the spot by some dark and compelling power. There is indeed something strange and contradictory in this wild creature, who serves the Grail by ranging distant

Richard Wagner

lands in search of balsam for the *King's* wound, yet abruptly, vindictively almost, repels proffered thanks, and is a sullen and unwilling listener to *Gurnemanz's* narrative. Furthermore, as *Gurnemanz* queried, where does she linger during those long absences, when harm has come to the warders of the Grail and now to their *King?* The Knights of the Grail do not know it, but it is none other than she who, changed by *Klingsor* into an enchantress, lures them into his magic garden.

Gurnemanz concludes by telling the *Esquire* that while *Amfortas* was praying for a sign as to who could heal him, phantom lips pronounced these words:

> By pity lightened
> The guileless fool;
> Wait for him, –
> My chosen tool.

This introduces an important motive, that of the **Prophecy,** a phrase of simple beauty, as befits the significance of the words to which it is sung. *Gurnemanz* sings the entire motive and then the *Esquires* take it up.

They have sung only the first two lines when suddenly their prayerful voices are interrupted by shouts of dismay from the direction of the lake. A moment later a wounded swan, one of the sacred birds of the Grail brotherhood, flutters over the stage and falls dead near *Gurnemanz.* The knights follow in consternation. Two of them bring *Parsifal,* whom they have seized and accuse of murdering the sacred bird. As he appears the magnificent **Parsifal Motive** rings out on the horns:

It is a buoyant and joyous motive, full of the wild spirit and freedom of this child of nature, who knows nothing of the Grail and its brotherhood or the sacredness of the swan, and freely boasts of his skilful marksmanship. During this episode the Swan Motive from "Lohengrin" is effectively introduced. Then follows *Gurnemanz's* noble reproof, sung to a broad and expressive melody. Even the animals are sacred in the region of the Grail and are protected from harm. *Parsifal's* gradual awakening to a sense of wrong is one of the most touching scenes of the music-drama. His childlike grief when he becomes conscious of the pain he has caused is so simple and pathetic that one cannot but be deeply affected.

After *Gurnemanz* has ascertained that *Parsifal* knows nothing of the wrong he committed in killing the swan he plies him with questions concerning his parentage. *Parsifal* is now gentle and tranquil. He tells of growing up in the woods, of running away from his mother to follow a cavalcade of knights who passed along the edge of the forest and

Richard Wagner

of never having seen her since. In vain he endeavours to recall the many pet names she gave him. These memories of his early days introduce the sad motive of his mother, **Herzeleid** (Heart's Sorrow) who has died in grief.

The old knight then proceeds to ply *Parsifal* with questions regarding his parentage, name, and native land. "I do not know," is the youth's invariable answer. His ignorance, coupled, however, with his naïve nobility of bearing and the fact that he has made his way to the Grail domain, engender in *Gurnemanz* the hope that here at last is the "guileless fool" for whom prayerfully they have been waiting, and the *King*, having been borne from the lake toward the castle where the holy rite of unveiling the Grail is to be celebrated that day, thither *Gurnemanz* in kindly accents bids the youth follow him.

Then occurs a dramatically effective change of scene. The scenery becomes a panorama drawn off toward the right, and as *Parsifal* and *Gurnemanz* face toward the left they appear to be walking in that direction. The forest disappears; a cave opens in rocky cliffs and conceals the two; they are then seen again in sloping passages which they appear to ascend. Long sustained trombone notes softly swell; approaching peals of bells are heard. At last they arrive at a mighty hall which loses itself overhead in a high vaulted dome, down from which alone the light streams in.

The change of scene is ushered in by the solemn **Bell**

The Complete Opera Book

Motive, which is the basis of the powerful orchestral interlude accompanying the panorama, and also of the scene in the hall of the Grail Castle.

As the communion, which is soon to be celebrated, is broken in upon by the violent grief and contrition of *Amfortas*, so, the majestic sweep of this symphony is interrupted by the agonized **Motive of Contrition,** which graphically portrays the spiritual suffering of the *King*.

This subtly suggests the Elegiac Motive and the Motive of Amfortas's Suffering, but in greatly intensified degrees. For it is like an outcry of torture that effects both body and soul.

With the Motive of the Sacrament resounding solemnly upon the trombones, followed by the Bell Motive, sonorous and powerful, *Gurnemanz* and *Parsifal* enter the hall, the old knight giving the youth a position from which he can observe the proceedings. From the deep colonnades on either side in the rear the knights issue, march with stately tread, and arrange themselves at the horseshoe-shaped table, which incloses a raised couch. Then, while the orchestra plays a solemn processional based on the Bell Motive, they intone the chorus: "To the last love feast." After the first verse a line of pages crosses the stage and ascend into the dome. The graceful interlude here is based on the Bell Motive.

Richard Wagner

The chorus of knights closes with a glorious outburst of the Grail Motive as *Amfortas* is borne in, preceded by pages who bear the covered Grail. The *King* is lifted upon the couch and the holy vessel is placed upon the stone table in front of it. When the Grail Motive has died away amid the pealing of the bells, the youths in the gallery below the dome sing a chorus of penitence based upon the Motive of Contrition. Then the Motive of Faith floats down from the dome as an unaccompanied chorus for boys' voices—a passage of ethereal beauty—the orchestra whispering a brief postludium like a faint echo. This is, when sung as it was at Bayreuth, where I heard the first performance of "Parsifal" in 1882, the most exquisite effect of the whole score. For spirituality it is unsurpassed. It is an absolutely perfect example of religious music—a beautiful melody without the slightest worldly taint.

Titurel now summons *Amfortas* to perform his sacred office—to uncover the Grail. At first, tortured by contrition for his sin, of which the agony from his wound is a constant reminder, he refuses to obey his aged father's summons. In anguish he cries out that he is unworthy of the sacred office. But again ethereal voices float down from the dome. They now chant the prophecy of the "guileless fool" and, as if comforted by the hope of ultimate redemption, *Amfortas* uncovers the Grail. Dusk seems to spread over the hall. Then a ray of brilliant light darts down upon the sacred vessel, which shines with a soft purple radiance that diffuses itself through the hall. All are on their knees save the youth, who has stood motionless and obtuse to the significance of all he has heard and seen save that during *Amfortas's* anguish he has clutched his heart as if he too felt the pang. But when the rite is over—when the knights have partaken of communion—and the glow has faded, and the *King*, followed by his knights, has been borne out, the youth remains behind, vigorous, handsome, but to all appearances a dolt.

"Do you know what you have witnessed?" *Gurnemanz* asks harshly, for he is grievously disappointed.

For answer the youth shakes his head.

"Just a fool, after all," exclaims the old knight, as he opens a side door to the hall. "Begone, but take my advice. In future leave our swans alone, and seek yourself, gander, a goose!" And with these harsh words he pushes the youth out and angrily slams the door behind him.

This jarring break upon the religious feeling awakened by the scene would be a rude ending for the act, but Wagner, with exquisite tact, allows the voices in the dome to be heard once more, and so the curtains close, amid the spiritual harmonies of the Prophecy of the Guileless Fool and of the Grail Motive.

Act II. This act plays in *Klingsor's* magic castle and garden. The *Vorspiel* opens with the threatful Klingsor motive, which is followed by the Magic and Contrition Motives, the wild Kundry Motive leading over to the first scene.

In the inner keep of his tower, stone steps leading up to the battlemented parapet and down into a deep pit at the back, stands *Klingsor*, looking into a metal mirror, whose surface, through his necromancy, reflects all that transpires within the environs of the fastness from which he ever threatens the warders of the Grail. Of all that just has happened in the Grail's domain it has made him aware; and he knows that of which *Gurnemanz* is ignorant—that the youth, whose approach the mirror divulges, once in his power, vain will be the prophecy of the "guileless fool" and his own triumph assured. For it is that same "guileless fool" the old knight impatiently has thrust out.

Klingsor turns toward the pit and imperiously waves his hand. A bluish vapour rises from the abyss and in it

Richard Wagner

floats the form of a beauteous woman—*Kundry*, not the *Kundry* of a few hours before, dishevelled and in coarse garb girdled with snake-skin; but a houri, her dark hair smooth and lustrous, her robe soft, rich Oriental draperies. Yet even as she floats she strives as though she would descend to where she has come from, while the sorcerer's harsh laugh greets her vain efforts. This then is the secret of her strange actions and her long disappearances from the Grail domain, during which so many of its warders have fallen into *Klingsor's* power! She is the snare he sets, she the arch-enchantress of his magic garden. Striving as he hints while he mocks her impotence, to expiate some sin committed by her during a previous existence in the dim past, by serving the brotherhood of the Grail knights. the sorcerer's power over her is such that at any moment he can summon her to aid him in their destruction.

Well she knows what the present summons means. Approaching the tower at this very moment is the youth whom she has seen in the Grail forest, and in whom she, like *Klingsor*, has recognized the only possible redeemer of *Amfortas* and of—herself. And now she must lure him to his doom and with it lose her last hope of salvation, now, aye, now—for even as he mocks her, *Klingsor* once more waves his hand, castle and keep vanish as if swallowed up by the earth, and in its place a garden heavy with the scent of gorgeous flowers fills the landscape.

The orchestra, with the Parsifal Motive, gives a spirited description of the brief combat between *Parsifal* and *Klingsor's* knights. It is amid the dark harmonies of the Klingsor Motive that the keep sinks out of sight and the magic garden, spreading out in all directions, with *Parsifal* standing on the wall and gazing with astonishment upon the brilliant scene, is disclosed.

The *Flower Maidens* in great trepidation for the fate of their lover knights rush in from all sides with cries of sorrow, their confused exclamations and the orchestral accompaniment admirably enforcing their tumultuous actions.

The Parsifal Motive again introduces the next episode, as *Parsifal*, attracted by the grace and beauty of the girls, leaps down into the garden and seeks to mingle with them. It is repeated several times in the course of the scene. The girls, seeing that he does not seek to harm them, bedeck themselves with flowers and crowd about him with alluring gestures, finally circling around him as they sing this caressing melody:

The effect is enchanting, the music of this episode being a marvel of sensuous grace. *Parsifal* regards them with childlike, innocent joy. Then they seek to impress him more deeply with their charms, at the same time quarrelling among themselves over him. When their rivalry has reached its height, *Kundry's* voice—"Parsifal, tarry!"— is wafted from a flowery nook near-by.

"Parsifal!" In all the years of his wandering none has called him by his name; and now it floats toward him as if borne on the scent of roses. A beautiful woman, her arms stretched out to him, welcomes him from her couch of

Richard Wagner

brilliant, redolent flowers. Irresistibly drawn toward her, he approaches and kneels by her side; and she, whispering to him in tender accents, leans over him and presses a long kiss upon his lips. It is the lure that has sealed the fate of many a knight of the Grail. But in the youth it inspires a sudden change. The perilous subtlety of it, that is intended to destroy, transforms the "guileless fool" into a conscious man, and that man conscious of a mission. The scenes he has witnessed in the Grail castle, the stricken *King* whose wound ever bled afresh, the part he is to play, the peril of the temptation that has been placed in his path —all these things become revealed to him in the rapture of that unhallowed kiss. In vain the enchantress seeks to draw him toward her. He thrusts her from him. Maddened by the repulse, compelled through *Klingsor's* arts to see in the handsome youth before her lawful prey, she calls upon the sorcerer to aid her. At her outcry *Klingsor* appears on the castle wall, in his hand the Spear taken from *Amfortas*, and, as *Parsifal* faces him, hurls it full at him. But lo, it rises in its flight and remains suspended in the air over the head of him it was aimed to slay.

Reaching out and seizing it, *Parsifal* makes with it the sign of the cross. Castle and garden wall crumble into ruins, the garden shrivels away, leaving in its place a sere wilderness, through which *Parsifal*, leaving *Kundry* as one dead upon the ground, sets forth in search of the castle of the Grail, there to fulfil the mission with which now he knows himself charged.

Act III. Not until after long wanderings through the wilderness, however, is it that *Parsifal* once more finds himself on the outskirts of the Grail forest. Clad from head to foot in black armour, his visor closed, the Holy Spear in his hand, he approaches the spot where *Gurnemanz*, now grown very old, still holds watch, while *Kundry* again in coarse garb, but grown strangely pale and gentle, humbly serves the brotherhood. It is Good Friday morn, and peace rests upon the forest.

Kundry is the first to discern the approach of the black knight. From the tender exaltation of her mien, as she draws *Gurnemanz's* look toward the silent figure, it is apparent that she divines who it is and why he comes. To *Gurnemanz*, however, he is but an armed intruder on sanctified ground and upon a holy day, and, as the black knight seats himself on a little knoll near a spring and remains silent, the old warder chides him for his offence. Tranquilly the knight rises, thrusts the Spear he bears into the ground before him, lays down his sword and shield before it, opens his helmet, and, removing it from his head, places it with the other arms, and then himself kneels in silent prayer before the Spear. Surprise, recognition of man and weapon, and deep emotion succeed each other on *Gurnemanz's* face. Gently he raises *Parsifal* from his kneeling posture, once more seats him on the knoll by the spring, loosens his greaves and corselet, and then places upon him the coat of mail and mantle of the knights of the Grail, while *Kundry*, drawing a golden flask from her bosom anoints his feet and dries them with her loosened hair. Then *Gurnemanz* takes from her the flask, and, pouring its contents upon *Parsifal's* head, anoints him king of the knights of the Grail. The new king performs his first office by taking up water from the spring in the hollow of his hand and baptizing *Kundry*, whose eyes, suffused with tears, are raised to him in gentle rapture.

Here is heard the stately Motive of Baptism:

Richard Wagner

The "Good Friday Spell," one of Wagner's most beautiful mood paintings in tone color, is the most prominent episode in these scenes.

Once more *Gurnemanz, Kundry* now following, leads the way toward the castle of the Grail. *Amfortas's* aged father, *Titurel*, uncomforted by the vision of the Grail, which *Amfortas*, in his passionate contrition, deems himself too sullied to unveil, has died, and the knights having gathered in the great hall, *Titurel's* bier is borne in solemn procession and placed upon a catafalque before *Amfortas's* couch.

"Uncover the shrine!" shout the knights, pressing upon *Amfortas*. For answer, and in a paroxysm of despair, he springs up, tears his garments asunder and shows his open wound. "Slay me!" he cried. "Take up your weapons! Bury your sword-blades deep—deep in me, to the hilts! Kill me, and so kill the pain that tortures me!"

As *Amfortas* stands there in an ecstasy of pain, *Parsifal* enters, and, quietly advancing, touches the wound with the point of the Spear.

"One weapon only serves to staunch your wounded side— the one that struck it."

Amfortas's torture changes to highest rapture. The shrine is opened and *Parsifal*, taking the Grail, which again

The Complete Opera Book

radiates with light, waves it gently to and fro, as *Amfortas* and all the knights kneel in homage to him, while *Kundry* gazing up to him in gratitude, sinks gently into the sleep of death and forgiveness for which she has longed.

The music of this entire scene floats upon ethereal *arpeggios*. The Motive of Faith especially is exquisitely accompanied, its spiritual harmonies finally appearing in this form.

There are also heard the Motives of Prophecy and of the Sacrament, as the knights on the stage and the youths and boys in the dome chant. The Grail Motive, which is prominent throughout the scene, rises as if in a spirit of gentle religious triumph and brings, with the Sacrament Motive, the work to a close.

www.ingramcontent.com/pod-product-compliance
Lightning Source LLC
Chambersburg PA
CBHW020228170426
43201CB00007B/359